Welcome
to the
Pleasuredome

Welcome to the Pleasuredome

INSIDE LAS VEGAS

David Spanier

University of Nevada Press
Reno • Las Vegas • London

THE GAMBLING STUDIES SERIES
SERIES EDITOR: WILLIAM R. EADINGTON

A list of books of related interest follows the index.

First published as *All Right, Okay, You Win: Inside Las Vegas*
in Great Britain 1992 by Martin Secker & Warburg Limited, Michelin
House, 81 Fulham Road, London SW3 6RB England

The paper used in this book meets the requirements of American
National Standard for Information Sciences—Permanence of Paper
for Printed Library Materials, ANSI Z39.48-1984. Binding
materials were selected for strength and durability.

LIBRARY OF CONGRESS CATALOGING-IN-PUBLICATION DATA

Spanier, David.
    Welcome to the pleasuredome : inside Las Vegas / David Spanier.
        p.   cm.   — (The Gambling studies series)
    Includes bibliographical references (p.   ) and index.
    ISBN 0-87417-213-6 (paper : alk. paper)
    1. Gambling—Nevada—Las Vegas. 2. Casinos—Nevada—Las Vegas.
I. Title. II. Title: Welcome to the pleasuredome.   III. Series.
HV6721.L3S65 1992
338.4'7795'09793135—dc20   93-20330
                                                                    CIP

University of Nevada Press, Reno, Nevada 89557 USA
Cover design by Patty Atcheson
Printed in the United States of America

9 8 7 6 5 4 3 2

For Suzy
  Because . . .

If it's worth doing,
it's worth overdoing.

—*Overheard in Las Vegas*

CONTENTS

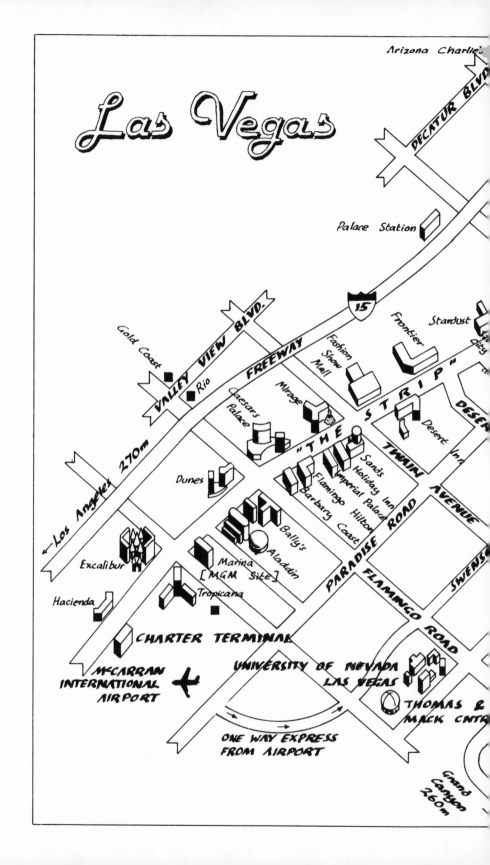

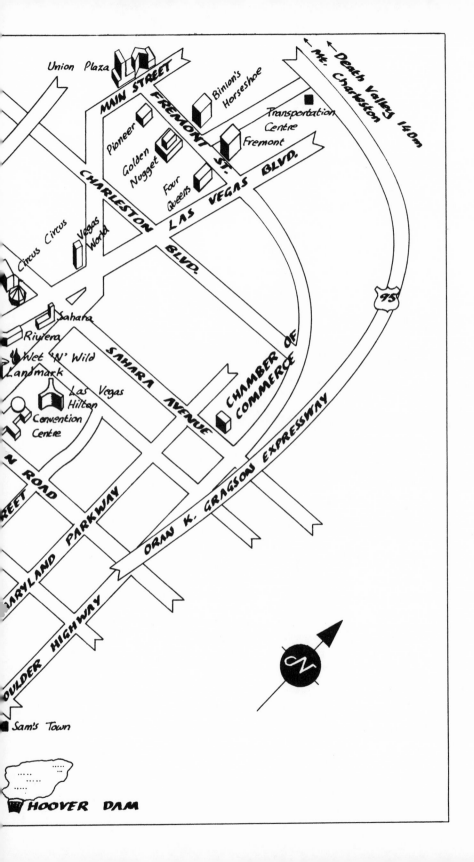

INTRODUCTION
Welcome to the Pleasuredome

I like Las Vegas. Admittedly, it is relentlessly vulgar, noisy, money-grubbing, deceitful and repetitive. Granted it screams bad taste from slot parlour to tower block, from gilded faucet to mirrored bedroom, inside and outside, day after night after day after night, glitz without end.

Despite all that, I like it. In fact I'll say it straight out: I LOVE LAS VEGAS. The point about it, which both its critics and its admirers overlook, is that it's wonderful and awful *simultaneously*. So one loves it and detests it at the same time. The fact that I keep going back, that I never miss the chance of making a detour from 'real' life, is convincing evidence that I like it a lot more than I dislike it.

It's not the gambling as such which attracts me. I've won, sure. Lots of times. Well . . . to be honest, I've lost quite a few times, too. More than a few times, actually, starting with my first visit back in my student days. I travelled into town by bus, carrying only a hold-all of dirty laundry and a typewriter, and very little money. I was sustained by a conviction, akin to a mystical belief, that I was endowed with an extraordinary inner power – an ability to reverse the iron laws of probability.

That very evening I started out at one of the gambling halls downtown. The system I had devised was simple enough. It was based on waiting for a long run of reds or blacks to come up at roulette before backing the other colour. Of course I knew about zero, and was momentarily discomfited to discover that here the casinos also sported a double-zero. But the hell with percentages! Why should that sort of mischance befall me, with my mystical power? My only anxiety, as I recall, was that there might not be a sufficiently long run of one colour that night to allow my staking plan to be put into action.

No need to worry, as it turned out. After a couple of hours, a run of eight reds came up and I started plunging on black. Red came up again, half a dozen more times. The bright tower of gaming chips which I had stacked up on the edge of the table came tumbling down. It now stood at a very modest height. The dealer, raking in my chips after each spin, was sizing it up like a demolition contractor, waiting for my next bet. But to double my stake, as required under my system, would take the rest of my stack, plus most of my travellers' cheques in reserve.

With the eyes of everyone around the table fixed upon me in wild surmise – Is this kid with his weird British accent going to blow all of his money? – a new thought, if not exactly a revelation, penetrated my over-heated semi-consciousness. This particular wheel was completely impervious to my system! It did not appreciate the fact that I had schlepped seven thousand miles by plane and train and bus to prove a seemingly logical mathematical point. What's more, there were still five weeks of my summer vacation left to run, and be paid for, somehow. I quit, pausing only to watch the next spin, noting with grim satisfaction that it, too, would have lost for me. I found a seat in the 25 cents ante poker game, where I even won a few pots.

We all learn the hard way, and Las Vegas is a hard teacher. So many people arrive with shining eyes – over 21,000,000 visitors hit town in 1991 (more than all the foreign visitors to London, a major capital city) – dreaming shining neon dreams, only to leave two and a half days later, purged. The great thing is to learn early in life rather than late. My lesson on that first visit, so I came to realise, was a bargain. It did not 'cure' me of gambling. As I have remarked about casino gambling in a previous book (*Easy Money*), I think gambling, in due proportion, is good for you. I like to cast myself as a *student* of gambling.

What I enjoy is the ambiance of gambling, and Las Vegas conveys that sense of risk, excitement, action, of anything goes and here it comes, more intensely than anywhere else. The whole operation is wound up and ready to go, any time, day or night, as fast or as slow as each customer wants it to happen. 'If it's worth doing, it's worth overdoing!' is Las Vegas' motto. Arriving at McCarran airport, the throngs of visitors are swept along the moving walkways into a timewarp, where life is lived in a faster register, away from jobs, mortgages, bills, taxes, bad news, TV ads, insulated from domestic chores, family trivia, social duties, the daily round and common task – a town without clocks.

McCarran airport, named after the Irish-American politician who ran Las Vegas in the post-war years, handles over sixteen million passengers a year. The airport greets the new arrivals in typically Vegan style, tempting the visitor to gamble via cut-price deals for hotels, offering shows, stars, music, girls, as if to go out and gamble were really to *save* money, and the big bucks were just waiting to spill out into the lucky players' hands. Chuckling voices speak out of the cool air: 'Hey hey hey! Welcome to Las Vegas . . . Keep a-hold of the hand-rail!' Rows of slot machines fill the airport lounges in flashing welcome; the ads promoting the big-prize jackpots offer a seductive challenge: 'One pull can change your life!' Why not? 'Enjoy your stay, Take time to play, Until it's time to part', rhymes an official welcome, 'Just remember when you leave, That Las Vegas does have heart.' A heart of gold, yeah.

Outside the terminal a wave of hot air from the desert slaps you in the face. The heat is too strong, round your collar, down your back; you take no more than a few steps without breaking sweat.

So how does one get into town? For the big players and established customers, enormous stretch-limos are purring at the kerbside. It's a wonderful way to ride in, reclining in the vast, cool interior of a limo, as the hoardings announcing the cabarets and the shows slip by, and the glittering pleasuredome beckons ahead. The sense of lolling in luxury, in delicious anticipation of everything ahead of you, is over all too quickly.

For workaday visitors, who do not care to waste precious gambling money on a taxi fare, airport buses ply the Strip and Downtown hotels,* for a fare of three or four bucks. The bus journey is fun because you share with all the different folks the same hopes and fears. Will they, won't they win? 'Ya know what,' avers a stout matron from the sunbelt, 'I gotta room and full board for twenny-seven fifty!' This self-same lady, bulging out of her rose-pink lurex pants, will be wagering ten times her room-rate in the next forty-five minutes. Never mind, with an 'All-you-c'n-eat' buffet for $2.99, she is not going to have to worry about where her next meal is coming from. None of us are.

Living is cheap in Las Vegas, it's the play which is expensive. The expectant gambler checks in, takes a shower, maybe calls home too, assuaging a final trace of guilt. Looks over the casino floor, saunters round. A quick pat of the wallet, to make sure it's still there, bulging the hip pocket, before venturing a few dollars in the slots or slipping into an empty seat at a blackjack table. Orders a drink from the cocktail waitress, on the house of course, then another (Okay, honey, keep 'em coming!) and gets stuck into the game. Then it's dinner time, followed by a show, and before the free-wheeling vacationer knows what's happening there's a gaping hole in his weekend bankroll.

People who play in Las Vegas find it hard, in retrospect, to disentangle winning from losing, the twin experiences become so

*The Strip is the two and a half mile section of Las Vegas Boulevard, on which most of the major hotel-casinos are situated; Downtown or Glitter Gulch is the area around Fremont Street, jammed with downmarket gambling halls and hotels.

mixed up. Inevitably everybody, or almost everybody, loses many more times than they win. Gamblers tend to operate a convenient little erasing mechanism in their memory, like a delete key on a computer, which allows them to wipe out, forget and – most important – *forgive* themselves past losses, so they can start again with a clean slate. As for myself, in subsequent visits to Las Vegas, and there have been many, I have spent no more than small change on the slots, and absolutely nothing at all on roulette with its iniquitous double-zero. Instead, that initial blooding in the saloons of Glitter Gulch confirmed in me a life-long addiction to poker, a gambling game where skill *can* put the odds in your favour.

Oh, I have seen dawn break over the desert and witnessed the glory of Elvis Presley before the cortisone got to him, I have thrown money around when I've won and wept silent tears when I've played badly. (Poker is a tough game.) But in truth, I had not actually gambled any sum over say twenty or thirty bucks until I returned some thirty years after that traumatic trip, with two of my young sons.

We had a most amusing time. Our plan was to make that 'one pull to change your life' and hit the million dollar jackpot. Half the fun was that the boys had to keep out of sight, peeping from the sidelines in schoolboy glee, because it is illegal for minors to take part in gambling, even indirectly. The thrill of anticipation, the razzle-dazzle of light and noise, were well worth the hundred dollars, or maybe a bit more, of family pocket money we stuffed into the ever-open jaws of those monster machines. 'It's quite difficult to go to sleep here,' noted Samson, aged eleven.

I don't know if my sons learned the lesson of Las Vegas from our venture the 'easy' way, but I think there is a fair chance they will have done. I tried to explain that even if we had hit the jackpot, it would not have changed our life in any significant way (though Dad might have bought Mom a diamond necklace as big as Caesars). Shouldn't children be initiated into gambling, along with other grown-up concerns, like a health innoculation?

Perhaps I am seeking a plausible excuse to justify making an extensive detour on a family vacation. When my wife Suzy accompanies me to Vegas, as she sometimes does, she makes just one condition. She regards gambling as an absurd and wasteful diversion of money that could be far better spent on clothes in Paris. Her precondition for joining me is simply that we find a hotel where the slots do not take up *all* the space – plus maybe a trip to Mexico on the side.

Hers is a point of view which I usually come to share, even before the week is up. One can take only so much of unreality.

I like the fleeting inconsequential moments of casino life which one experiences every day. In the press of the casino floor, for instance, running into John, one of the old-timers of the poker room: he's as thin and white as a sheet of waxed paper now, but he still manages to stop by almost every day to feel the living hum of the place where he has spent most of his life. As he shuffled slowly across the crowded floor at the Mirage, I asked John what he thought about the frenetic activity on all sides. 'They just keep on comin'!' he whispered.

'Do you think it will last?' I asked.

John looked around: 'It better had!'

I took a shoeshine from another John, an old-fashioned shoeshine man, who slapped and cracked the cloth across my feet like Art Blakey on a drum solo, a virtuoso performance. He inclined his head gravely when I gave him a five dollar bill. This was four o'clock in the afternoon, and from the open doorway I could see two Japanese in suits and ties playing $100,000 hands at baccarat, squeeezing out the cards, nodding and half-smiling politely when they lost, shouting when they won.

Or an example of style in gambling, in the old tradition. One afternoon downtown, I was gossiping with one of the long-time casino managers, Rod Morris, in his office at the Union Plaza, when one of his staff stuck his head around the door in a hurry. 'Scuse me! There's a guy over at the craps table winnin' $20,000!' he announced agitatedly.

Rod Morris unclamped a very large cigar from his mouth. 'Yeah? Who is he?'

'Looks like a young guy, he just walked in off the street.'

Morris bit on his cigar, glanced up at the TV monitor showing the dice game, puffed airily, and turned back to me, 'Okay.' As I was only wasting his time on a journalistic interview, I volunteered to postpone our talk. 'Na, don't worry about it.' So about five minutes later, the same assistant, now even more agitated, reappeared at the door: 'He's up to $28,000!'

Again I offered to stop, but Morris, drawing on his cigar, feet up on the desk, insisted we finish the interview in our own good time.

Finally I rose to go and we shook hands. No sooner was I out of the door than Morris' beetle-like figure swept past me on the casino floor. Without actually breaking into a run, his arms swinging up and down like an olympic walker entering the final lap, he raced over to the dice table to check out what was happening. No one minds a winner, so long as he can be persuaded to stay on the property and go on gambling.

Then there was the sight of the dealer's jaw dropping in disbelief at the journalists' poker game when it was explained to him how the media liked to play. The press game, played for minimal stakes, is a social event held annually, courtesy of Binion's Horseshoe, the night before the million dollar World Poker Championship. Across the floor half a dozen former world champions were involved in a cash game – players like Doyle Brunson, Johnny Chan, Berry Johnston, Stu Ungar, Bobby Baldwin, household names in this milieu – playing for such dizzying stacks of dollar bills that an armed guard was posted twenty feet from the table. One of the players tossed him a $100 chip by way of thanks. There we were, the gambling press, open a dollar, raise three dollars, no wonder the dealer thought we were kidding. At such moments the coincidence of random events is curiously pleasing.

But my favourite moment came at the end of a bad losing week, when I enjoyed the kind of coup you only dream about. It was my last morning, I couldn't sleep, so I went down to the poker room at about six a.m. The guys who had been playing and drinking all night were slumped around the table in various stages of weariness and disillusionment. I was showered and aftershaved, as fresh as a daisy – if you could ever find a daisy in Vegas. I came over to an empty seat, enquiring in a cut-glass British accent: 'I say, fellows, is this seat open? What is this game, anyway?'

Everyone around the table jerked upright as if a bolt of lightning had been shot down their spines. Here was a real live one! At last! The heavy-eyed dealer did not break the sequence of his shuffle: 'Twenny-forty, Hold 'em – deal ya in?'

First hand, under the gun, I found a pair of threes in the hole, which is of course a useless little pair, but I raised at once to establish my image as a complete sucker. Everyone called and lo and behold the flop came up with the other pair of threes. I checked, there was a lot of raising, which I called meekly, and then I re-raised like Old Glory on the last two cards. No one believed me – how could they? As I stacked up the mountainous pile of chips the dealer shoved across to me, the old Vegas proverb seemed so sweetly true: 'What goes around, comes around.'

Among all the variety of people who work in Vegas, the one who made the most vivid impression on me, for good or ill, was a host – hosts being the guys who look after guests and make them feel welcome, perform any little services the players want, and generally keep them happy. Although I don't want to name him I can't resist giving his nickname, because it says so much about him, and hosts in general: Jam-up. Jam-up is what happens in a poker hand when everybody piles into the pot, raising and re-raising, and the betting bubbles over.

Jam-up reminded me of a great St Bernard dog because he was so enthusiastic about his job, so raring to go, he just lapped good will all over you.

'Every employee who comes into contact with a customer is a

representative of the establishment, and he should host customers by being pleasant and helpful,' says Bill Friedman in his classic *Casino Management*. 'If a player is treated well by a host, even if he only spends a very short time with him, he is likely to become a regular customer. Personal attention is the main quality that makes an establishment hospitable and a desirable place to be.'

Jam-up is special because he thrives on his role, he loves customers, he can't get enough of meeting and greeting, he can't even pass a pretty secretary – they scatter through the executive offices like confetti – without calling her by her first name, grabbing her by the hand or blowing her a kiss, and enquiring after her mother or boyfriend or weekend trip. Being friendly is an occupational disease with this man.

Out on the crowded casino floor, Jam-up tracks down a new customer. He is betting in $50 units at a blackjack table. The man hits a blackjack and the host jumps in to pump his hand. 'Got ya tickets for the show, Mr B. How ya doin' Mrs Brown? Nice dress you're wearin' tonight! Say, can I book you folks a limo if you're goin' downtown? Here's my card, just give me a call! Any time!' It takes half a minute, the next deal is already rolling – but here is a new customer, hooked for life. Such an apparently simple routine makes the difference between a big winning casino and an average winning casino.

Then something happens which sums up, for me, the whole Las Vegas experience. Jam-up's beeper goes. There's a call on the line. He grabs the house phone. 'Wow! Great to hear from you! How are you? Hey that's wonderful, come on over! I'll book a table in our Eye-talian restaurant! You'll love it! Oh boy!' The reason the host is so pleased, so thrilled, so almost beyond words, is that this customer is a big hitter, who has called him from a rival casino on the Strip. Jam-up, as a host, could not himself call this man, although he knows he's in town, to invite him over from the casino where he is staying, because that would be against the etiquette of hosting. But if the client calls *him* – 'I'll get the chef on to it, you're gonna love this! How many are you? Seven, that's great, I'll join you! Oh this is so marvellous you've called me, I can't tell ya.'

The meal is going to cost, he confides, hand cupped over the phone, $1,500! They'll be drinking Dom Perignon and Chateau Latour. This is something special, because this is a wonderful guy who plays off a million dollar credit line. The host sounds like a man might sound when he hears his son has won the top scholarship to Harvard and his daughter is engaged to a movie star, when at that very same moment a call comes through to say he's been promoted vice-president of his company. Oh boy, oh boy, oh boy.

When he hung up I asked whether this particular high roller was a nice fellow to know, just on the personal level? The host gave me an incredulous look.

'YOU GOTTA BE KIDDING! THIS IS THE THIRD RICHEST MAN IN HAWAII!'

Everyone on the casino staff is on the make. It's one of those things about Las Vegas which one senses even on a first visit, is irritated by, and then comes to take for granted. The doorman, the bell captain, the cocktail waitresses, the dealers – it's not that they have their hands out (well, they do in many cases) it's rather that it is expected. As a consequence, wages are low for many staff, which makes them still more predatory for tips, or tokes as they are called. The visitor not only has to gamble all his money away at the tables to support the industry, he is more or less required to top up the wages bill. At the high stakes tables, big players tip in proportionate amounts – hence the eagerness of dealers to work at the richer casinos like Caesars. Some of the baccarat crews are paid entirely on tokes, rather than salaries. On the other hand, some services remain cheap, notably valet parking at a dollar a time.

This eternal chase after spondulicks is not confined to the dealers and waitresses, the other ranks. The officer class, the managers and pit bosses, is just as bad, in the sense that if the table is down, if the shift registers an abnormally low hold, everyone is aware of it, and feels jumpy; and if it happens two or three times in a row, everyone is damn nervous. What's happening? Why are we losing? HELP!

The management will try anything – prayers, lucky charms, curses, changing the dice or the cards or the tables, switching the staff around, *anything* to put a crimp in the laws of probability. In the last resort, the Las Vegas Hilton dismissed an entire blackjack crew – a decision which cost them several million dollars in compensation to the dealers who sued the casino for wrongful dismissal.

All those millions upon millions of visitors can't be wrong, all of them, can they? Why do so many people return to Las Vegas year after year? It must be, can only be – the truism is worth repeating – that they like to gamble. All the other reasons – tourism, conventions, trade shows, entertainment, sports, sex – are so much flim-flam around the edges. These things have their appeal, indeed they do, and Las Vegas has made huge efforts to present itself as a resort, a centre of family entertainment, which certainly attracts new people who otherwise would not gamble.

But how many of the millions of visitors and tourists keep their hands in their pockets as they pass by the tables and the slots, as they must do many times every day during their stay? Not very many. The average gambling budget in 1988 was $389, with 7 per cent of people allocating over $1,000 for gambling. According to a study in 1991, the average Las Vegas visitor is a Californian male, age forty-seven, who earns between $20,000 and $40,000 a year. He drives to Vegas, stays three nights, has a non-gambling budget of $356 and a gambling budget of $533 used mostly for play in quarter slot machines.*

Gambling, more precisely risk-taking, is a basic human instinct. Las Vegas gratifies it in abundance. So do other places,

*Visitor Profile Study by Las Vegas Convention and Visitors Authority.

like Reno, which became a tourist centre in the 1920s, or Atlantic City which did not see its first casino open until 1978. Reno in the north of the state, has grown in a haphazard way, and failed to exploit the opportunity it had of becoming a destination resort. It has long been outshone by Vegas. Atlantic City, though it serves a huge population area, has remained, so far, a day-trippers' place. In Europe, there is London, Cannes, Monte Carlo, all of which have their following. But for round the clock action there is only one place to go.

There are an awful lot of ways to lose money in Vegas. On 1 January 1990 the total number of slot machines was about 86,000, as follows: 102 penny slot machines, 16,388 nickel slots, 537 dime slots, 49,559 quarter slots, 754 fifty cent slots and 17,545 dollar slots. Above that level, there were 696 $5 slots, 114 $25 slots, 17 $100 slots and 4 $500 slots, plus 273 Megabucks outlets (see p. 191). At that time there were also 1,875 blackjack tables, 267 craps tables, 163 roulette wheels, 75 keno games and 39 wheels of fortune.

One statistic says it all. Twenty years ago, in 1970, the casinos' gross gaming winnings (which means the net amount of money lost by the punters) in Clark County, the area of Las Vegas, was $369m. This figure has risen every year, often by double-digit percentages. It hit the $1,000m. mark in 1977, $2,000m. in 1984 (now including Laughlin at the southern tip of the county) and $3,000m. in 1988. Is there any business which can even approach that record in the whole of the United States? The figure for the casinos' gross winnings in 1990 was over $4,000m. At this rate of progress it will be close to $5,000m. in a year or two, and could easily top that by the middle of this decade.

Such expansion can't go on for ever, can it? One day, presumably, Las Vegas will peak. All one can say is that there is no sign of it yet. On the contrary, the place has been expanding at the start of the new decade with unprecedented vigour. Nine of the ten largest resort hotels *in the world* are within screaming distance of each other on the Strip. Following the recent spate of expansion (during which time the figure changed from month to month according to which new extension or tower block was completed) the pecking order has now stabilised as follows: the Excalibur 4,032 rooms, the Flamingo Hilton 3,530, the Las Vegas Hilton 3,174, the Mirage 3,049, Bally's 2,832, Circus Circus 2,793, the Imperial Palace, 2,637, the Stardust 2,500 and the Riviera 2,273. On a rule of thumb that each hotel room requires 1.6 employees, the 11,795 rooms added in 1990 meant jobs for nearly 19,000 people. Provided, in turn, that sufficient numbers of suitable workers could be found. The pressure on the labour market is intense: but the unions in this town, whose workforce comprises so many individuals hoping to get lucky, moving in and out of jobs, have never cut much ice. Only once were the hotels nearly brought to a standstill, in the culinary union strike of 1984.

The pleasure of gambling is many things, but primarily it is a way of paying to enter a super-charged mood of excitement. After all, some people do win. Everyone has heard of big winners, million dollar jackpots, fortunes won as well as lost. You see it and hear it all around you, as you venture your own little pile of gaming chips across the baize. So why not you?

The gamblers who enter this pleasuredome are beguiled. Sometimes Lady Luck smiles on them but when most in need she turns her back. She is not merely fickle, she is not even in charge! Behind her stands an impersonal force, which answers to no name. Probability is inexorable, impervious to either blandishments or threats. Probability does not bestow favours, it embodies mathematical laws. Assuming that everyone who comes to Vegas can read and write (though Benny Binion who founded Binion's Horseshoe could not) they all know the odds, near enough. Yet most of the time everybody deliberately ignores them.

Why? Because the thrill of it all is the true pay off. Win or lose, everyone feels the thrill. Vegas' success, the millions of visitors, is attributable first and foremost to the town's comprehensive indulgence of this basic human desire to gamble, against the odds, and its dedication to stimulating and gratifying it, one hundred and one per cent. Here there are no doubts, moral reservations, second thoughts. The casinos, in any case, do their utmost to speed up the process, with their hypnotic mix of light, noise, alcohol and day-into-night, night-into-day indulgence, to infuse in the gamblers and vacationers a hazy, dazy sense of letting go . . . But like the law of gravity, the laws of probability are always present.

How does Las Vegas get away with it? It is a thought which crosses many people's minds. Moments of sombre reflection do occur, surprisingly enough, during a three-day gambling trip. Such experiences tend to come after a self-destructive session at the tables, as the luckless player heads back to a hotel room which, all of a sudden, looks awfully expensive, despite its cut-rate price. Las Vegas is a place to get away from it all, but it is also a place where one is assailed by disturbing thoughts about what one is doing there, in a fundamental way. Losing seems to induce a state of mind which prompts introspection and the exchange of deep confidences with other comrades in misfortune. This self-questioning is an inevitable side-effect of playing with chance, of exposing oneself to these stomach-churning reversals of fortune. One feels things more intensely in Las Vegas.

In this book I have sought to explain Las Vegas' unique success. I describe the most flamboyant operator in town, and the biggest enterprises to date in the opening chapters, and go on to survey other aspects of the gambling capital which have intrigued me. I do not claim to have found all the answers, because there is more to Las Vegas, no doubt about it, than any individual can uncover. Win some, lose some, as they say. In the end, Las Vegas itself is always going to wind up the winner.

I
Men
&
Casinos

1 MIRAGE MAKER

If you wanna make money
in a casino, own one.

Steve Wynn

If any one man can be said to have created modern Las Vegas, in
the sense of showing the way ahead, it is Steve Wynn. He has a
clear, individual view, a vision if you like, of gambling. And he is
ready to take big risks in realising it.

He did it first at the Golden Nugget downtown, transforming a
sleazy gambling hall in Glitter Gulch into a sophisticated hotel-
casino for high rollers. He did it again, in a flanking movement,
when he replicated the Golden Nugget out east, in Atlantic City.
And he set out to do it a third time, on a super-colossal scale, by
constructing the Mirage, centre-stage on the Strip, at a start-up
cost of $620m., and rising. This was the man once accused by
Donald Trump, in a dismissive aside, of being a classic under-
achiever.

Wynn is still in the middle of this latest and biggest gamble, to
make the Mirage pay. To do so, he needed to generate a 'nut', as
the net profit on a casino is called, of a million dollars a day, and
probably a bit more, every day of the year, just to pay the costs
and interest charges. In the first year of its operation, the Mirage
has proved that this feat – which far surpasses any other casino's
record – can be done. In its first full year, the Mirage's gaming

revenues exceeded $409m. and its hotel and other income $251m.
But, as Wynn puts it, running the Mirage is like driving a high-
powered racing car at top speed: fantastically exciting, but
another bend in the track is always rushing up to meet you.

Wynn is a showman first and a businessman second, a showman
who likes to dazzle with his extravagance, to show off, to make the
seemingly impossible happen. Like his first big coup playing, if
you please, Howard Hughes.

Back in 1971 when he was thirty and just another bright young
guy making his way in Vegas, Wynn was trying to run a liquor
distribution business. One way or another it got into difficulties.
Bob Maxey, then a senior executive of a finance company, recalls
his first meeting with Wynn. A young fellow burst into his office,
in sports shirt and tennis shorts, without an appointment, and
started jumping all over the place shouting: 'I need help! You
gotta help me!' Maxey did help. He later became one of Wynn's
partners: he worked with him on the launch of his casino in
Atlantic City and then collaborated in the opening of the Mirage.
Wynn had no wish to dally with the liquor business. From the
start, he was fired by the ambition to get into casinos. His big
chance came with a property deal.

If there was one thing everyone knew about Howard Hughes it
was that he didn't sell property; the elusive multimillionaire
bought up everything in sight, and never sold to anyone. Wynn
persuaded him. It happened this way: While looking for a bigger
house for his wife Elaine and two baby daughters, he met a real
estate associate of Hughes, Herb Nall, and got talking. Wynn had
his eye on another piece of property, a parking lot which Hughes
owned next to Caesars. He asked Nall what Hughes intended to
do with it. Wynn knew that Hughes had refused every offer made
by Caesars, but an intriguing piece of inside information had
come his way – namely, that Hughes was renting another parking
lot, at $10,000 a month, next to the Landmark, a casino which he
had rescued from bankruptcy. Yet Hughes was only getting

$1,000 a month rent from the lot next to Caesars, which Wynn estimated had cost him $1m.

It was a narrow, awkward piece of real estate, with power lines down its full length, which meant there was very little space to build. Wynn asked Hughes's agent if they would sell it, and offered a million for it. He knew it was worth much more than that, but Herb Nall had inadvertently let slip another useful bit of information: that the property had originally been acquired for Hughes by the previous management team, now out of favour and out of their jobs, in one of Hughes's periodic blood-lettings. 'Steve, if you've got a million dollars, enjoy yourself,' Nall told him. 'This man doesn't sell, he buys. Been with him for twenty-three years, he's never sold anything.'

Still, Wynn asked him to make an offer to Hughes, who was then living in the Bahamas. He made the point that if Hughes had paid $1m. for the Caesars' lot, that meant it was worth $80,000 or $90,000 a year at current interest rates; yet they were only getting $12,000 from Caesars, so they were losing between $70,000 and $80,000. At the same time, Hughes was paying $120,000 a year to lease the lot at the Landmark. By taking Wynn's offer, they could buy the Landmark parking lot, saving the rent. 'It's a big pick-up,' so Wynn claimed. 'Instead of losing 6 per cent on your money, you'll make 12 per cent.' (Even multimillionaires, perhaps especially multimillionaires, count the pennies.) 'Don't hold your breath,' Nall told him, 'you'll turn purple.'

Ten days later, the Las Vegas *Sun* blazoned the news on the front page that Kirk Kerkorian was going to buy the Bonanza, a derelict casino opposite Caesars, and build the world's biggest hotel there, to be renamed the MGM Grand. Whoops! thought Wynn, there goes the corner lot at Caesars. He had thought it was worth a million and a half when he bid for it, now it must be worth at least two million, and Hughes would never sell. But come Sunday afternoon, Wynn was sitting around at home when a call came from Hughes' estate agent. 'If I'm with this guy another twenty years,' Nall said, 'I won't understand him. I'm instructed under certain circumstances, strict circumstances, to sell you the corner.' Hughes wanted a million one, in order to show a profit on his original purchase. Cash. Wynn agreed. What next? he asked.

'The second condition – you better listen to this real good. They don't want you to talk about it. They don't want any publicity. And to make sure you don't, there's no preliminary agreement, just a meeting and an exchange of cash for the deed.' Is that it? Wynn asked. That was it, the agent confirmed, and asked when he wanted to do the deal. Wynn suggested the coming Friday at two p.m., before Thanksgiving. He hung up and danced about the house in glee. Then he called his banker, whose response was brief: 'Thata' boy,' he said. They met as arranged, Wynn handed over a cashier's cheque and was given the deed, which he registered at the county clerk's office and put in his safe-deposit box. He then caught a plane to Denver for a weekend's skiing with his family. After breakfast on Sunday morning, in the ski shop at Aspen, a fellow looked up from reading the Denver *Post* and asked Wynn, 'What are you going to do with the parking lot?' *What?* Wynn looked around the ski shop as if this was a joke. He hadn't even told his secretary about the deal. But there it was: 'Hughes Sells Las Vegas Strip Property to Liquor Owner.' It turned out that Hank Greenspun, the late editor of the Las Vegas *Sun*, kept a reporter on regular look-out at the county clerk's office in those days when there was so much property changing hands in Nevada, and they had picked up registry of the deed.

Overnight Wynn became a celebrity, a position which he revels in. 'Your first big deal,' as he later recalled, 'is the sweetest deal of your life.' Everyone was calling him, wanting to know if he knew Hughes, the man of mystery, and what was going on. The more he refused to talk, the more the speculation bubbled. For the next few months, hardly a day went by without an offer coming in for the Caesars' lot. After ten months – during which time Wynn had never had so much fun – giving Caesars the impression he was actually drawing up plans to build his own little casino right next door to them – he sold the lot to Caesars, for two and a quarter million. Two-thirds of the profit, $766,000, was his. The deal meant that Wynn now had the chance to get into the casino business as an operator.

The place he set his sights on was the Golden Nugget, in those days a hurdy-gurdy grind joint on the neon crossroads of Fremont Street in the heart of Glitter Gulch. It faced the grinning cowboy figure of Vegas Vic, outlined sixty feet high on the front of the Pioneer, winking down every five seconds, 'Howdy po'dner'. Wynn told his broker to buy shares in the Nugget every day he could. It was not long before he owned more stock than anyone else. He then took the precaution of getting licensed as a casino operator by the State of Nevada. Now he was a serious contender; he could stake a claim to a seat on the board. As he had suspected, the place was extremely inefficiently run: money was slipping through the cracks, and there was also a lot of cheating. A bar owner downtown, whom Wynn had once helped out, repaid the favour: he told Wynn that every morning around three or four a.m. a group of employees from the Nugget, dealers, floormen, shift bosses, met at the bar to divide up 'a ton of cash'; even the parking attendants were cheating on tickets. Eventually 16 casino supervisors were caught, and 160 employees lost their jobs. Even today, with all his responsibilities, Wynn sees red if he finds so much as a pair of sheets has gone missing, instituting maniacal searches and counts of the entire laundry stock.

After a couple of weeks' investigation of the state of play at the Nugget, Wynn went to Buck Blaine, the sixty-three-year-old President, and told him and the people running the place: 'Look, we've been friends, and we've known each other a long time. There is no reason to argue and fight . . . I've got 170,000 shares of stock out of one million eight . . . I've got 10 per cent of the company, and what's more, I speak for another 20 per cent.' This was July, and the next stockholders' meeting was not until the following May. 'I'm going to make a lot of fuss about what's being done here and then we're going to have a big fight and nobody's going to come out on top. But why don't you just let me take a crack at running it now and we can do it real nice?' Bucky, sitting in his presidential chair, just caved in. With the backing of influential friends, like the banker who had underwritten his parking lot bid, the Nugget's board was rapidly prevailed upon to see it Wynn's way. He was elected vice-president in June 1973; a special board meeting was called; almost everyone stepped down. Wynn appointed his own directors in their place and was himself elected chairman, president and chief executive (he is not a man to do things by halves) just forty-five days after he moved in.

At the end of his first year the Nugget's profits, which had been a meagre million pre-tax on assets of $18–20m., had risen to $4.25m., on an 8 per cent increase in revenue. After construction of a 579 room hotel tower in 1977, the Golden Nugget's profits rose to $12m.

So how did Wynn turn the Golden Nugget around so fast? It so happened that he knew something about casinos, from the inside. As a ten year old, back in 1952, Stephen had been brought to Las Vegas by his father Michael, who had got a job running a modest bingo parlour at the Silver Slipper. The young boy stared at the star-spangled showgirls and the cocktail waitresses, breathed in the western mystique, and thought to himself . . . *what a town!* There was magic in the place. Unfortunately, Poppa had got it bad for the dice. He used to sneak out, after putting his son to bed, and gamble away at the craps tables all the profits he had earned from managing the bingo. In fact he would bet on anything that moved. A rival bingo parlour had been opened by a popular gambling hall with more money – that place happened to be the Golden Nugget. Within a few weeks, father and son were hitting the road, broke, back to Maryland.

'When you see a person crumble and lose his self-confidence, it's a very horrible experience,' Wynn recalls. 'But one thing my father's gambling did was to show me, at a very early age, that if

you wanna make money in a casino . . . the answer is to own one.'
Wynn attended a military academy near Syracuse, and in 1959
entered the University of Pennsylvania; originally he had ideas of
becoming a doctor, but switched to English Literature. He also
attended classes at the Wharton School of Business. There he met
Elaine Pascal (a former Miss Miami Beach) whose father likewise
had a taste for gambling – he happened to be Michael Wynn's
partner at pinochle. Their first date, accompanied by both sets of
parents, was a spree to a jai alai game in Miami. 'What attracted
me to Steve? It was his intelligence. I don't mean street smart, but
a kind of serious approach,' Elaine says. 'I knew right away he was
someone special.'

Today the couple have an affectionate but curious relationship.
They were divorced (the decision was said to have been taken for
financial as much as amorous reasons), but still shared the same
home; Steve just never got around to moving out, an aide
explains. Then they remarried, quietly. Elaine has played a close
part in running the Golden Nugget, where the gourmet restaurant bears her name. At the Mirage, where her office is next
to Steve's, she has a free-wheeling role, like a minister without
portfolio. She is a director of the board of Golden Nugget Inc,
the main company. 'Steve is a brute forcer,' says Elaine. 'He
takes everything on his shoulders and barges down the hall. He
can be spoiled and petulant. If you don't stop what you're doing
and drop everything and do what he wants, he can get testy.'

In his senior year at university Steve flew back nearly every
Sunday to Washington, to help his father run his bingo parlour in
rural Maryland. 'Since the day I took my first breath I have been a
kid who has never had a meal, a dollar for tuition or a piece of
clothing on my back that didn't come from gambling.' Michael
Wynn died suddenly in 1963 and Steve took the business over on
his graduation a month later. It was a great blow to Wynn; his
father (born Weinberg) is still a hero to him. If Steve could have
one wish it would have been to take his Dad through the Golden
Nugget, the place that busted his old bingo parlour, to show him

that everything had worked out OK. The bingo parlour proved a
successful venture under new management: as one report put it,
Steve called the numbers, Elaine counted the money – they were
married a month after completing university. 'We did not have
the luxury of choosing a career,' Elaine says. 'We just had to pitch
in.' Wynn ran the bingo for three or four years; his income rose
substantially. But he had been dazzled by the stardust of Las
Vegas and in 1967 he moved his family out there.

As so often happens in gambling, Wynn's shining hopes
quickly turned to dust. He joined a small casino called the
Frontier, which turned out to have hidden mafia ownership.
According to a Federal investigation, casino profits were being
funnelled to a mob family in Detroit. Though unaware of this
connection, Wynn lost his investment and his job. But through
this involvement, he met the man who was to change the course of
his life, E. Parry Thomas, principal banker to Howard Hughes,
with close connections to the Teamsters. 'I've got to see that this
community stays healthy. I'll take dollars from the devil himself if
it's legal,' Thomas, himself a Mormon, was quoted in the local
press, 'and I don't mean anything disparaging toward the
Teamsters by that.' A mover and fixer, a keeper of secrets, a man
who knew the good fellas and the bad fellas behind the green
baize, a banker – this was the point – who wasn't afraid of making
loans to the gambling industry, Thomas was the power broker of
Las Vegas at that time. Through bankrolling casinos and hotels,
he had become enormously wealthy. And he evidently marked
down the ambitious young Wynn as a good risk. Thomas it was
who got Wynn his job as a liquor supplier, Thomas it was who
backed him in the crucial parking lot acquisition, as described
above, and who helped secure the deal, and Thomas it was who
propelled him, immediately after that, in his lightning strike to
seize control of the Golden Nugget. Thomas had the know-how,
Wynn had the flair. He was the father figure Wynn needed.

In 1978 Wynn took another big step, buying into Atlantic City.
While visiting Resorts International, then the only casino in

town, he was bowled over by the crowds of players, surging five-deep round the tables. 'I had never seen anything like it,' Wynn said. 'It made Caesars Palace on New Year's Eve look like it was closed for lunch.' As the story goes, he walked over in sandals, shorts and Willie Nelson T-shirt to the Strand Motel on the boardwalk and offered the owner $8.5m. for the property. Twenty minutes later the deal was done. Up went the Golden Nugget in Atlantic City, a 506-room hotel-casino, at a cost of $140m. It opened in December 1980 and was profitable from the start. Wynn gave it his designer touch, in the style of the Nugget in Las Vegas: vaulted, mirrored ceilings and mirrored walls; crystal chandeliers, stained glass and marble pillars; even gold-tinted slot machines. In short, the imprint of luxury. 'We perceived that the East Coast experience was basically a gray one,' said Wynn. 'If Atlantic City was ever going to be exciting and successful it was going to be because . . . it offered the people a big dose of color.' And in a town where most of the gambling was tacky and tawdry, the Nugget had class.

In a comment which expresses the heart of Wynn's thinking, he observed: To a certain extent, every facility reflects what management thinks its customers want and are. These tacky, unexciting, unimaginative places are a representation that these decisions were left to people who were ill-equipped to understand the relationship between design and ambiance, and the customer's emotional and psychological needs. When a person is in a nice place, he feels complimented.' It took Wynn several months to get his New Jersey casino licence in 1981, but after he took charge, the earnings soared. One venture that did not pay off was his acquisition of a leasehold on a London hotel. The British Gaming Board, ever wary of foreign ownership, refused to grant him a licence, making it painfully clear that he was not the kind of chap, actually, one would welcome to one's club.

Another man who took a look at Atlantic City around the mid-1970s was Donald Trump. Trump's rivalry with Wynn explains a great deal about the modern casino business. It was a matter of personalities as much as properties. The thought of going into casinos first occurred to him, so Trump recalls in his auto-biography *The Art of the Deal*, when he heard on his car radio that Hilton stock was plummetting because of a strike in its two casinos in Las Vegas. Although Hilton owned 150 hotels worldwide, these two properties accounted for more than 40 per cent of the company's net profits. At that time he was wrestling with planning approval for a new hotel in New York: even if he got the hotel built, Trump realised, it still would not be nearly as profitable as a moderately successful hotel-casino in a small desert town in the south-west. Trump looked around Atlantic City, but decided to wait for the referendum on gambling. As soon as gambling was approved, however, land values soared, so he waited a while longer. It was not until late in 1980 that he found the site which – after multifarious negotiations, including partner-ship and then a public split with Holiday Inn – eventually turned into Trump Plaza. Despite one or two problems with the licensing authorities, Trump claimed that after he took over the enterprise, profits soared, from a projected $38m. to $58m. in 1986. Trump Plaza, he declared, would make substantially more money than the top ten office buildings in New York, combined.

At that time the casinos on the boardwalk – the boardwalk being that tatty, salt-water stretch of gimcrack souvenir stores and down-at-heel snack bars which fronts the beach – were regaled as a flock of golden geese, roosting along the New Jersey shore. Encouraged by his early success, Trump succeeded in cutting a deal with Barron Hilton in April 1985, to buy the property designated to become the Hilton casino on the marina. The Hilton group had been refused a licence and lost its way. Purchase of the Hilton casino, which cost $320m., was especially sweet to Trump, because he got the better of Wynn, who was trying to buy the entire Hilton chain. Dubbing his victory 'Wynn-Fall', Trump summed up his rival as follows: 'He's got a great act. He's a smooth talker, he's perfectly manicured, and he's invariably dressed to kill in $2,000 suits and $200 silk shirts. The problem with Wynn is that he tries too hard to look perfect and a lot of people are put off by him.'

The new purchase was made almost entirely on gut feeling, so Trump claimed afterwards, because when he made his bid he had never even walked through the hotel. The place was immediately re-named Trump Castle. (But Wynn refused to sell him a 26-acre site he owned next door.) Instead of hiring a manager from inside the industry, Trump put his wife Ivana in charge. The 'nut' or gross gaming revenue on the first day of operation was $728,000. Inevitably, given Trump's abrasive style, a dispute arose with Hilton, over costs. But apart from that, boasted Trump, the story (back then) was almost entirely positive. In words which were later to rebound with a vengeance, Trump declared: 'Much of the credit has to go to Ivana. No detail escapes her . . . great management pays off . . . It pays to trust your instincts.' Ivana was a firebrand as manager, sharp on costs and inventory, but rather too sharp with people; she later moved to the Plaza hotel in New York. Trump, however, had no experience of casinos. He had made his fortune in real estate in New York. He came to Atlantic City as an outsider, attracted to casinos simply and solely by their amazing cash flow, which made real estate look so slow. He made some costly mistakes, as he was bound to do, for instance not building an underground garage at Trump Plaza, which was essential for customer flow. Only after three years of losses did he finally act to put in parking, at a cost of $28m.

Wynn, on the other hand, knew casinos inside out. The top performer in Atlantic City, in terms of gross revenue, month after month, was the Golden Nugget. It had become the hottest property in town, out-performing Resorts with only two-thirds of the latter's floor space. Wynn was becoming recognised not merely as a flamboyant operator – the gimmick of presenting new cars to his casinos managers, all 377 of them, attracted nationwide publicity – but the rising star of the gaming industry. To promote the Nugget in Atlantic City he cast himself in a series of humorous ads on TV, alongside Frank Sinatra. In a typical scene, Sinatra was shown strolling through an elegant suite at the hotel. Mistaking Wynn for the valet, he stuffs a ten dollar bill into the chairman's palm, telling him to make sure he has enough towels. An incredulous Wynn turns full face to the camera: *'Towels?'* Unfortunately, ol' blue eyes had a flaming row at the blackjack table. The dealer, an oriental girl, obviously terrified out of her wits, refused to deal the cards from a single deck as Sinatra vociferously demanded, because it was against house rules, and insisted she had to deal from the shoe. After incurring the censure of the New Jersey Gaming Control Board, the casino was fined $25,000, and Sinatra was chastised for his boorish behaviour. He vowed never to perform again in a State which, so he felt, did not appreciate his special talents.

Wynn quite clearly was number one; he was the man to beat if, as Trump did, you react solely in terms of personal rivalry. This feeling ran deep: it explained the little jibes about Wynn, which the Donald (as Ivana liked to call him) chose to vent from time to time. He accused Wynn of being a carpet-bagger, who took money out of Atlantic City and spent it in the south-west; while down on his yacht, Trump would demand of his guests: 'It was never like this at Steve's, was it?' In reality, it was a one-sided challenge, because Wynn never saw Trump as a rival: that isn't the way he views the casino game. 'There's only one way to make money,' Wynn believes, 'and that's to work hard at your own business.' Trump invited Wynn to a showy lunch in New York, with singer Diana Ross as a trophy, but the occasion was a disaster.

The expansion of casinos made Atlantic City hard going. The central question was (and still is): Why would anyone go there? Most of the visitors to Atlantic City are day trippers and 'bus people', a high proportion of whom are senior citizens eking out low incomes. The place which looked so good on the map, so close to the great centres of population in the east, has never measured up to Vegas, which is a destination resort. Meanwhile the results at Trump Castle have gone from discouraging to terrible: from a peak of $3.8m. in 1986, income fell by over a half the following year, and showed a loss in '88 and '89. In 1990 the result was worse still: the Castle lost over $43m. in the year to March '91. In the general gloom which descended over Atlantic City, the Plaza was hit too, losing $10.5.

At the same time, Trump hankered after a property in Vegas, if the right opening should ever come up. He opened a Trump Nevada office downtown and appointed a former chairman of the Nevada Gaming Control Board to run it. Despite a succession of rumours in the press, Trump did not manage to get in. In mid-1987 he claimed he owned 4.9 per cent of Golden Nugget stock – given to exaggeration, as Trump always was, the true figure was thought to be substantially less. Perhaps he wanted to get a stake in the Nugget, if he could, perhaps he just wanted to rile Wynn. In any case, it gave him considerable leverage in the media as a prospective player. Wynn, meanwhile, maintained that the company was not for sale and never had been. 'There is more than money involved here, you've got two gigantic egos on the line,' a financial analyst commented on this episode. When Wynn acquired the 80-acre lot on the Las Vegas Strip – the vast stretch of wasteland out of which the Mirage was destined to arise – Trump, who also coveted it, lost out again. Wynn paid $57m. for it (a man who knows what he wants and goes for it, he also paid off a couple of motel operators to acquire the sole right to the name 'Mirage'). Trump proposed that they develop the site jointly, but again Wynn turned him down.

This rebuff, coming on top of everything else, was perhaps the turning point. It was certainly significant in hardening Trump's commitment to Atlantic City, and it helps explain his ambition to build something bigger and bolder and brasher than anyone else. From hostility, his attitude towards Wynn turned into a kind of long-distance admiration: Trump out East, Wynn out West, leaders of the industry. Wynn did not see himself in that role, in fact he went out of his way to mollify Trump. When Donald and Ivana flew into town, needing somewhere to stay, the Wynns responded by offering them a suite at the Golden Nugget. And when Trump called up (he rang not once but a dozen times) to ensure that he was seated as befit his status at a world heavyweight boxing match, Wynn deliberately sat him in front of himself – in this glamorous gathering of star names and high rollers that was a tribute to die for.

By this time Wynn was off and running in another direction. In the mid-'80s, he took a fresh look at the Golden Nugget in downtown Las Vegas, and came to a typically idiosyncratic decision: he decided to take the place up-market, despite its location in the middle of Glitter Gulch. His plan was to transform the Nugget into an elegant resort hotel, to rival the palaces on the Strip. In a top to bottom refurbishment of the property, all the neon and glitter and exterior signs were swept clean away. Not even the name of the place was left over the entrance. 'If they don't know who we are, they shouldn't be here!' was Wynn's attitude. The result was a cream and green skyscraper, built around a palm-fringed pool, a sleek oasis in the urban blight of downtown. But to bring in the high rollers, he also had to change the reputation of the place, which was not one of high stakes and conspicuous consumption. How did he do it?

If there is one individual who personifies style in Las Vegas, it is Frank Sinatra. Wynn made Sinatra the kind of offer, to lure him away from Caesars, which even he couldn't refuse – $10m. for three years, plus handsome stock options. The aim was to entice the high rollers down to the Nugget by trailing the aroma of luxury under their opulent noses. The appearance of Sinatra, even for people who know Las Vegas well, is a tremendous draw. His presence means, or has meant these many years past, the patina of high action gilding the casino floor. No matter that Sinatra was well over the hill and couldn't always hit the high notes and seemed to have a puffy orange hue under the spotlights. Everyone from out of town wants to see him and hear him. A crowd of acolytes and big spenders hang around Sinatra, who often gambled for high stakes himself. When the performance in the show room ends, and the audience streams out straight into the gaming tables, as it has to, there being no other exit, it is ready to go wild. The whole atmosphere is charged up like an electric storm. As part of the upgrading of the Nugget, Wynn also poached top personnel from rival casinos: dependent as good casinos are on the personal touch, hiring the right staff is crucial. That lesson he learned from his first experience with the Nugget.

Wynn went further than bringing in Sinatra and other entertainers like Diana Ross, Kenny Rogers and Willie Nelson, simply to perform. 'One day I had this idea,' he explained. 'Suppose I could sell discriminating people the idea of being involved in an atmosphere almost like a concert in the East Room of the White House – like a private show with Frank Sinatra . . . And suppose as part of the weekend, these people could meet him. And we had special parties, and we did the whole weekend, and the show was only part of that weekend . . .' Wynn talked to Sinatra's people about the idea of the star being a kind of host, and he agreed. He did it a dozen times: it made a change from sitting in his suite all day doing the crossword puzzle. 'Come for a special weekend – a theme party at the Nugget,' as Wynn put it. 'Have a cocktail party in Dallas, and say: Steve Wynn and Frank Sinatra request the presence of your company. See if anybody comes! Try it with Diana Ross and see if it works. In Dallas, the Hunts showed up.'

Wynn's image as a celebrity in his own right, partly thanks to his TV commercials alongside Sinatra, was not undeserved. I recall an annual general meeting in the ballroom of the Golden Nugget in Vegas at which Wynn took the floor for over an hour. He set out the results, he analysed the figures, he responded to shareholders' questions, displaying the kind of sassy humour that a stand-up comic employs while improvising before an audience at a dinner show. Radiating confidence like a sun lamp, Wynn clearly loved every moment of it. As he roamed up and down the aisles with his portable microphone, some six or seven directors of the group, including Elaine, sat in a line on stage behind him; not one of them was required to say a word. Sinatra himself could hardly have put on a better show.

Wynn has a handicap, which he bears with courage. He suffers from an incurable, degenerative eye disease called retinitis pigmentosa, diagnosed twenty years ago. He sees well enough in daylight, but his field of vision is slowly narrowing. In casino lighting he is sometimes in difficulties and needs a helping hand. 'He's fine, for the most part,' says Elaine. 'His condition is stable. It's only if someone holds out a hand to shake hands, he doesn't see it because it's too low, that you get an awkward moment.' The failure rate is different for each individual: in the worst case, Wynn risks losing his sight completely.

Meanwhile Wynn had packed his bags and fled Atlantic City. It looked like good judgement, getting out while the going was good. In fact it had nothing to do with expertise at all, he admits, it was just good luck. He saw that Atlantic City was facing a rocky period, with new casinos stepping up the competition for what was essentially a 'service-the-day' market. What's more the civic administration was ludicrously under-powered, and beset by a succession of venal mayors: despite much fine talk, and vast taxes paid by the casinos, nothing was done to improve its housing, its streets or its amenities. One of the major casino groups, Bally – half-scared out of their wits by Trump, who was buying up their stock and threatening an unfriendly take over – made a huge bid for the Nugget. Bally paid a high price for the property, $440m. The idea was to take on so much debt that Trump could not afford to pursue his bid. The Nugget was worth perhaps half that much, given a realistic view of Atlantic City's prospects and the regulatory constraints of the market; or it might have been worth it, if the magic ingredient of Wynn's management flair had been included in the deal. Without that it was just another big pile on the boardwalk. At the same time he sold his land out on the marina to Kirk Kerkorian, resisting any temptation to build a second hotel.

If he were to do it all over again, Wynn reflected, reviewing his original decision to go into Atlantic City, he would design a different kind of building. 'First of all I've got more money. In 1978, I had to design what I could afford. We could afford to do a project now that's correct, regardless of its cost, so long as it's got a good return on its investment.' The question, as he sees it, is whether by building better facilities, the market itself can be changed: on the one hand, buildings are passive, they cater to the business that is there; on the other hand, the buildings do have a significant impact on the customers. He had had a dress rehearsal, in transforming the Golden Nugget in Las Vegas; the real test would come with his next venture. The sale of the Atlantic City property provided the cash for his dream-project, this new challenge, which was dramatically to upstage everything he had done before.

'It's what God would've done,' Wynn liked to quip to chamber of commerce audiences, enthusing about the construction of the Mirage, 'if He'd had the money.' A good one-liner, because the money was big. The $30m. Wynn spent on the volcano – 'the only volcano in Nevada!' – in front of the Mirage was more than Caesars Palace next door had spent on its entire construction. 'If one of my people wants to spent $10m. or maybe $20m. more, to get something right, I wouldn't even hesitate,' Wynn would boast. As he explained, there were two types of casino: cost-driven, like Circus Circus, where the whole effort was directed towards saving expenses; and revenue-driven, where the idea was to generate income, and the hell with the cost. Counting the millions has never bothered him. 'What do you do when you owe the bank $500m. and on the first of the month you can't meet the interest charges?' Wynn would demand, pausing theatrically before answering himself in triumph: 'Absolutely nothing!' The Mirage cost around $620m. to open, and that of course was only the initial cost. Additions in the first year took it up to $700m. Costs will go on rising as other changes are made – it's a living process.

The whole town was agog, after three years of hype, to see what the Mirage would be like. The opening on 22 November 1989, was staged, deliberately, as a local affair, a unique occasion in Las Vegas' merry, tinsel life when the town looked in on itself. And it was a day which lived up to its advance billing. I arrived early that morning, to be greeted by a shoal of pretty girls darting about the hotel check-in counter like tropical fish against the blue-green aquarium, which ran along the back wall. A three-foot tiger shark, mottled in grey and black, swam up and down, oblivious of the special role assigned to it in this scheme of creation. Hotel guests would henceforth have something to look at while waiting in line to register. The press had already been given a conducted tour over the 3,000 square feet of floor space on 'play day', a dress rehearsal the previous day. We had even been issued with 'play' money, like monopoly dollars, for trying out the gaming tables. Now, a day later, these brief hours before the public crossed the threshold were the first and probably the only time that the interior of the Mirage would be empty and hushed, apart from men on high ladders adjusting spotlights and workmen adding a last dash of paint or plaster. On the street outside, crowds were lining up behind security guards, hours before the official opening at noon. The new parking lots were overflowing, casino staff had to pick their way through, the sense of expectancy was crackling.

In the basic Y-shape of three towers, 30 storeys high, in white and gold, the hotel complex contained 3,044 suites and rooms. No less important, for its immediate impact, was the lighting, designed by David Hersey, the man who lit *Cats* and *Les Misérables*. 'We've got enough lighting out front,' he revealed, 'to light three Broadway shows.' First there was the volcano, and the lagoon around it. To prevent any noisome odour from the tongues of fire, which were to erupt at fifteen-minute intervals into the night sky, the volcano had been impregnated with the scent of pina colada. (In reality the volcano was only a waterfall with fire and lighting effects: it should have been more dramatic, higher and larger, according to architectural critics.) Then there

was the causeway over the water to the porte-cochère; immediately beyond the foyer, with its sea-green aquarium, guests
were cocooned in a tropical rain forest. Like a green screen,
steamy and wet with spray, trees festooned with orchids and
creepers, the foliage curved around the path, inside a 90-foot high
glass atrium. The tropical motif was inspired by the famous resort
hotel in the shape of a pyramid, the Princess in Acapulco.

What a way to enter a casino – it was like stepping through a green
looking glass into a realm of make-believe. For what emerged after
the forest was the whole casino floor, glowing light-and-dark, with
its 2,250 slots and 118 tables, its 9 restaurants, its multi-screen
sports book like a computer bank for a space-launch, its ballrooms,
convention centre, shopping arcade, health club. The cleverest
aspect of the design was that each section of the casino floor, opening
out from red pathways curving across and around, had a sense of
intimacy, of its own locale, despite the vast space. Slatted wooden
ceilings, suspended below the casino lights, brought the gambling
down to a human scale.

Let there be gambling! After all, no one had ever opened a
casino of this super-colossal size before – *snap!* – just like that;
casinos tend to grow gradually, from small beginnings, extending
their floor space out of cash flow, budgeting for expansion step by
step. The Mirage sprang to life fully grown, all of a piece, it hit the
Las Vegas Strip at full tilt. The 7,500 staff (over-recruited by at
least 1,000 in order to shield customers from the rough edges of
the launch) had been practising running a full-scale hotel-casino
for three weeks, from serving breakfasts on the top floor down to
raking in the chips at the tables. The show room was not yet
ready, nor the swimming pool lagoon, with its islands and
waterfalls, nor the landscaping of the grounds – which would
include all in all over 3,000 exotic trees* – and the five bottlenose

---

*For the record: 460 canary palms, 614 washingtonia palms, 275 pine trees,
947 canopy trees including carob, photinia, cherry, lingustrum and sumac,
131 sago palms, 106 chamaerops, 213 trachycarpus, 26 pindo palms, 44
cordyline, plus thousands of shrubs. It would need an arborculturist to
identify them all.

dolphins were not due until next year. Nonetheless, the Mirage was ready to roll.

Wynn looked as svelte as an ad for aftershave, as befits a man with 32.8 per cent of the action. It was his day, but inwardly he was shaking. What if nobody showed up, after all this! He had woken in the night a bundle of nerves. Wynn had insisted from the start on a 'soft' opening, without national publicity, just in case. Elaine was there, trim in dark green, as were daughters Kevin (who was working for the company in marketing) and Gillian, both in their twenties, and Wynn's younger brother Kenny, director of the design and construction division. Wynn had met with the entire staff, in three separate meetings in the ballroom (seating for 3,000), during the preceding days, to tell them, with all the pzazz of a broadway producer: 'We got a beautiful building, sure. But it doesn't mean a thing without you. The Mirage is only going to be as good as the people who run it.' He must have dealt with a thousand queries in the week before. Now he seemed unhurried. It was all going to be put to the test of the real experts, the only people, as Wynn kept on saying, whose judgement really mattered: the customers.

'Fantasy becomes reality!' Wynn announced (it was the cliché of the day) in an opening ceremony staged outside the main entrance. He stood at the centre of a semicircle of employees – a bus boy, a chef in a white hat, a cocktail waitress, a keno runner in a miniskirt, a blackjack dealer in an apron, a security man in a green uniform, faces shining like the chorus line from an operetta. 'It started off as mine and Elaine's fantasy. I can remember clearly the moment in history when it took a giant leap towards becoming reality. It was the day I met Mike Milken. He saw the possibilities and the doors opened for us in the gaming industry . . . It is as much his fantasy as mine.' It was a surprising opening tribute. The inventor of junk bonds, Mike Milken, standing there with the Wynn family, was then facing myriad charges of larceny (and was later convicted). The Mirage was a shining exception to the rule, it was living proof that junk bonds could work.

The day that Wynn met Milken has been recorded in *The Predators' Ball*, a graphic account of the rise and fall of junk bonds by Connie Bruck. In order to build in Atlantic City, Wynn had needed to borrow $100m.: yet his Las Vegas casino, five years after he took control, was worth only about a tenth of that, with a minimal income. So how was it to be done? How could he borrow the kind of money he needed? There was only one guy who could do it, a friend told him. Wynn flew to New York and was introduced to a young kid wearing jeans, a plaid sports shirt and black loafers. The kid asked Wynn brief, terse questions about Atlantic City and for annual reports of the Golden Nugget. Then he gave his verdict: 'You think you need a hundred million. I think you need a hundred twenty-five million. I don't like people to be under-financed. The firm [Drexel Burnham Lambert] has turned down Harrah's, Bally's and Caesars – they don't want the gaming industry, don't want the association.' Milken told Wynn he would introduce him to the chief operating officer of Drexel Burnham Lambert. 'Wear a regular suit,' Milken added.

The heads of the firm persuaded themselves to take the gamble. Wynn had a track record, and the fact that he had sunk almost all of his own money into the Golden Nugget, about $2m., was convincing. The gaming industry was at that time without investment banking services, because no one in Wall Street wanted to risk the taint of gambling (though of course all of them were gambling their heads off every day). This was the opportunity which Milken, in his clairvoyant way, foresaw. It took almost two years for Wynn to raise the money. He criss-crossed the country, making his pitch to mutual funds and other institutions. No one could make a more snappy public presentation than Wynn, with his stand-up cabaret style, but he had to work at it. Milken told him simply to tell his story: 'If the deal works, as it will, inside of five years you'll be able to do five hundred million over the phone.' Over the next two years Drexel raised not $125m. but $160m. for Wynn's project. The capital came largely from mortgage debt, with some subordinated debt and small equity offerings, so Wynn's ownership stake, roughly 20 per cent, was barely diluted. And six years later, when he sold the Golden Nugget in Atlantic City, Wynn's original $2m. was worth about $75m.

Milken was proved right. Wynn had made the deal work. The Nugget made more money every single quarter than any other casino in Atlantic City, until Wynn left; the only issue was who came second. And over the next six years, Drexel raised about $1 billion for him. On this occasion, the grand opening of a project which really existed, which everyone could see, compared with the paper transactions which characterised the wheeling and dealing in junk bonds, Milken was entitled to feel justified. He showed no emotion, however, at Wynn's expression of loyalty. As he had predicted, when it came to raising new money to finance the Mirage, Wynn simply picked up the phone. He may not have felt that confident, but he sounded confident. Wynn's private motto for himself says a lot about him: 'Runnin' scared, straight ahead.'

The design of the Mirage – 'Fantasy becomes reality' – was crucial. Kenny Wynn – a slighter, vibrant, younger brother version of Steve – is not an architect himself, but he runs Atlandia Design, the design and construction arm of the corporation. He has worked with Steve since he left school – in the casino business you can trust family. Atlandia's offices are situated on the edge of the Mirage property. His architect is Joel Bergman, a fast-talking southern Californian who has some good buildings to his name. He designed the Golden Nugget in Atlantic City and much of the Golden Nugget in Vegas. Bergman knows about casinos: as a young man he was project architect for the team which built the MGM Grand. After the infamous fire he gave extensive evidence to the inquiry on how safety precautions had been skimped, against professional advice, to save costs. That experience, which seared him, was a lesson to all planners of high-rise buildings on the paramount importance of fire safety.

The design of the Mirage was a team effort in that Wynn knew he wanted something special, something extraordinary, but wasn't sure what. There was a lot of improvisation; they kicked ideas around for hundreds of hours, making drawings and scale models, until one day Bergman got close to the vision – a long curving front, with pillars at the porte-cochère, and water, and palm trees . . . That was the beginning, which after much experimentation led to the final version. 'The unique thing about working for Steve is that he is prepared to support his demand for excellence with the money to pay for it,' says Bergman.

The structure of the hotel was only a small part of the design. There was the casino, the rooms, the restaurants, every little thing right down to the fresh and distinctive logo: five little palm trees – in mauve, yellow, orange, pink and, slightly to the right, a green one, forming a group. The palm trees logo, which is repeated endlessly throughout the decor, hints at tropical gaiety rather than casino gambling. The concept of the Mirage was defined by Wynn in autumn 1986 and the first drawings done in summer '87. 'This is not going to be like the rest of Las Vegas. No neon. We're doing something else,' he told the design team. 'But don't think for a moment we are going to forget who we are or where we are. This is the highest energy midway in the world. We are going to be elegant. But we're going to have a ton of punch. We have got to compete with the environment or we'll get lost like a black hole.' Hence David Hersey for the lighting. It was Kenny who after seeing the spectacular lighting of his musicals in London persuaded Hersey to come to Vegas. 'He was very reluctant, at first. Wouldn't even take his coat off. Then we showed him the drawings.'

The place turned out very much how they'd planned, Kenny says, the gold, the glass, the shape of it, the high-rise structure with its outstretched wings, the attempt to create intimacy in a large space. With hindsight, if they had realised how popular it was going to be, they would have built the atrium wider and had a better throughput for handling the crowds, moved some of the facilities one floor up, and so on. Changes are being made all the time, as suites are remodelled, restaurants revamped, the lay-out of the casino rejigged. Above all, the aim is to keep the synergy going.

'It's more than just a business opportunity,' Wynn wound up the opening ceremonial. 'It's a much deeper thing. It's a judgement about the place, in this case Nevada and Las Vegas. It's a judgement about the potential state of the economy. It's a judgement that this is the place to be for a long time . . . It's a vote of confidence by people who say such an enterprise will be safe and secure for many many many years in the future . . .' Governor of Nevada Bob Miller applauded. 'That was the spirit which inspired us. It's a statement about where we live and what we are up to.' Everyone applauded. Wynn is a man who makes speeches like that. I preferred his humorous comment backstage: 'For all those who were critical . . . I forgive you!'

The first RFB guests ('complimentary room, food and beverage', those precious initials which touch every gambler's heart) then drew up in a Rolls-Royce. Siegfried and Roy, resident entertainers, stepped out accompanied by two sleepy white tiger cubs, one of which, gathered in Wynn's arms, curled itself around his neck in a proprietorial way. Illusionists with animals, Siegfried and Roy had been hired by Wynn from the Frontier casino to stage their show on a permanent basis ($58.5m. for a five year contract). 'Mr Vinn,' said Siegfried feelingly, 'you followed the melody.' Inside the hotel a special 'habitat' had been created for their troupe of Siberian tigers. It was located behind a wall of glass, at the end of a moving walkway, next to an arch leading to Caesars Palace. The walkway was designed to draw pedestrians in from the street, first of all to see the tigers and then to go on into the casino. (Wynn's disembodied voice, 'Welcome to the Mirage . . . Stay as long as you like', greets visitors as they glide in.) The two entertainers disappeared, shortly to lead their tigers into this kitsch abode of fake rocks and statuettes of elephants in white plaster. The tigers, sleepy for all their coiled power, paced around, blinking slowly behind the glass wall.

At five minutes to twelve, unwilling to hold back the crowd any longer, the thin green line of security guards gave way. And at five past twelve, the place was jammed. The people began at a fast walk, then broke into a run over the last few paces, and raced through the swing doors – baseball caps bobbing, bomber jackets billowing, T-shirts flapping over day-glo bermudas, sneakers thudding below pale pink pants, white pleated skirts and blue jeans – the whole rag, tag and bobtail of a holiday crowd on the spree. All of a sudden the air was filled with noise: the slots were whirring and chunking, line after line of them, the coins were rattling around like sea shells in the tide, this heavy metal rhythm overscored by a sort of moaning siren-like scream from a bank of super-slots, shouts, greetings, laughter, and above it all, snatches of rock music, loudspeaker announcements, bells ringing, metal clashing. The sweet sound, in my instant judgement, of success.

Before it opened, a lot of people were sceptical about the Mirage, particularly top executives at rival casinos. 'You can't make a nut of a million-plus a day with that set-up,' I was told. 'The ratio of staff to guests is too high, the costs are enormous, Wynn's borrowed up to the eyeballs.' Others estimated that even a nut of a million a day was too low, that the Mirage would need to clear at least a million and a quarter. Even at Caesars, the market leader for two decades, the nut was probably only around three quarters of a million a day. So how was Wynn going to pay off his accumulated debts and make a profit? Wynn's rivals thought he had taken on an impossible task.

'They want to believe that!' said Wynn through gritted teeth, late at night, or rather early in the morning at the end of that Thanksgiving weekend, after some sixty hours of non-stop action at the Mirage, when I spotted him on the casino floor. 'They only wish it would be true. We made a million dollars in the first ten hours we opened. That was just our expenses, in ten hours. Yesterday we made two million. Of course we're a hit. I knew we would be.' Wynn, in white windjammer and slacks, his usual electric smile somewhat dimmed, was looking battered, as if he had just come ashore after a long sail in rough water. 'I can't enjoy our success. What upsets me is all the things we're doing wrong, all the mistakes we're making. I want to get them right, and I want them right now.' For example, on the second morning the slots area had run out of coins for giving change – something of a calamity for a casino. He frowned as another aide came up, reporting some new glitch. Yet the opening itself, whether the huge investment in the Mirage turned out to be a winner or a loser in the long run, was a triumph. To open up a place that size, from nothing, so that at noon it stood empty, and by midnight it had a win of a million dollars, with everything clicking and jumping and glittering on cue, was an astounding coup. It dazzled a city well used to exaggeration and hype. In the first few days, the crowds were so dense – families with children well to the fore – that the walkway from Las Vegas Boulevard had to be closed. And it has remained a 'must see' place for every visitor in town.

Nearly all the major casinos were rebuilding for the 1990s, as a wave of confidence in the continuation of Las Vegas' apparently inexorable rise took hold. This confidence was based on the growth of visitors and gaming revenues described earlier. But it was also, to a significant degree, a reaction to Wynn's own plans. Just as his renovation of the clapped-out old Golden Nugget had proved beneficial in raising standards in Glitter Gulch, so the same process looked like being repeated up on the Strip. Circus Circus' new project, the Excalibur, 'a mediaeval castle with jousting knights', would be even bigger than the Mirage. All over town, blood-orange cranes were cutting the skyline, as teams of workmen in hard hats scrambled around the scaffolding: they worked in three shifts, round the clock, just like the casino staff. Time is money.

I stayed at the Mirage three times in its first year and it was usually jammed. Even on a weekday afternoon, even at four in the morning, it was ticking over. The image that struck me most was the crowd of young kids standing around the Wheel of Fortune.

This is an old fairground device, a huge wheel like a weighing machine, which turns around slowly, stopping finally at one of the numbers marked around the rim, which the players bet on, like a primitive form of roulette. Casinos like to keep a Wheel of Fortune near the front entrance as a colourful memento of the old days rather than as a gambling game. The edge against the player, at 11 per cent, makes it such a bad gamble that even Jack Binion at the Horseshoe feels a slight pang at operating the device. But at the Mirage, the players, mostly kids out of college on a date, did not seem to give a hoot about odds. The betting on the Wheel of Fortune and the shrieks of youthful glee as it turned around went on at all hours. So far as the house was concerned, the machine was living up to its name. If even the Wheel of Fortune was so much in demand, it boded very well indeed for the rest of the operation, I thought.

According to the leading authority on the economics of commercial gaming, Eugene Martin Christiansen, the Mirage was 'a masterpiece of creative finance', despite its being such a high-risk venture. Almost all of its borrowings are from itself, so to speak, the subsidiary company which owns and runs the Mirage, leaving its parent company, Golden Nugget, Inc., virtually unencumbered. Despite much high-flying speculation in the press, interest payments on the Mirage are only $65m. a year. On the day the Mirage opened, its appraised value was $675m. and its 'estimated street value' $1,000m.* 'An extra-

---

*Golden Nugget Inc., (GNI), through GNS Finance Corp., borrowed $535.1m. to finance the Mirage, placing all but $75m. of this sum privately. These borrowings, plus a $107.1m. equity contribution from GNI, produced a pre-opening capital structure for the Mirage of $535.1m. debt and $72.5m. shareholders' equity, for a total facility capitalisation of $607.6m. All of the $535.1m. debt is secured by the Mirage-Casino-Hotel (MCH), a wholly-owned subsidiary of GNI that owns and operates the Mirage. In other words, as Christiansen put it, payment of this debt, both interest and principal, depends on the operating result of the Mirage itself, not on operating results of the parent company. Of the various securities used to finance the Mirage, only one issue (maturing 8.1.98) was unconditionally guaranteed by GNI (these figures are taken from an article by Christiansen in *Gaming & Wagering Business Magazine*, May 1990).

ordinary operation, quite brilliant,' Christiansen told me, 'even if the eventual outcome cannot be foreseen.' As director of a casino consultancy firm in New York, he has wide experience of these ventures.

What it came down to was that in financing the Mirage, Wynn had not bet his company on a single facility, like a single roll of the dice. It had all been much more carefully structured and thought out. GNI itself remains a highly leveraged company, with an estimated $900m. of debt on a capitalisation of $1,000m. But it has a track record as the best operator in the business. On the evidence of its popularity in its opening weeks, the Mirage was already a hit of major proportions, Christiansen thought, which had profound implications for the rest of the industry. 'The Mirage looks beyond Las Vegas gambling halls to other kinds of leisure consumption, to the alternative realities offered by Disney theme parks, Hollywood spectacle, popular music and travel in foreign lands. It is a quantum leap forward in the evolution of casino hotel resorts.' I think one could make the point the other way round: can you imagine how fabulously profitable Disney-land might be, if it also had casino gambling.

Success of course was not assured. Wynn and his aides trembled in anticipation, in those first weeks and months at the Mirage, as the figures came in. When they saw the net win for the first month, $39.8m., however, they breathed huge sighs of relief. The win on the slots was $13m. an unheard of return. January, usually a slack month, racked up $38m. The win for the first half of the year was over $1m. a day. Wynn kept thinking: 'This can't go on, now it's off-season, it's got to back off, we'll just scramble it next month.' But it did go on, right through the opening of Excalibur, the new rival, in June, with 97 per cent occupancy of the hotel in the heat of summer. In October, the win rose to a colossal $48m., despite a Japanese punter winning $2m. on the last day. In December, always a lean month, occupancy was running at 84 per cent and come December 27, when Vegas wakes up after Christmas, the crowds hit the place like an express train.

You could hardly draw breath on the casino floor. That month the Mirage made almost $19m. profit after meeting all expenses.

Wynn couldn't sit back and relax because this was still a gamble – a gamble in the best sense, when you put your money and expertise and reputation on the line and see if your judgement is right. The way you keep score, in the casino industry, is by the print-outs which land on your desk every morning, showing the net result for each table and each game, in each part of the casino, for each of the three shifts the day before. The casino manager scans the sheets, like a military commander studying aerial photos. 'The place causes me anxiety, all the time. I was never concerned about capturing the public's fancy. We spent a lot of money, we hired a ton of people, we made a pile of promises,' Wynn said. 'This is an *extraordinary* place. It's fine and dandy if we keep our promise. But keeping our promise puts pressure on management. Will we be able to do it consistently? A year later, our standards have to be more exacting. If we're not consistent, we begin to slip back. If we don't attract repeat business, word of mouth, then all of a sudden, real problems come up. The Mirage can't just hold its own.'

To be nervous is a way of not taking things for granted. Wynn insists that the Mirage must do more, must keep on surprising the public. If the experience for people who come back isn't better than on their previous visit, then the Mirage is failing. And if it fails, it starts going backward. In his view there can be no standing still. A lot more money was spent in the first year, $50 or $60 or $70 million, says Wynn airily, as if the numbers are small change. The dolphin pool came in, at a cost of $14m., and it is indeed an example to zoological displays anywhere in the world (in contrast with the white tigers' plaster habitat). There are two pools, linked, allowing the dolphins room to disport themselves, or to be separated for health care and breeding (a sixth dolphin was born in the spring). There are no tricks or aquatic per-formances. Instead, the visitor gets a close-up view, especially from the gallery below the water level, of these mammals in their natural habitat. (A daily programme is run for school children.) Wynn is now considering building a shark pool, for forty sharks, with a glass tunnel for spectators underneath.

But the really big surprise came on the new accommodation for high rollers, known as the Villas. The Villas are a series of eight super-luxury apartments, built at a cost of about $3m. each. They are located off a hallway as long as the corridor in the Palace of Versailles, and almost as grandiose, at the far end of the casino beyond the ballrooms. For once the expression 'no expense has been spared' seems justified. Each villa offers everything in interior decoration that money can buy – in the foyer, high ceilings, inlaid marble floors and oriental carpets; in the living room, an open fireplace, chandeliers and hand-crafted period furniture; in the 'library', overstuffed sofas and club chairs, plus a high-tech sound system; in the bedrooms, four-poster beds as in a seventeenth-century château, with the convenience of electronic-ally operated draperies. The pièce de résistance, for those who choose to take a villa, is the his-and-hers bathrooms: 'Each master suite includes two separate private bath and dressing facilities for both the lady and gentleman. Marble walls soar to a 12 foot height . . . Her bath and dressing room offers a spacious whirlpool, extravagant make-up and lav vanity, walk in closet and private safe . . . Bidet and commodes are secluded in their own chamber behind hand textured European glazed doors . . .' Outside each villa, a strip of artificial lawn adjoins a private pool, flanked by statuary and fountains in Florentine style – plus a miniature putting green – the whole space, lined by tall Cypress trees, nestling under the towering height of the rear wall of the hotel.

Wynn takes an inordinate degree of pride in this accommoda-tion. He wants people to see it as surpassing any hotel, anywhere in the world. 'If Queen Elizabeth and Prince Philip came here,' he summed up, 'the Queen would say: "My dear, we are at home." ' And who are these sumptuous villas, which rent at around $3,000 a night, designed for? For the high rollers, mostly Asian; who must surely feel, under the high ceilings, a little like miniatures in a treasure chest. The baccarat tables in the salon privé are about a three minute stroll away, and the house commission on the first couple of bets by such guests more than takes care of comping their overnight stay in a villa.

The cream of the gaming revenue, as with all upmarket casinos, has to come from the high rollers. To a large extent the place depends on their patronage. That is the point of the villas and bungalows with their pools and patios, and the extensive suites on the top floor of the hotel. The baccarat pit is the heart of the gaming operation. In addition to the four games which are continually in action, rising to a dozen tables at peak holiday weekends, Wynn set up a salon privé. This ingenious little oubliette, just off the main baccarat pit, was conceived of as a cross between a French salon and an English gentleman's library. On the marble mantelpiece stands a row of leather bound volumes (a Japanese high roller might soothe his fevered brow with a quick perusal of the 'Ode to a Nightingale'), and high-backed, brocaded chairs ($7,000 apiece) are set around as in a drawing room. The furniture is completed by a shiny new roulette wheel, a blackjack table and a baccarat lay-out, and a private kitchen. (No need ever to move.) An armed guard stands always at the door.

Entry to the salon privé is open to anyone, anyone that is with a credit line of a million dollars. The minimum bet is supposed to be $1,000 though that would be regarded as no more than a 'walk on' bet, to warm up. The Mirage is in direct competition with Caesars and one or two other big casinos (not to mention London and Monte Carlo) in seeking the patronage of high rollers. A player who is prepared to gamble half a million or a million over a long weekend is bringing manna from heaven, compared with the slow-grind operation on the casino floor. From time to time the gods of chance will ensure that the high roller beats the house out of a lot of money. Everyone smiles. The bountiful player tosses chips to the dealers like so many after-dinner mints in recognition of their part in his good fortune. And rumours of the big win, which puts a sharp crimp in the baccarat pit's returns, whisper their way across to the executive offices. But the management trusts to another rule, the law of probability. In the first eight months of the Mirage's operation, the baccarat pit drop was $140m. and the house, which 'got lucky', held about 40 per cent.

Wynn has experience from Golden Nugget days of the different species of high roller. The Texans, for example, who fly up to Las Vegas in their DC-9s. 'They come for the weekend with the wife or the girlfriend – in some cases both – and they want to raise hell.' They have a routine, as Wynn recalls. 'When they arrive on Thursday, the first thing – this comes first – is gambling. They like to gamble. Before they get ready for dinner, there's the Thursday afternoon, two hours. Later the routine is: Get up in the morning at eleven o'clock. Go down for breakfast, shoot the dice a little bit, maybe go play golf (the Mirage has built its own private course 'Shadow Creek' ten miles north), get dressed for dinner, go to the gourmet room, take in a show, come back around eleven o'clock, gamble till two in the morning.' These sort of players would have a quarter of a million credit, but an acceptable sum to lose, at the back of their minds, would be $100,000. (For people who do not play craps, I must explain that if you are playing dice for several days on end, you need both a tremendous run of luck and the true grit to hang on to it: only about 8 per cent of players will come out ahead.)

Nowadays the high rollers who are prepared to drop two or three million over a weekend are mostly Asian, from Japan, Taiwan and points east, but there are also a number of wealthy Mexicans and Latin Americans. Why do they do it? They don't play to make money, according to Wynn. They just love to gamble, it's a particular form of rich man's fun. 'Winning is good, because now they can play some more with *our* money. It's inventory.' With the economic downturn in 1991, credit got stretched and bad debts increased. That is the real risk in building villas for high rollers (see Chapter 7).

Meanwhile out on the east coast, 3,000 miles away, a frenzy of wheeling and dealing in casinos was also going on. In fact, measured in decibels of publicity, it was no contest: Trump was a runaway winner. The Taj Mahal, his new venture in Atlantic City, was to be the eighth wonder of the world – if it was ever finished. It was being dubbed the 'Taj Mirage', not as the counterpart of Wynn's new casino but on the assumption that the whole gigantic leviathan might fade away and dissolve in the sea mists along the boardwalk. The saga of Trump and the Taj Mahal makes an interesting contrast to the fairytale success story of the Mirage: it proves the point that there is a lot more to running a casino than sitting back and letting the money roll in.

In acquiring the Taj Mahal Trump set out to show what 'the art of the deal' was all about. The opportunity came with the decline in fortune of Resorts International, the first casino to open in Atlantic City. At the start Resorts had been incredibly profitable, though not without its troubles, mainly over Mafia connections and infringement of gaming regulations. But by now the good times were well and truly over. The company was in debt and facing fierce competition all along the boardwalk. It was still, potentially, a great property, which included in its assets – this was the attraction – the mammoth, over-expensive, heavily indebted project for building what was intended to be the most lavish casino yet seen. Trump began buying up the voting shares in the company and rapidly secured control. He warned that the company was overvalued and the Taj could run into hundreds of millions more costs, beyond the $600m. Resorts had already sunk into it. The share price plummetted, the company seemed to be falling into Trump's hands – it comprised, roughly speaking, $1 billion of assets and $600m. in debts, which Trump was proposing to acquire for about $200m. – when a joker jumped out of the pack, in the genial form of Merv Griffin.

Griffin was the best known TV host in America. In *Wheel of Fortune* and *Jeopardy!* he had created the two most successful game shows ever seen on TV. He was more than a successful performer. In 1986 Coca-Cola bought out his company for

$250m. Overnight he became a tycoon. Out on the West Coast, lulled by the rhythms of Hollywood, far away business deals tend to be seen through technicoloured specs. Griffin got the notion of taking over Resorts himself. This was in March 1988 when Trump was just about to close the whole deal. Griffin was more than tempted: he went and upped the bid for Resorts by a leap and a bound, from the $24 a share Trump had bid, to $35 a share – a price which amazed the gambling community and mesmerised Wall Street.* What followed was several months of acrimonious negotiation between Trump in New York and Griffin in Los Angeles. Griffin seemed to be making the running, setting deadlines and then extending them, issuing ultimatums via his lawyers and rescinding them – there was a sense that at long last someone had come along, straight out of Hollywood, who could handle the loud-mouthed city slicker.

The essentials of the deal were cut in a six minute confrontation in Trump Tower. Trump kept some land and the uncompleted Taj. Griffin got the rest of Resorts International – the hotel and casino, some undeveloped New Jersey real estate, and Paradise Island, comprising a casino and four hotels in the Bahamas. Trump was to pay $273m. for the Taj, which had cost Resorts, so far, the best part of $600m. Griffin was to buy Trump's voting shares at cost. The press whooped that Griffin had come out on top. 'The Resorts deal marks Merv Griffin's first foray into the world of takeovers and is especially impressive given that analysts initially thought he had little chance of succeeding', an analyst noted in the *New York Times*. 'Merv Griffin's Outrageous

---

*In financial terms, the jump in price made no sense. It was not until many months later that a different, more sinister, explanation was offered. Doubts were raised about the probity of Griffin's main financial advisors. Inquiries revealed that the two men concerned were not quite the trusted and independent advisors he had always supposed; a link was even alleged with a member of the Genovese family in New York. The suspicion arose that the extraordinarily high price Griffin was persuaded to bid for Resort's shares might have been – albeit unknown to him – part of an insider share-dealing scam. (*Barron's*, September, 1990.)

Fortune', screamed the tabloids. The headlines annoyed Trump, who insisted that his former rival broke the golden rule of the art of the deal, which was that 'You shouldn't be trumpeting'.

Wynn was under no illusions about the disaster facing Trump and begged him not to chase after Resorts. Though not exactly friends – 'What is it with you and me? All that is over,' Trump had told him. 'You are the greatest, I am the second greatest' – they were on long-distance telephone terms. Here, with Griffin's bid, was a heaven-sent opportunity for Trump to get out, unscathed. 'It was one of the most ironic transactions in the history of casinos,' Wynn concluded. 'Trump was going to make a profit. But he felt he was going to be bested by Merv. This was a deal so warped and distended that both men got the worst deal of their lives. It's like the Kenny Rogers song – "You gotta know when to hold 'em and know when to fold 'em." ' Wynn was not a competitor in this scenario. Indeed, in his public statements he did what he could to build Trump up. 'Only a man of Donald Trump's energy can overturn the image of Atlantic City,' he declared.

It did not take long for the tinsel to fade from Griffin's purported victory. When the casino people took a look at Resorts close-to, they found the place in a state of advanced dilapidation – the heating and cooling systems were clapped out, the elevator cables frayed, even the roof leaked. Why didn't Griffin's team take a good look at the place before they bought it? Well, why didn't Trump look at the Castle before buying it? The answer is that businessmen often act on impulse. Within ten months Resorts International halted payment on its $925m. in bonds. Two months later, the company went into voluntary liquidation under Chapter 11. But the outlook was hardly any better at the Taj. By this stage costs had got so far out of hand that they easily outstripped the Mirage. Back in 1979, construction of the project was budgeted at something over $175m., only one-fifth of the final bill. Inflation, changes of plan, higher building costs – 'Some of the numbers we'll never find,' commented one of

Trump's aides. The Donald (telling his reflection in the mirror each morning 'OK baby, you're the greatest') refused to be put off. His claim, when he took the project over from Resorts, was that he had the expertise required to get the job done. An operator like Wynn was spending hundreds of millions in building his dream-casino, was he not? But Wynn, with a lifetime's experience of the ups and downs of gaming, and an intuitive sense of what makes a casino take off, had a vision. Trump's main talent lay in screwing down building contractors.

Moreover, Trump's plans were hit by a tragic stroke of misfortune. His three top executives died in a helicopter crash: there could in an obvious sense be no recovery from that sort of disaster, no matter what new appointments were made to fill the gap. So when the Taj Mahal finally opened its doors, on 2 April 1990, it was a great day, a triumph of will and effort and personal ambition, regardless of expense. Trump had finally made his mark in the casino world. Certainly the opening caused far more bally-hoo than the opening of the Mirage four months before, which was a village fête by comparison. This was a spectacle which attracted the media worldwide – and not simply because the Taj had cost a billion dollars. Trump's recent and highly publicised split with Ivana, following his romantic entanglement with a starlet named Marla Maples, gave the tabloids the juiciest copy they had had in years. This amorous tangle, saucier than any TV soap, topped it all. (Marla had to stay away from the opening: her mere presence would have diverted all media attention from the casino and caused absolute pandemonium).

The Taj, like a huge decorated shed, stranded on the beach, was jammed, indeed the crowds were so desperate to gamble that when the slots – all 3,008 of them, each bearing the Trump logo – were fully operational, the counting staff could not move the sheer weight of coin. Under New Jersey regulations the money had to be counted after the machines were emptied, before being re-set for play. For two days the slots had to be shut down, gradually returning to full operation in the course of the month.

This frenzy of gambling was an encouraging sign, even if it showed that in some basic respects the Taj was not geared up. It took several weeks before the procedures for handling the hard count (as coin is called) were put right. Still, in its first four weeks of operation the performance of the Taj exceeded its projections. The total win was $34,205,869, which was well above the nut, variously estimated to be over $1m. a day. Business flattened out during the succeeding months, and remained flat during the summer – which did not bode too well for the winter months, when the boardwalk is such a dismal prospect.

I took a look at the Taj soon after it opened and found the comparison with the Mirage revealing. Driving into Atlantic City the first thing one sees is Trump's name, in huge red letters, across the skyline. His name seems to be everywhere; as if one were in Trumptown rather than Atlantic City. Along the way Trump had also acquired a fourth hotel, the Atlantic Regency (formerly the Atlantic casino), which gave him 40 per cent of the city's hotel rooms. A cheeky sign at the entrance to town, promoting the new attraction, proclaimed in bold letters: 'The Taj Mahal – More than a Mirage'. The Taj is big, certainly. Its ninety minarets shine out over the ocean like coloured onion domes. A fleet of limos could stage a cavalcade around the entrance, while the hotel foyer, stretching out in empty space, is like a railway terminus. What all this space is for, considering that the Taj, as an hotel, is relatively small at 1,250 rooms, is another matter. Maybe to instil in the visitor a proper sense of awe at the sheer scale of it. The casino floor covers 120,000 square feet, which is the basis of Trump's claim that the Taj is the world's biggest casino (it all depends how one defines casino size, but let that pass – small it isn't). With its serried ranks of slot machines, like a painted metal army rooted to the drill-square, the casino floor stretches out in a huge square, bright with Indian motifs and decoration. Overhead a line of 24 crystal chandeliers, which cost Trump $250,000 each – a typical extravagance – gives the place a slightly old-fashioned look. The dealers and cocktail waitresses are costumed in jewelled

uniforms and mock-Indian saris. To an Indian, perhaps to anyone who has breathed in the ethereal yet imperishable magic of
the Taj Mahal at Agra, the overall effect might be offensive, if it
wasn't so obviously kitsch.

Yet for all its Indian ornamentation and detail, the Taj seems
outdated, the last of the old-style casinos rather than one of the
new. The endless banks of slot machines, the long, long
corridors, the vast convention rooms, the restaurants with their
tired old themes, are all of a massive piece, with little or nothing
added to enhance people's enjoyment. Lacking personality or
warmth, or any touch of humour, its basic message is: 'Big is
Beautiful'. By mid-June, 1990, less than three months since the
Taj's glorified opening, the financial crisis threatening his empire
broke over Trump's head. The immediate cause of trouble was
his failing to meet interest payments due on bonds at Trump
Castle totalling about $73m. The press got worse and worse
through the first half of the year. From merely being over-
stretched, which can happen to any financier and any company,
Trump was written off as being, simply, incompetent.

The glossy magazines announced that the decade of greed was
over. The changing times were epitomised by the collapse of junk
bonds, which put a sudden stop to the Las Vegas casinos' flow of
easy money too. The public was swept up by a rising sense of hope
as the Cold War came to an end (before the Gulf War started). A
gentler, greener America was opening up, which someone like
Trump, it was implied, with his relentless pursuit of profit, was
not attuned to. In the nick of time, Trump's creditors cobbled
together a rescue operation. Expressing his appreciation, Trump
declared: 'I have gained a great and deep respect for the banking
system and those who make it work.' In former times, this used to
be known as kissing the rod. Clearly Merv Griffin was not the
only loser in Atlantic City. At the American Booksellers
Association in Las Vegas in July, Trump drew a record 2,300
people to a breakfast meeting, to hype the second volume of his
autobiography, entitled *Surviving at the Top*. It came out in the

autumn and hit the bestsellers lists only briefly. This time Trump was not in a position to order thousands of copies as gifts for his casino customers. 'Anyone who makes it to the top of his profession will tell you,' he wrote, 'if he's honest, that his worst potential enemy is himself.' In its first full year of operation the Taj reported losses of $120m.

The times are changing in Vegas, too. The Mirage remains the market leader but it is a bit beyond Wynn's ability to forecast future performance. The cloud over the national economy is considerably bigger than a man's hand, and he is wary. The Mirage's first annual report noted that the Gulf War had caused 'a general decline in interest in entertainment-related activities and an increased level of concern over terrorism aimed at international and domestic travellers.' If such factors continued, they could hit the Mirage, Wynn warned. How do you keep up? 'Any place that has this kind of raw vitality, this kind of unbelievable energy . . .' he told me, 'is expensive to operate. The casino grossed $409m. in our first year and the hotel $251m., after paying all the comps. But it cost $1.2m. a day to operate. You've got to take it seriously. I mean, $450m. a year to crank this baby up! You miss by 20 per cent and you're losing $90m.'

The only way is to pay close attention to the business, and keep on paying close attention. Savings have been made. The hotel and casino staff, deliberately over-manned at the opening, has been slimmed, but are still nearly 7,000 strong. As market leader, however, the Mirage is not price sensitive. People are prepared to pay over the odds for rooms and restaurants. Behind the gloss, Wynn's expertise shows in unexpected ways, in the kitchens, for example, which he sited centrally next to the food storage area. To him, the kitchens are a thing of beauty – 'a chef like Girardet would rave about my kitchens'. Room service has its own bank of elevators: one day they did 4,100 room service meals, five times more than planned. Tough times may be coming. (For starters, the Gulf War reduced tourist traffic on the Strip by about 7 per cent, which for the Mirage, less vulnerable than most, spelled a 5 per cent loss of revenue.) The management team tries all the time to sharpen the operation, by switching casino personnel around to overcome the boredom factor in dealing the same game day after day, and in encouraging staff to take vacations at off-peak periods; special attention has been given to making the slots areas feel light and attractive; and so on. Wynn wants to reduce the debt and increase the equity: then if there is a day of reckoning, the Mirage will be strong enough to ride it out. You don't need a Ph.D. to know exactly what you have to do, he says.

The most impressive aspect of the Mirage (in my view) is the attention given to staff relations. After all, how do you suddenly hire 7,000 personnel? The recruitment and training programmes, based on a detailed study of the demographics of Las Vegas, and the new people moving in month by month, were most effective, besides being 'applicant friendly'. 'You can take the best you can possibly find – and really make that commitment – or you can flush it. There's nothing in between,' according to Artie Nathan, who has the title of Director of Human Resources at the Mirage. College recruitment was spectacular: 42 graduates from university hotel courses at Las Vegas and Cornell were taken on, and given further training to become supervisors and managers. 'You can give speeches and pep-talks until everybody wants to throw up,' says Wynn. 'It's not what you say – it's what you do! And if you want employees to think like customers, then I want them to feel like customers . . . It's the only thing that really makes us different, not the palm trees, or the little volcanoes or the silly rain forests. That's just stuff, it's just money. A little imagination and patience, anybody can do it – really anybody can do it. Big deal!'

The size of the place is the crucial factor. It takes time to review all the different operations. And a long lead time before changes can be carried out. Unlike running a hotel like Claridge's, Wynn says, where all you need is one manager in the foyer. What matters in a resort is people. 'The Mirage and the Golden Nugget in the end will be known by the personality of the staff. That is the impression that will last and be enduring with each of the guests that experiences these places. To the extent that that impression is enduring and positive, we win; we win everything – the biggest tips, the greatest occupancy, the greatest resistance to economic downturn, the greatest safety in hard times.' He has hired talented people but he has also lost good people, such as his casino manager at the Mirage and Dennis Gomes from the Golden Nugget (see Chapter 3), both lured by sky-high salaries by Trump to move to Atlantic City.

Wynn has a reputation for bawling out senior staff, but he can also be a very generous employer, who knows the value of loyalty. At board meetings, what Wynn says goes, even if it's wrong. He takes decisions quickly, leaving the implementation to Bobby Baldwin, president and chief executive of the Mirage, known in his previous incarnation as a professional poker player as 'The Owl'.

Baldwin reached the pinnacle of his (former) career when he won the World Poker Championship, held annually at Binion's Horseshoe, in 1978. 'He's so super-aggressive that I sometimes wonder why he doesn't get a sore arm from shoving all his chips to the centre of the table so often,' another world champion, Doyle Brunson, observed admiringly. He was still 'a true Southern gentleman', Brunson added. Certainly he is one of the few people who have made the transition from professional gambler to chief executive. He is tall, wears a dark suit and rimless spectacles and carries a quiet authority. On a night off he may be seen sneaking out in white windjammer to a poker game downtown. What he learned about people through playing poker, Baldwin says, has stood him in good stead in his business career. 'You need to have a general understanding of probabilities . . . but it's worthless if you don't understand people, and the way you should interact with people and how people behave.' Baldwin's fine-tuning of everything going on at the Mirage complements Wynn's fast-lane driving. All the vice-presidents report to him, and all the department heads, supervising 550 managers, report to the vice-presidents. Bobby Baldwin holds regular staff meetings in the ballroom – with elegant buffets set out on white table-cloths – to spell out in detail every phase of the operation, with flow charts and slides, to hundreds of managers and supervisors down the line. The biggest danger is that the various parts of the business get disconnected.

If executives start making excuses for low returns, Wynn once declared, testifying at the New Jersey Control Commission, 'I don't listen to them. I don't care about their stories. I dump them. That's it.' 'Difficult? The man's impossible to work for,' a former colleague claimed. Another observed, without rancour: 'I was friends with Steve before we got together. And I'm friends again now that we don't work together.' Wynn's style is inspirational and intuitive: he goes for the big decision – like suddenly ordering a clamp on high roller credit just before a holiday weekend – and leaves the practicalities to others. He's been known to call staff out from home after midnight, because a marvellous idea has just struck him. 'The only time he's not demanding,' Elaine adds, 'is when he's asleep.' In his defence Wynn demands: 'What hard-driving, ambitious person is not egocentric? What's wrong with that anyway?' On the other hand he has the kind of magnetism and sexual energy which attract women and a reputation for dalliance.

In the end, it all depends on Wynn himself. 'We mustn't appear to try too hard. And yet we must appear to try hard. In the end, the public knows how hard we are trying. We want to say, "Come on! This is the best there is!" But we're not allowed to trumpet too much, we mustn't be too commercial. We would like to be relatively subtle. But the key word is relatively. Subtlety here would be unabashed promotion in any other environment.' Wynn picks up a recent instance, it's irritating and gratifying at the same time. 'On New Year's Eve, twelve more million-dollar customers showed up than we expected. Four of them went off down the street. We want to know why they left! We thought we only had nine. Now we have twenty-one. Why not twenty-two? You start to covet everything. We're not greedy so much as victims of our last success.' At the annual meeting of 1991, shareholders approved a change of corporate name from Golden Nugget Inc. to Mirage Resorts Incorporated. And at the end of the year Wynn, wearing a pirate hat, announced plans to build a 3,000-room family-oriented theme hotel to be called Treasure Island on 17 acres of parking lot on the Mirage property: cost $300m.

The front of the new property will be designed as an outdoor theatre, depicting a seascape from Stevenson's novel. Each hour a pirate ship and HMS *Sir Francis Drake* will engage in a cannon battle. Who will win? After much thought the management decided that the pirates will be victorious.

The Mirage, Wynn admits, is running him as much as he is running it.

2   TRAILBLAZERS

> Ours was the first and will doubtless be the last party
> of whites to visit this profitless locale.
>
> Lieutenant Joseph Christmas Ives, on sailing
> up the Colorado river to a point near the
> present location of Las Vegas, 1857.

Why did Las Vegas start here, just here, of all places? Looking up
and down the Strip from the great crossroads at Flamingo, the
skyline of enormous buildings lit by flashing signs and illumina-
tions looks unreal. A trick of the light in the desert, a random
construction of enormous blocks, surrounded by a ring of
mountains. People from another age, discovering it, would surely
be mystified by its presence. Why here?

The success of Las Vegas, at its start as now, lies in its position
as a link to more important places, notably Los Angeles to the
south-west. Indians had lived in the region of Nevada for
thousands of years before the first whites appeared. 'They came
like a lion, yes, like a roaring lion,' one of the few Indian accounts
of the intruders reported (*Life Among the Paiutes* by Sarah
Winnemucca). The chief of the Paiutes nation believed that the
arrival of his white brothers happily fulfilled an ancient prophecy.
He travelled out to welcome them. But distrustful of him, they
kept him at a distance.

Violence soon followed. 'The land . . . was held in low regard
as a place for serious settlement, even unfit for habitation,
possibly a place of exile,' historian William D. Rowley has noted.

But along the trails which ran east to west through this desolate land the whites and the Indians fought and killed each other through the 1850s. 'The white men are like the stars over your heads,' warned Chief Numaga, counselling prudence. 'You have wrongs, great wrongs, that rise up like the mountains before you; but can you, from the mountain tops, reach and blot out those stars?' The chiefs who continued to fight in the 1860s were hunted down with their followers and killed. The Indians were driven back, and herded into reservations. (In a curious turn of the wheel of history, gaming on the Indian reservations is one of the most controversial issues in the U.S. today, though there is little possibility of Indian gaming in Nevada itself.)

Originally a stopping point on the oldest trail across Nevada, known as the Spanish trail – 'the City of Las Vegas owes its existence and success to transportation,' affirmed David Thompson in his finely wrought *Nevada: A History of Changes* – the place was called Las Vegas Springs. Men, horses, mules and oxen could find rest and water. Travellers liked to stop at Las Vegas (the word in Spanish meaning a marshy place) because it was at the edge of a fifty-five mile wide desert – the *jornada de muerto*, journey of death – that had to be crossed to reach Los Angeles to the south-west, Salt Lake City to the north-east and Santa Fé to the south-east. A Mormon settlement came and went in the 1850s. Describing his crossing of the California trail, the northern route, by stagecoach in 1861, Mark Twain wrote in *Roughing It*: 'From one extremity of this desert to the other, the road was white with the bones of oxen and horses. It would hardly be an exaggeration to say that we could have walked the forty miles and set our feet on a bone at every step!'

Most of the early mining towns in Nevada developed during the two great mining eras, the Comstock bonanza from 1859 to 1898 and the discovery of silver at Tonopah in 1900, which reached its peak in 1918. The first settlements were tents, soon to be replaced by wooden log or framed gabled buildings with rectangular 'false fronts'. They were lined up on both sides of the trail, which remained open-ended, a way in and a way out. Almost simultaneously, came the saloon keeper, the small merchant, the bartender, good-time gals, and all kinds of gamblers and adventurers. A single good prospect often started a camp, and soon after came the promoters, to buy up land for development or resale through stock companies.

In 1904 the Union Pacific Railroad built its tracks across the *jornada de muerto*, over the central section of the Spanish trail, which ran from the Muddy river south-west down to Las Vegas Springs. Freight traffic carried supplies to the silver mines. A year later the town was on the main railroad line between Salt Lake City and Los Angeles, and then came electric power. On Christmas Day 1905, only eight months after lots in the railroad township were sold at auction, one traveller reported that he saw the notorious Block Sixteen going at full blast, with crowds – all men – thronging the bars and gaming wildly at faro, roulette, blackjack and poker. Senator Clark of Montana (after whom Clark County is named) had intended Las Vegas to be a model town. But the entrepreneurial spirit soon found a loophole. Anyone who chose to open a hotel was entitled to run a bar, and a bar could have gambling; this led to the building of saloons with a few rooms upstairs – well supplied, no doubt, with female company. Block Sixteen was already renowned for its painted ladies.

The sale of lots was a tremendous gamble. An engineer named McWilliams, who had bought 80 acres to the north-west, beyond the railhead, took over the name Las Vegas. His site, the original settlement, had become a thriving tent city for mining supplies. It already boasted a bank, two hotels and half a dozen stores. He conceived a scheme to outflank and outsmart the Railroad Company. Its township, then hardly more than a flattened space in the desert, was to be built around the goods yard along Fremont Street. McWilliams' Las Vegas Townsite Company, on the wrong side of the tracks, offered the public lots from $100 to $300. 'We know these prices are ridiculously low as compared with what the Railroad Company expects to get for their lots at auction, but we have built the town of Las Vegas on broad gauge, liberal, live-and-let-live ideas and have public opinion entirely in our favour. . . This is the last opportunity you will ever get to buy Las Vegas property at such low prices. Get into line early, buy now, double your money within 60 days . . . We want the town built and not the profit on the lots.' McWilliams' site speedily declined, in later years fading into West Las Vegas, still a problem area.

Meanwhile, there was such a huge clamour from local people, miners, saloon-keepers, gamblers and all manner of other investors, from Los Angeles as well, wanting to buy lots that Clark's Las Vegas Townsite, representing the railroad company, put off its sale. The move only heightened the enthusiastic mood of the public. The day was hot, the beer was cold, a thousand-strong crowd thronged the auctioneer's platform set up under a mesquite tree. The bidding went on for two days. Prime lots on Fremont Street went for $1,750, others for about half that figure. 'Las Vegas had made the map as a town,' summed up a local historian, Stanley W. Paher, in *Las Vegas: As it began – as it grew*. The message was amusingly expressed in a cartoon strip from 1907 put out by local businessmen, entitled 'He Came, He Saw, He Stuck'. 'May the Lord have pity on your soul, you poor fool, going out to a place like Nevada,' advises a plump, bankerly figure to the prospective traveller. 'There's nothing to eat, no place to sleep, rattle snakes, wild cats, bank robbers and murder . . . You'll need 6 or 7 guns,' he's told. 'Got yer life insured?' On arrival, the newcomer finds a hotel, bank, general stores, an opera house in the making. The waiter in the restaurant apologises that there's nothing left on the menu but chicken, trout and quail. 'To Whom It May Concern,' writes the new arrival, 'I'm here to stay.'

For three decades the railway dominated the development of Las Vegas in virtually every regard. Most of the resident population, which grew from 945 in 1910 to 5,165 in 1930, depended one way or another on the railway, noted John Findlay in *People of Chance*. When the State Legislature created Clark

County in 1909, Las Vegas became the centre for administration. The highway, built roughly along the line of the Mormon trail (the Nevada section of the route between Salt Lake City and Los Angeles) between 1914–24, opened up the town to tourism. Construction of the Hoover Dam, which caught the imagination of the nation, completed the process. The dam drew thousands of workers to Las Vegas looking for recreation – hard liquor, women and gambling.

Gambling was by no means the main business. When the State Legislature legalised gambling in 1931, Findlay adds, it was viewed as secondary to the notion of the Old West. Vegas was a side trip. It was the dam which was the big draw. Easy divorce, granted on the nod after six weeks' residence, was another attraction. The town was given nationwide publicity thanks to Clark Gable's wife Ria divorcing him there in 1939. 'Las Vegas impressed me as being different from any other American town,' noted another traveller in those days. 'There was a lack of formality in the air and absolute disregard for social distinction. The people were friendly and money was loose and plentiful. The bars and gambling halls were packed to capacity.' In the mining camps social distinctions hardly counted, noted Paher. 'Mineral fields held a special fascination for romantic people of culture. Teachers, retired army officers, lawyers, judges and other educated men came in good numbers and might be found digging together in a rocky hole.' In such company a first name was enough by way of introduction.

On the eve of the Second World War, gambling was still small time. Nothing suggested the boom that was to come. The war saw the establishment of Nellis Air Force base to the north of Vegas, and a host of servicemen looking for a quick fling. The town has benefitted greatly, over the years, from the military presence and all the federal spending that went with it. A lot more people came to see Vegas. Its reputation spread. And the war, as was natural, served to loosen the moral inhibitions of the great American public against gambling. Geographically, it was still a small town, spreading out from the railway station either side of Fremont Street. But from its rough-and-ready frontier beginnings, the essential characteristics of Vegas seem to have been determined from the start – gambling, sex; easy money, good times.

A major change of direction came with the building of Bugsy Siegel's Flamingo in 1946–47. This was the first of the new casino-hotels. Wartime shortages and priority lists for building materials proved little obstacle. Using his influence with political friends like Nevada Senator Pat McCarran, his close ties with the Hollywood studios, and his access to black market supplies, Siegel was able to proceed at a frenzied pace. Criticism from local veterans groups, whose need for postwar housing was being shoved aside, was ignored, noted historian James Smith (in his paper 'Bugsy's Casino and the Modern Casino Hotel'). As chairman of the appropriations committee in Washington, McCarran had the clout to get round official restrictions: building materials were urgently needed, he claimed, to house 'thousands of people in the southern Nevada area who are aiding the war effort'. Siegel got his finance, directly or indirectly, from Meyer Lansky and friends. The little matter of materials delivered to the Flamingo being stolen overnight from the construction site, and sold back to Siegel the next day, escalated costs. He was soon heavily in hock to the mob. Costs rose from a projected $1–2m. to $6m.

In fact, El Rancho Vegas, the first hotel out on Highway 91, the road to Los Angeles, was built before the war. It was a motel, sporting a neon windmill on the casino roof, with white adobe bungalows around it, located three miles out from downtown. Two miles further on, the Last Frontier, built soon after, was likewise a ranch-style gambling hall (though some people doubted the area could support two casinos). It was these gambling joints which inspired Siegel to build his own place, but go one hell of a lot better. The Flamingo set a style, despite its initial failure, which over the next generation was to transform

Las Vegas: it was not just a hotel, not just a gambling hall featuring entertainment, it was a *resort*. Siegel told gambling writer John Scarne: 'I figured it this way. If people will take a trip out into the ocean to gamble, they'll go to a desert too – especially if it's legal and they don't have to worry about getting pinched. So one day I drive into Nevada looking for a nice desert spot and I picked this one because the price is right and it's on the main road to L.A.' (*Scarne's Guide to Casino Gambling*)

The casinos which followed through the 1950s gratified the postwar urge to live it up, the gambling equivalent of the baby boom. The Flamingo had landscaped lawns and gardens studded with palm trees, an elegant waterfall by its front entrance, plus a variety of distractions for its guests including a pool, health club, tennis and golf, stables for forty horses, show room and shops. The hotel, low and spacious, had only 105 rooms but reeked of luxury – it could never be confused with a mere motel. 'For the grand debut of Monte Carlo as a resort in 1879 the architect Charles Garnier designed an opera house for the Place du Casino, and Sarah Bernhardt read a symbolic poem. For the debut of Las Vegas as a resort in 1946 Bugsy Siegel hired Abbott and Costello,'* noted Tom Wolfe, 'and there, in a way, you have it all.' (The immortal Sarah Bernhardt was wont to gamble away her fees at the gaming tables, which shows that the Monegasque management was not altogether blinded by culture.) The only thing wrong with the Flamingo was that Bugsy had no cost control or management skills. The place wasn't finished when it opened and more or less everything went wrong. After heavy losses in the first two weeks (Siegel must have been cheated left and right), it had to close its doors.

Where Siegel was smart was in recognising the crucial importance of the link with L.A. Highway 91 was the way visitors drove in. The bright lights above the casino were the first sign of welcome to the people who had sweated out the 273 miles across

---

*The headliner at the opening was Jimmy Durante, but the point is valid.

the desert. All the new casinos were built in a line along this route, in marked contrast to the gambling halls of downtown which were clustered around the railroad station, in a gridiron plan. This short stretch of highway, two and a half miles long, became known as the Strip, after Sunset Strip in L.A. Siegel himself was shot before he had a chance to see the Flamingo transformed into the money-making machine he had anticipated, so vindicating his judgement. Its success encouraged a number of showbiz people, such as Frank Sinatra and Mae West, to consider building their own places; Roy Rogers talked of a dude ranch. 'I'm going to build a hotel', became a stock phrase among celebrity visitors. Through the postwar years, around two-thirds of all visitors to Vegas came from southern California. By the mid-1950s the population of Vegas had risen to 50,000. Tourists came pouring in, the great majority by car. Southern Californians, suggested John Findlay in *People of Chance*, had developed a type of leisure which revolved in part around fantasy – movies, TV, Disneyland. To some extent, of course, everyone who gambles enters into a make-believe world. Vegas presented it in living technicolour.

Within minutes of Siegel being gunned down in the living-room of his girlfriend Virginia Hill's home in Beverly Hills, three former associates arrived at the executive offices of the Flamingo. They announced that they were now in charge. Siegel's real crime, in the eyes of the mob, was that he was no good as a businessman. He was succeeded by an array of gangsters who were. In due course one Gus Greenbaum was brought in from Phoenix to run the Flamingo, where he turned a handsome profit in his first year. He had 'grifter sense', a gambler's instinct seasoned by experience, and ran a no holds barred operation. Dealers found cheating were taken to a soundproof room and taught the error of their ways with a baseball bat.

Greenbaum also hired star entertainers such as Joe E. Lewis, Nat King Cole, Pearl Bailey, Lena Horne, Dean Martin and Jerry Lewis, for the Flamingo's show room. The quality of such shows was appreciated by a performer whom one might not immediately associate with Las Vegas, Noel Coward. 'I am so fascinated – and helped – by the professional "expertise" in all departments,' he noted in his diary after 'one of the most sensational successes of my career' at the Desert Inn in June, 1955. 'Here also there is a genuine respect for, and understanding of, light music . . . Light music has been despised and rejected in England for years . . . Here, light music has its own genuine values, which are recognised not only by the public, but the Press. The orchestral arrangements and variations are incredible – vital and imaginative.' For Coward's opening night, Sinatra chartered a private plane and flew in Judy Garland, the Bogarts, and the Nivens; also present were Joan Fontaine, Zsa Zsa Gabor and the Joe Cottens. But what really gratified Coward was his talent to amuse ordinary audiences, 'dinner shows, filled with people from Kansas, Nebraska, Utah, Illinois, etc.'

Greenbaum's tenure of the Flamingo, which was highly successful, lasted seven years. Thus began Vegas' dark period: Meyer Lansky, regarded as the brains of the mob, exercising control at a distance; his partner from New York, Frank Costello, dubbed the prime minister of organised crime, a kind of chief operating officer; Moe Dalitz, the bootlegger from Cleveland, known affectionately as the godfather of Las Vegas; plus a retinue of consigliere, soldiers, skimmers, hitmen and lesser lights. The Mafia, or Cosa Nostra, bound the Italians together. The gangsters of Jewish origin could never be accepted as full members, initiated in blood, but they worked hand in glove with them. Such men set the style of Vegas, in those formative years, rather like the cowboy set the image of the West. 'The townspeople took it quite calmly,' recalled Robbins Cahill, then head of casino licensing, 'and rather bragged about the fact that, "that fellow from Murder, Inc. has come to Las Vegas and is going to build the most fabulous place that anyone ever heard of . . ." The only attitude I ever got out of the town was, "Hooray! He's going to bring money into the town." ' Tourists, too, have always been fascinated by the gangsters in their midst, half-wary and half-enraptured by their nefarious glamour.

Organised crime figures played a major role in hotel financing, speeding up development of the Strip, particularly at the Dunes, Stardust, Flamingo, Riviera, Tropicana and Sands, noted another modern account, *Resort City in the Sunbelt* by Eugene Moehring. 'The various gangland factions made and lost millions, first building and then overbuilding the Strip in the late forties and fifties. In turn, these huge capital investments invigorated the town's relatively small-scale resort industry, exerting a substantial multiplier effect upon the community's economy.' Better yet – casino executives linked to the mob had an instinctive feel and flair for gambling, acquired via illegal bookmaking. They emerged, in legalised gambling, as keen exponents of civic development, supporting improvements in roads, sanitation, schools and other services. Gus Greenbaum was elected chairman of the town board of Paradise (the township which covers the main part of the strip), styling himself 'mayor of Paradise'. All this was of direct benefit to Vegas as a resort and, more immediately, to their own properties.

Moe Dalitz and his associates moved in on the Desert Inn when its owner Wilbur Clark got into financial straits in 1949. This set a pattern for casino management, which the regulatory bodies found hard to break: the owner's name might be emblazoned over the marquee, but he was only a front man, behind whom the mob ran the show, skimming and scamming and corrupting virtually without hindrance. In the process, Vegas surged ahead, though the Kefauver hearings on organised crime in 1950/51 sent a shiver through the community. In 1957, when Frank Costello was shot in his New York apartment, the police found in his pocket a note of the current financial returns for the Tropicana. Costello survived the hit but was forced into retirement. There is a piquant irony in the mob's involvement in casinos, however: which is that its operations, on the 'legitimate' side, tend to be extremely efficient. Gambling is unique compared with other areas of criminal activity, because it is the only one where a prime objective of the crooked owners is to make the business work –

skimming (unlike say, robbing banks) takes place out of the profits which have been earned on turnover. The bigger the turnover, the richer the skim. How much money Lansky and others creamed off over the years is a matter of guesswork – certainly tens of millions.

The Chicago 'Outfit' moved in around the mid-'50s (see Chapter 8). It seized overall control, treating Vegas as a prize fiefdom. So far as the public and the players were concerned, none of this was visible apart from the occasional spat of bad publicity in the papers and the periodic gangland murder. The wheels spun and the slots clicked, faster and faster: through the '60s visitor volume rose year by year to an annual total of six million. The new resorts along the Strip were transforming the desert town into a national playground. Far from being the 'profitless locale', which the trailblazers had surveyed when they crossed the *jornada de muerto*, the very name Las Vegas became a symbol for extravagance.

In January 1951, a brighter light, even, than the neon blaze on Fremont Street was to rise over Las Vegas. The US Atomic Energy Commission conducted its first above ground nuclear test in southern Nevada, at the proving grounds of Nellis air base. Far from objecting to the test, the people of Vegas hailed the event. The little white puffball which rose in the sky over the edge of Glitter Gulch was another 'happening' in town. It put Las Vegas in the news yet again.

Gamblers rushed out of the casinos to watch the desert sky glow in the light of an artificial sun. Buildings shook, windows shattered. Swimsuits and wedding cakes were fashioned after a mushroom cloud. Overall a certain western pride was evinced in Nevada's contribution to strengthening the nation's defences. Though a more nervous, human reaction is shown in the fine movie *Desert Bloom* (1985), depicting those 1950s days, when schoolchildren were taught to cover their heads and shade their eyes against the unearthly light of the explosions. The nuclear tests brought more business and more prestige to the town. No event could symbolise more dramatically the transformation of the Wild West to the Space Age, though after 1962 the testing was done underground, which spoiled the show – and by 1982 1,100 people had sued the government for compensation, as the effects of exposure to fall out from the tests became evident (Howard Ball, *Justice Downwind*).

The picture was transformed again by the arrival of Howard Hughes in 1966. Hughes proceeded to acquire several properties – the Desert Inn (which he bought as a residence rather than vacate his suite on the top floor), the Sands, the Frontier and the Castaways, all on the Strip, and a block behind it, the Landmark, a building 340 feet high, shaped like an airport control tower. Hughes was seen as a white knight riding in to rescue Las Vegas, the only man rich enough to buy out the old mobsters, who were already well dug in and therefore immune from the new licensing regulations. By then the city had come to realise – it was a period of self-awareness like a bad gambler coming to his senses – that if it failed to clean up its act, it risked Federal prohibition of gambling. Hughes spent $300m. in Nevada, buying quantities of real estate in and around Las Vegas and myriad mining claims, plus two airlines and a TV station. He became at the same time the largest employer in the state and its most reclusive citizen. The law was widened to allow corporate ownership of casinos, as distinct from individual operators, partly to attract new capital, in 1969.

Whatever mania consumed his personal life, Hughes understood the essential appeal of Vegas and was indeed prescient about its future development. 'The Corporation did not look upon Las Vegas or Nevada as a gaming Mecca, but rather as a total environment in which gaming was one part,' his Summa Corporation explained its investment policy some years later – a short-vacation oriented get-away resort, offering sports, climate, entertainment, hotels, plus a unique attraction – gaming. 'Nevada was also close to a large metropolitan customer population; and properly developed, could expand from the close-proximity California market to draw from the entire world, particularly with the increased facility made possible by the jet airplane. This assessment continues to be verified each day.' Thus spake Hughes in his incorporeal voice from immurement in the Desert Inn. He lived long enough to see the main part of his prophecy fulfilled. In 1976, when Hughes died, Las Vegas was drawing nearly ten million visitors a year. His analysis of Vegas' appeal would certainly be endorsed in every detail by any casino president today. The enigmatic presence of Hughes, who would have bought even more casinos if anti-trust restrictions had not thwarted him, may be seen as an interregnum between the good ol' boy operators, who had hustled their way in, via illegal gambling, and the new-style corporations, run by boards of directors reporting to shareholders.

Hughes' sphere of influence was challenged by another powerful and individualistic entrepreneur, Kirk Kerkorian. He had, like Hughes, made his first fortune out of aviation, and then bought into Hollywood, with the acquisition of MGM. In 1969 Kerkorian broke with conventional wisdom by building a casino-hotel, the International, then the largest in the world, half a mile behind the Strip, beyond the Landmark. But he did not sit still long. A year later, in a deal with the Hilton Corporation, which marked a significant change in the pattern of casino ownership, Kerkorian sold the International and the Flamingo (which he had acquired briefly after various changes of ownership) to raise money for a new project. This was the MGM Grand, to rise on the fourth corner of the great crossroads, flanked by the Flamingo, opposite the Dunes and diagonally facing Caesars Palace. (The rise and fall of the MGM is detailed in Chapter 3.) Kerkorian has remained an influential figure, moving in and out of Vegas ever since; even now, in his seventies, he has grandiose plans for a bigger project than anything done before. (In terms of ambition and ego required, there is an affinity between making movies and running casinos, it seems.)

The modern era, in effect, began a year or two earlier with the opening of Caesars Palace. This casino-hotel marked a new dimension in showiness and luxury. Set back from the road by an ornamental garden and lines of statuary, Caesars stood in imperial isolation at the head of the Strip. It cost $22m. in 1966, which at the time was an unheard of extravagance. The original owners, who had raised their money via the corrupt Teamsters' Union, were of extremely dubious reputation. Ovid Demaris, not a man to pull his punches, declared that Caesars was 'a mob-controlled casino from the day it opened its doors' (*The Boardwalk Jungle*). To take just one instance of sleazy practice, the man appointed chief casino executive had served a twenty-month prison sentence on a conspiracy conviction, arising from an attempted fix of a football game. (Nonetheless he got his licence.)

In need of a face-lift, Caesars was taken over in 1969 by Clifford and Stuart Perlman, who (so Demaris put it) had parlayed a hot-dog stand in Miami Beach into a restaurant chain. They paid $60m. for it, which showed how casino values were moving (though the price may have been inflated as part of a stock manipulation) and changed the name of their company from Lum's to Caesar's World. Things got rapidly worse. For the Perlman brothers, too, had all kinds of undesirable connections – 'with persons of notorious or unsavoury reputations or who have extensive police records', as the Gaming Commission put it – and were continually upbraided by the regulatory authorities, whose strictures they simply ignored. When various charges of stock fraud were brought against the company in 1971, the owners and principal employees all took the Fifth. After one scandal over dubious loans, Clifford Perlman protested: 'What's happening is that we're being accused of associating with a guy who's accused of associating with a guy. And we are getting more newspaper coverage out of that than the Second World War.'

Such malodorous scandals sullied Caesars' marble brow hardly more than a puff of sand blown off the desert. With its glitz and glamour, and reputation for high action, Caesars Palace led the party. It was the hang-out of the mob, of Sinatra and the rat pack, of the high rollers, the movie stars and the new jet set, it set the standard by which every other casino judged its own performance. Finally, however, the time came when even the Perlmans judged it wise to jump: in 1981 they sold out their 4.8m. shares for $99m., which was more than twice the market value. The Gaming Commission approved the transaction, but barred Clifford Perlman from continuing as chairman and chief executive of Caesars Palace. Thus the decade which had begun with the arrival of the Hilton Corporation as a major casino operator, and ended with the management restructuring of Caesars, encompassed a complete sea-change of the casino industry from private to corporate ownership.

Las Vegas owed its original success to its location as a transit point: now the position was reversed. It had become a destination resort. The convention centre, built in 1955–59, and frequently modernised, is located beyond the Strip, next to the site of the present Las Vegas Hilton. It was a success from the start, enabling Vegas to rival any city in the country. In 1970, 269 conventions totalling 269,000 delegates came to town. Very few among all those worthy salesmen and buyers, or their spouses, would be likely to leave town without first venturing a few bucks at the tables, so close to the meetings halls. And the city strove mightily to bring in the people. By 1980 the conventions total had risen to 449 and 656,000 delegates; and by 1990 to over 1,000 meetings and 1.75 million conventioneers. Bookings currently run several years ahead, into the next century. The airport – a fun place – has been expanded, as traffic rose through the '80s to nearly 50,000 passengers a day.

Its reputation for excitement emanated like an aura. Scores of movies and TV series of the 1970s and '80s beamed Las Vegas round the world. Among many brilliant images, James Bond's car chase around Glitter Gulch in *Diamonds are Forever* (1971) stands out. The police cars race around the block, up and down car ramps, in and out of garages, against a backdrop of casino fronts, shown again and again with glittering verisimilitude. Such publicity outdid any official PR, not that the Convention and Visitors Authority was backward. By this time Vegas had established itself as one of the leading resorts in the country. But no film could match Tom Wolfe's evocation of the *sound* of downtown Vegas, in his piece entitled 'Las Vegas (What?) Las Vegas (Can't Hear You! Too Noisy) Las Vegas!!!!', first published in 1963. It begins, you may recall, with the word 'hernia' being repeated over and over and over again. Hernia, hernia, hernia, HERNia for a whole paragraph. This is the only noise which Raymond, standing at the craps table, zonked out of his mind after two and a half days without sleep, can hear at that point.

'Hernia, hernia, hernia, HERNia, hernia . . .'

It still *is* the characteristic background blur at the tables, in the middle of the casino floor, when you are that far gone. Wolfe caught Vegas at the beginning of its upswing, a surge which has continued into the 1990s. The resort could expand along the Strip because there was so much land. Even today, there are huge empty lots ready and waiting (at a price) for development, between the big casinos. Each period of expansion has been followed by a pause, as the industry adjusts to the new level of competition. After the Stardust opened in 1958 there was an eight year gap before the Aladdin went up, at the southern end of the Strip. There was a mild recession in gaming at the end of the '70s and early '80s, reflecting a decline in the national economy, (exacerbated by the apparent challenge from Atlantic City). And today, after the opening fireworks of the Mirage and Excalibur, another pause is due, with a probable shake-out of weaker companies.

But people are still flooding into Vegas, to work and live, at an astounding rate. Through 1989 and 1990, as the Mirage and Excalibur were recruiting their staff, and 5–6,000 people a month were moving to town, to fill jobs in the new casinos, Las Vegas became the fastest growing city in America. There is space for the town to expand, all around. Housing tracts, in a sunny Spanish-colonial style, are going up for the middle-income groups at bargain prices (from the high $80,000s to the low $100,000s for smaller two bedroom homes, from the mid-$100,000s and upwards for three or four room houses). For the less well-off, mobile homes, nestling head to tail in huge trailer sites, dot the inner suburbs. These people, who work in the big casino-hotels, and play in the local casinos, are the descendants of the first settlers who rushed in to bid for building lots.

Hopeful people, like Harmony, the not-so-young showgirl in Larry McMurtrey's novel *Desert Rose*, come to Vegas in search of work. This story, overly sentimental as it is, shows people as they are, working, rushing their coffee breaks between shows, trying to get their cars fixed and do their household chores, enjoying fast friendships like fast food, the daily round set against the non-stop action of the Strip casinos, which are not, for these people, places of entertainment but places of work. The heroine of this tale has a special quality 'the ability to see the bright side'. She likes to think about the good kinds of things that could happen rather than the bad kinds of things – one of the good things being that Vegas enabled her to find a glamorous job on stage. All the new people rushing into town are a little like Harmony: full of hopes and dreams, turning Las Vegas into a new frontier.

3 GUYS ON THE BLOCK

ON THE STRIP

If a man can . . . make a better mousetrap than his
neighbour, though he build his house in the woods,
the world will make a beaten path to his door.

Ralph Waldo Emerson (Attributed)

Driving north to south on the Las Vegas Strip, just before you
reach the Desert Inn, still glowing faintly in its half-life as
Howard Hughes' final refuge, is an enigmatic road sign which
proclaims: Town Limits: ENTER PARADISE.

Back to the right is the huge pink and white striped tent of
Circus Circus. It appears to billow slightly, not from a wind off
the desert but from clever lighting – and also, perhaps, from the
waves of pulsing energy given off by the mass of gamblers
crammed beneath its canopy. In a laconic aside, the writer
Hunter S. Thompson remarked that Circus Circus was what the
whole hep world would be doing on Saturday night if the Nazis
had won the Second World War. It is true that when you stand in
the balcony below the big-top at Circus Circus, and look up at the
half-naked acrobats performing desultory swings on their ropes,
and then gaze down at the abandoned throngs jamming the slots,
while simultaneously one of your ears is assaulted by a drum roll
and the other ear by the amplified blare of pop music, an
overwhelming sense of nihilism takes hold.

But Circus Circus must be doing something right. Its room
occupancy rate is a staggering 99.7 per cent. In an obvious way,

Circus Circus *is* the Strip, it has touched the soul of mass taste in America. The Strip is barely two and a half miles long. Circus Circus brackets it. At the other end stands Circus' new enterprise, Excalibur. It is the first big image which hits the new arrival, coming in from the airport or driving from LA, even before reaching the ultra-bright, overwhelming crossroads on Las Vegas Boulevard South marked by Caesars Palace, Bally's (the renamed MGM Grand) and the Flamingo. Forget town planning, forget commercial architecture, forget good taste: these massive structures radiate to the skies an awesome vitality.

Caesars Palace has been the market leader, the most extravagantly luxurious, the name to conjure with in Las Vegas for over two decades. Caesars (no apostrophe) had that elusive quality, style. No matter that this style, at least in some eyes, was a ridiculous mixture of bad taste and fake history, epitomised by – well, epitomised by its swanky drive-way lined by white columns and mock-Roman statuary, by the larger-than-life imitation of Michelangelo's David which adorns its central lobby, by the relentless kitsch of its decoration, from the mini-toga costumes worn by the casino staff down to the signs once painted in latinate script on its washroom doors – 'Caesars' and 'Cleopatras'. No matter, Caesars had an unmistakeable identity, and the revenue to prove it paid. Through the twenty years of its sway over this mighty crossroads of gambling, Caesars stood out, not alone, but first. To the media, Vegas meant Caesars. The shows, the stars, the money, the aura of extravagance, gave it unique status. An estimated ten million people a year visit the property. But the day that the Mirage opened its doors, Caesars paled. Suddenly it looked out-moded.

Caesars' reputation was not always above suspicion. From the day it opened in 1966, the wrong people had got in there. Built by a notorious gambler called Jay Sarno, with loans provided by Jimmy Hoffa's Teamsters' Union, it became a favourite hang-out of the mob. Many of Caesars' executives were known to have direct links with Mafia families, imparting a sinister undercurrent to the action, and over the years many of these people, from owners and executives down to managers and employees, had been investigated, and often indicted, for stock fraud, skimming, conspiracy and other offences. As related in the previous chapter, when the company applied for a licence to operate in New Jersey in 1978, the New Jersey Casino Control Commission insisted that the two principal owners, the Perlman brothers, dissociate themselves from the corporation (without admission of any wrong-doing). New management took over. And like the misspent years of a profligate youth, the resort's shady past was – formally – consigned to nostalgic memory.

Chairman Henry Gluck, who has headed the company since 1983, was aware of the challenge from the Mirage. He decided to meet it, not by reckless expansion, vying with all the other properties on the Strip, but by upgrading their existing facilities – Caesars, with a mere 1,600 rooms, has no ambitions to giganticism. As the suites, with their mirrors over the beds, their sunken bathtubs and gold-plated taps were re-vamped, the room total was actually reduced. Even so, small it isn't. Plans include an extension of the casino floor to allow space for a total of 2,200 slots (the same as the Mirage), a shopping forum modelled on an ancient Roman village (more accurately Rodeo Drive in Hollywood) and a Temple of Caesars with triumphal arches, approached via a walkway or 'people mover', ferrying the shoppers in (plus tunnels off the Strip leading to free parking). The new people mover was constructed next to the Mirage's own walkway, to lure customers in the Roman way. All this at a capital cost of over $300m. for 1989 and '90, to be completed by the end of 1992.

It was an ingenious approach, yet Caesars seemed a little slow off the mark. In the first few weeks after the Mirage opened, the place looked empty. The baccarat pit took a terrible beating at the end of the year, though the loss of several million was attributed to a run of good luck by a big punter, as can happen. Several hosts at Caesars – whose job is to take care of high rollers, like gardeners tending prize roses – were summarily dumped from the payroll. Their dismissal, whether a cause or effect of the downturn, accentuated the decline. The casino staff looked unhappy and underemployed, the gourmet restaurant was half empty. No doubt about it, Caesars was hurting.

'When there's a new kid on the block,' explained vice-president Don Guiliemino, then director of publicity, 'everyone wants to play with him. Everyone expected Steve [Wynn] would attract the crowds at the start. We don't feel Caesars will lose its place as the front runner in the industry. The company is very, very strong.' Guiliemino, who had an elegant office surrounded by pictures of the prize-fighters who have blitzed their way in and out of Caesars – Ali, Liston, Leonard, Hearns, Hagler – has a relaxed and persuasive manner. Caesars might be hurting a little, he implied, but if so it was no more than a bruised shin.

This was the general reaction up and down the Strip, in the weeks after the Mirage opened. In fact, opinion in the executive offices in the casinos immediately opposite – notably Bally's, the immense mausoleum which used to be the MGM, and the Flamingo Hilton, which soars up over Bugsy Siegel's first extravaganza, and the downmarket Imperial Palace – all claimed they saw the opening of the Mirage as a plus. 'Good luck, Steve,' said Michael Gaughan, owner of the cheap and cheerful gambling hall the Barbary Coast, which fills a long narrow strip on the corner, in a message of congratulation, 'and thanks – you've added $50m. to the worth of my property.'

The argument was that the electric wave of publicity which the Mirage set in motion gave Las Vegas a new sparkle in the public eye. Everyone who came into town wanted to see the new place, sure. But the crowds who thronged the Mirage would not stay there all day and all night; they would be milling out all around the crossroads and along the Strip, spending their money on the attractions of rival casinos too, in effect turning Las Vegas

Boulevard South into a shopping mall of gambling. A good point: but in January 1990, out of a total revenue of $125m. reported by Strip casinos, the Mirage took $40m., a staggering share. At this rate, Wynn was going to get his investors' money back pretty fast – though others pointed out that there was no way of knowing what the Mirage's opening expenses really were. Promoting the middle-weight title fight between Leonard and Duran (which turned out to be a dismal anti-climax) had reportedly cost Wynn some $10m.

Caesars World, the parent company which owns the Caesars casinos in Atlantic City and Lake Tahoe as well as Las Vegas, noted in its annual report for 1989: 'Our strategy is straightforward: Caesars World has a long-standing commitment to preserve its reputation for maintaining the finest gaming . . . and other resort amenities available anywhere. Our financial condition is excellent. Cash flow from operations far exceeds debt requirements.' Whereas the Mirage (it was implicitly understood) was carrying a colossal debt burden of $500m. or $600m. or more – who knew the true cost? A year later, Caesars' annual report for 1990, by its own admission, made 'disappointing' reading. Operating income in Nevada declined by $43m. from the previous year, primarily due to a decline in casino revenue. Net income of the group fell from $66m. to $36m.

Marketing, which is the key to casino success, is strong at Caesars World. The name itself, with its pointy Roman lettering, is a world-famous logo. Abroad, a network of offices in 21 countries, reinforcing sales offices in 17 cities in the USA (there were 28 and 19 respectively the year before), attests to the underlying strength of the operation. Caesars in Vegas claimed it had more revenue from international customers (high rollers from Asia predominating) than any other casino-hotel in the country.

All the same, Caesars was left standing by the high-speed opening of its next door neighbour. Did the trouble stem in part from the fact that the headquarters of the group is off-centre, out in Los Angeles? Decisions made out there, designed to cut costs and straighten out the bottom line – such as the sudden dismissal of so many experienced casino hosts – were not just short-sighted, they were critically wrong. Good hosts are the vital oil in the wheels of a high-rolling casino. In accountants' beady eyes, cutting such a big ticket item out of the salaries bill might look like a saving; but such decisions, whatever the motive, seem to lack any appreciation of what makes a top casino work. One long-serving (but not long-suffering) host who walked over to the Mirage was re-employed inside fifteen minutes.

It took another month or two before Caesars' board got the message. Caesars Palace's hold on the market had been chal-lenged and to prove it, its revenue had been hit. As in boxing, a new guy had popped up and socked it to the old champ. Caesars was winded, but it was certainly not out. New managers were appointed, others sacked, staff were switched around, the enterprise was given new vigour.

In 1992 Caesars opened its Shopping Forum, a Roman street sporting columns and arches with colonnades of fashion stores and cheap boutiques. Overhead, a vast dome of a ceiling, painted to resemble a Mediterranean sky, shone down all the colours of dawn through dusk. In the central piazza the statues, on the hour, came to life. *Stupendo!* The only way people can make their way out of Caesars' shopping extravaganza is (of course) via the casino.

Caesars, no doubt, will remain a force in Vegas. It has a superb property and the gloss of luxury. There are always going to be plenty of rich people for whom one of the 'fantasy suites' at Caesars is the ultimate experience of heaven on earth.

Like a pair of colossi, the white and yellow blocks of Caesars Palace and the Mirage stand side by side. Their illuminated signs, proclaiming manifold attractions such as cabaret, tigers, dolphins, boxing, buffets, jackpots, soar over the petty mortals on the sidewalk, as if trying constantly to upstage each other, day and night. Set back in their own grounds, the two casinos give an ample sense of space and leisure all around.

By contrast, the other side of the road is cramped, on one side by the twin slabs of Bally's, and on the other by the Flamingo Hilton, and the Imperial Palace, and then the Holiday Inn, now called Harrah's, Las Vegas. This short stretch of the Strip packs in over 16,000 hotel rooms.

Bally's is so vast it would make a Mayan temple look like a gazebo. It is a solid block, relentlessly unimaginative in design, both outside and in, where the main casino floor just goes on and on and on. Bally's was originally the MGM Grand, built by Kirk Kerkorian. Kerkorian spotted the potential of Las Vegas early on. The son of Armenian immigrants, raised in California during the years of the depression, Kerkorian achieved his first business success buying up surplus aircraft after the war, during which he had served as a flight instructor. He saw (like Howard Hughes) the coming expansion of air travel and from a small start launched his own airline. He bought land on the corner of the Strip and Flamingo Road. This lot became the site of Caesars Palace, no less. When the time came to sell his then highly successful Trans International Airlines, he used the money to buy into hotel-casinos, first the Flamingo (a snip at $15m. in 1967) and then the International, which he built himself. At 1,500 rooms it was at that time the largest resort hotel in the world.

In the '70s Kerkorian acquired a controlling interest in Metro-Goldwyn-Mayer, the most famous name in Hollywood. A new casino in Vegas was a natural continuation of his showbiz interests. To finance the MGM Grand he sold off various assets of the movie studios, which upset cineastes and sentimentalists alike. But here again, as in his fledgling airline, Kerkorian was ahead of the game. He foresaw that casino gambling as a total-leisure activity was likely to prove far more profitable than conventional movie-making. All the contractors involved in the new project were impressed with the need for speed: the hotel, covering two and a half million square feet, was completed from start to finish in nineteen months. From its opening day it was a box-office hit. The name MGM has a special magic for Americans. In its first full year of operation in 1974, the new hotel-casino was like a crock of gold. It contributed $22m. out of $28.6m. to its parent company. This was the highest revenues and profits MGM had ever made in its entire history – which just showed that there *was* one business even better than show business.

Fast forward to 21 November 1980. It is early morning. Smoke is seen rising above the colossal front of the MGM. The alert is slow in coming. Inside the casino, crystal chandeliers crash down and ceiling panels crack and fall, while above, so far unseen by anyone, a second fireball races towards the front entrance (as recorded in *The Day the MGM Grand Hotel Burned* by Deirdre Coakley et al). Pipes, conduits and insulation material ignite and burn relentlessly. A moment after the wall of fire crashes through the restaurant end of the casino, a second, more violent fire reaches the hotel's main entrance, dropping a blistering wall of flames that consumes everything in its path. Carpeting, gaming tables, light fixtures, furniture, ornaments, and wall coverings are all engulfed in seconds.

According to this account, in just ninety seconds life ceased in the casino and surrounding areas. Fourteen people were already dead. As the fire roared through the casino, a cloud of toxic smoke poured up through the ceiling. The smoke rose up through every crack, every duct, every open door, through elevator shafts and stairwells. Escaping into the open air, the smoke rose in a column nearly one mile high. Most people were asleep, others panicked. By the time the fire was out, 85 people had lost their lives, one of the worst hotel fires in American history. The MGM was closed for eight months, 3,750 casino workers were left without jobs, and Las Vegas' reputation as a leave-your-cares-behind, get-away-from-it-all resort went up with the flames. The fire was traced to faulty wiring above the ceiling of a deli on the ground floor. It had smouldered for several hours before breaking through the kitchen ceiling; then the sudden rush of oxygen, acting as a back-draught, sent the whole place up like a vast torch.

But the show, as everyone knows, must go on. The employees found new jobs. The gaming went on across the street. Every major hotel moved to install up-to-date smoke detectors and generally to modernise its fire precautions. All the lawsuits against MGM across the country were consolidated under the same jurisdiction in Las Vegas. And Kerkorian set a deadline of July the following year for its re-opening. The public, perhaps reassured by the new hotel's 'state of the art' fire-safety system, began to make reservations in record numbers. On 29 July 1981 the MGM was born again, but quietly. 'The hotel looks just about the same,' remarked a cocktail waitress, summing up the prevailing view.

The MGM always had something of an identity problem. It was big, sure. But that was all. The casino lay-out, designed in a vast open square like a football field under chandeliers, was, to me, ineffably boring. In those pre-disaster days, the management tried to gild the place with an aura of Hollywood, by posting up pictures of movie stars of the golden days. But the massive structure of the place resisted all attempts to implant a human dimension. Though I recall a striking picture of the MGM lion in full roar, over the desk of the public relations man, captioned 'Here the Customer is King'. Bally's Manufacturing Corporation took over MGM Grand Hotels Inc. in 1986 at a cost of $440m., plus $110m. of company debt. Kerkorian, shrewd as ever, kept the rights to the name MGM Grand. Bally's was a manufacturer of slot and pinball machines and computer games – it was the company which devised the phenomenally successful Pac-man. But its dominant position as supplier of slots to the gaming industry was under challenge from new competition. Likewise, its chain of health and fitness clubs had begun to peak.

Bally's casino in Vegas remains entertainment oriented: its Jubilee Spectacular, featuring show-girls in talcum powder and ostrich feathers, includes tableaux such as the Sinking of the

Titanic and Destruction of the Temple by Samson. The show, at a start-up cost of $10m., ran to capacity audiences throughout the decade but needed updating. The Celebrity Room presented entertainers like Frank Sinatra (he has in his time played most of the hotels on the Strip), Dean Martin, whose cabaret gigs go right back to the start of Vegas, and Sammy Davis Jr. (When Sammy Davis died in 1990, all the strip casinos dimmed their lights for ten minutes as a gesture of respect. The late entertainer being out of funds – evidently he enjoyed gambling a bit too much – Sinatra paid for the funeral.)

Overall, Bally's gave the impression that although its four casinos were a major earner – on total revenue of over $2 billion in 1989, $948m. came from its two casinos in Vegas and Reno and its two in Atlantic City – the company was drifting. Operating income from the Nevada casinos declined by one third in 1989 – and that was before the Mirage or the Excalibur opened. The basic trouble was that on the Strip Bally's had not quite found its niche in the market or settled on a distinctive image. The whispers and rumours came to a head in the fall of 1990. While Bally's board of directors gathered in Scotland, to ponder policy in the relaxing setting of the Gleneagles hotel, a blood-curdling cry came over the heather: the company's shares were tumbling on Wall Street, on reports of dividend cuts and imminent bankruptcy. Bally's chairman Robert Mullane, was shaken enough to offer to resign, then agreed to stay on, then resigned the next day.

A wholesale reorganisation of the company's top management was announced, together with plans to restructure its huge $1.86 billion debt – meanwhile a scheduled interest payment of about $18m. was postponed, pending a review of its financial condition. Arthur Goldberg, a businessman from New Jersey, elected to the board as Bally's largest shareholder, rapidly set about restoring confidence. He said the company would not be filing for bankruptcy – 'It's not even an option. We want to look at every aspect of the business and see how it fits into the picture. The board fully intends to have the company's Nevada operations continue as a viable entity.' The fact that Bally's share price could lose nearly 90 per cent of its value in a year, tumbling from the mid-20s to 1.87, showed how even the mightiest casino edifice could seem paper-thin. Bally's went into bankruptcy at the end of 1991. Its survival was said to depend on funding improvements to the property, which in turn depended on restructuring its debt.

Size isn't everything: opposite Bally's, tucked into the sidewalk, runs the narrow strip of the Barbary Coast. It's an old-fashioned gambling joint, run by Michael Gaughan, who learned the casino business from his father Jackie Gaughan, one of the good ol' boys still in business. The Barbary Coast knows what it's doing and does it well, sans frills. Gaughan also has the lucrative concession on running the slots of McCarran airport, where there is no need to spend a cent on bringing in the customers.

Its prime location on the corner means that Bally's Casino Resort remains a highly attractive property. If the new management team can hold on to the wide-ranging clientele it has built up over the years, while upgrading the casino and hotel, it may yet pull through. With the head of Bally's casino operations paying himself a higher salary, $4m. a year, than any other executive of a publicly traded casino company, it should do something. I was only sorry that in the reorganisation, Bally's decided not to proceed with its acquisition of the Clermont Club in London, an eighteenth-century jewel-box of a casino, badly in need of livening up. Its two little salons (patronised by a couple of languid English gentlemen or an Arab sheik) comprise three blackjack tables, two roulette wheels and a Punto Banco (baccarat) table. Bally's, in comparison, has over 100 table games and more than 1,000 slots.

The Flamingo Hilton, opposite Bally's and facing Caesars, is *on* the Strip, flush with the sidewalk. Its glittery entrance is designed to attract walk-in customers. The Flamingo has of course long since shaken off the blood-stained dust of its founder Bugsy

Siegel. In one version of the story he and his financial backer
Meyer Lansky chose the name in memory of the flamingos which
they had so often seen flying and dancing over the infield at
Hialeah racetrack in Miami; another version is that Flamingo was
Bugsy's pet name for his girlfriend Virginia Hill. (The flamingo
was also supposed by the Indians to be a symbol of good luck.)

Anyone who has ever heard of 'the syndicate' must feel a little
shiver of excitement as he enters the Flamingo's doors. This was
where it all started, this was where Bugsy's murderous career
reached its apogee. One half expects a mean-eyed guy in a zoot
suit, with a bulge under the shoulder, to emerge from behind the
door, to give each visitor a quick once-over. Well, not quite.
There used to be a little plot of garden, out by the pool, known as
Bugsy's Rose Garden, in memory of the founder – but no more.
'They dug it up when they built the new tower. I guess you could
say the mystique has gone,' explained an attendant. The
Flamingo has become a big place, but it is impeccably organised.

It is run, unusually, by a European-born and trained hotelier,
Horst Dziura, who has been successful in giving the Flamingo a
family feeling. He is credited as the man who saw the opening Las
Vegas offered for promoting tourist and family-style vacations.
Under his presidency the Flamingo has grown from 700 rooms to
over 3,000. For a few weeks, in early 1990, it was the biggest casino-
hotel in the world, with 3,530 rooms, before the Excalibur arose out
of the desert. The Flamingo sign on the new tower cost $1.6m.
Dziura has a clear idea of his patrons' tastes and needs. The average
amount of money the Flamingo's customers have to spend on
gambling, he told me, is $375 a head (implying a budget
approaching $2,000). Such estimates are only a rule of thumb but
they illustrate the kind of calculation a modern casino can make, in
order to tailor its gaming to its clientele. A prime feature, for
example, has been the 'Pot o' Gold' slots with a jackpot of $250,000.
At $3 a pull this is not cheap, but well within a vacation budget. The
Flamingo's shrewd approach can also be seen in its running a
casino-within-a-casino, next to its main entrance, called O'Shea's:

the Irish motif gives customers a change of scene. The answer to the question: How much of his or her gambling budget will each player lose? depends on the size of bet and rate of play for each individual. Overall, the casino's hold, the proportion of money staked which it wins, has declined (Dziura says from 21 per cent to 17 per cent) because the public has got smarter and learned more about 'money management'. Increased competition from rival casinos on the Strip puts pressure on everyone to 'sharpen the pencil' when it comes to costing rooms and meals, Dziura adds. Nevertheless, in fiscal year 1990 the Flamingo had a record profit of over $76m.

Next to the Flamingo, but set back from the street so you might pass by without even noticing it, is the Imperial Palace. With 2,700 rooms, this is not a small place either. The main entrance, below street level, is via a car-turning circle. It leads into an extended, up-and-down barn of a property, with an oriental touch: it is not much of a palace and not at all imperial. In fact it looks as if it had been tacked together with string and scotch tape. The explanation is that the Palace has just grown, at the behest of its owner, an entrepreneurial builder named Ralph Engelstad. Cheap and downmarket, the casino windows advertise hot dogs at $1.25 side by side with 'Win a New Mercedes-Benz'.

The Imperial Palace earns its keep thanks to its fortunate location in the heart of the Strip. Its show features impersonations of Marilyn Monroe, Elvis and Liberace. It also has an antique automobile collection with 200 cars on display, including Al Capone's Cadillac and a bullet-proof Mercedes-Benz made for Hitler. A propos of which, Mr Engelstad achieved notoriety a year or two back by holding a party to celebrate Hitler's birthday. This is not the kind of publicity Las Vegas needs, to put it mildly. He was fined $1.5m. by the Nevada Gaming Control Board, which also imposed certain conditions on his gaming licence, notably a ban on parties or displays of memorabilia that would glorify Hitler or Nazi Germany. Engelstad's attorney defended his actions, as the party was held in private. The Board contended that he had damaged the reputation of Nevada and its gaming industry. The Imperial Palace has done well thanks to maintaining strong margins. According to a business colleague, its hard-hat owner is not anti-semitic, 'just a bit goofy'.

On the fourth corner of the great crossroads marked by Caesars, Bally and the Flamingo is the site of a famous name from the past, the Dunes, which for some time seemed to be sinking into its own sand. The casino, called the Oasis, is shaped like a gold plated onion, right on the corner, fronting the hotel – a location to dream of. Everyone coming down the Strip, north, south, east or west, must pass the Dunes; the trouble was that so few people were stopping there. The property was bought out of bankruptcy by Japanese businessman Masao Nangaku in 1987, since when the place has languished. His intention, so he claimed, was to restore the Dunes to a 'leadership position'. One idea was to convert the present Top o' the Dunes into a Japanese style 'Karaoke', where guests would sing along to musical hits displayed on a video screen. But Mr Nangaku refused to carry out the renovation and expansion as promised without being granted a full licence; and for their part the gaming authorities refused to go beyond a temporary licence, without clear proof of sound management. Meanwhile the Dunes remained three-quarters empty, losing $2m. a month and offering living proof that location is not everything either.

Ahead of new licence hearings in spring 1991 Mr Nangaku succeeded in finding a first-rate casino manager, Larry Clark, whom he recruited from the Taj Mahal in Atlantic City (casino executives switch between the two resorts like an employment bureau). 'The Dunes has the greatest potential of any property on the Strip,' Clark stated, probably correctly, given its low starting point. A lightweight professional boxer in his early days, and a three-time recipient of the Bronze Star in Vietnam, Clark is used to fighting his way out of tight corners. 'I learned that when you're hurting, you become very creative and work hardest,' he says. His approach to casinos is based on the formula $SC = M$, meaning success in a casino depends on its marketing. His first task at the

Dunes was to rebuild this department, run-down in cost cutting, but he did not stay long. Concerned above all for stability (six different management teams had been in and out of its doors) the Nevada State Gaming Control Board still refused to grant Nangaku a full licence. But its decision was overruled by the Nevada Gaming Commission so Nangaku finally got his way. His other project, the $100m. Minami tower, designed as a business centre downtown, looked impressive in drawings but appears to be stalled in mid-construction.

The Sands, another favourite haunt of Sinatra and the Hollywood set, is another great name from the past. One can catch a vibrant echo of those days from listening to old recordings of Nat King Cole live at the Sands or Sinatra swinging with the Count Basie orchestra. The Sands may be picking up the beat again. Located further down the Strip, it too has a marvellous site, opposite the southern exit of the Mirage; all the thousands of people coming out by the Mirage volcano have only to cross the road to find a welcome at the Sands. The question is whether the Sands is ready for them. The property was bought by a successful businessman, Sheldon Adelson, who made his name in running the Comdex exhibition, which is the world's biggest computer conference, attracting 50,000 delegates. Adelson conceived the idea of shunting the whole show to Vegas, where it has continued to run successfully for several years (though not so popular with other casinos, who complain that computer people don't gamble).

Adelson decided that the business principles he learned in running the Comdex exhibition could be applied, without undue difficulty, to managing a modern casino. Accordingly he is building his own convention centre, at the rear of the Sands, which will eventually have the largest exhibition space of any hotel in town. These delegates, however, will not be gambling at the Sands, which remains a small place of only 700 rooms, albeit with a distinctive 1950s charm about it. The personal touch is provided by Adelson's brother Zachary, who roams around the property like a bemused koala: 'When I came out here I thought I was going to be a big shot,' he laments, 'but it's just work, work, work.' He acts as a soothing influence on Sheldon, whose abrasive style has led to clashes with fellow operators. If he is right about making the Sands the hub of a new convention centre, Adelson will make a big name for himself in Vegas; if, as some people of experience believe, he is doing things the wrong way round, he may fall flat.

By contrast, the Las Vegas Hilton, towering in monolithic isolation, is the only major casino-hotel off the Strip. Its bulk is so huge it looks as if it's only a few steps from Las Vegas Boulevard: but it's half a mile out, adjacent to the Las Vegas Convention Center. When the site was chosen, opinion in the gambling business was sceptical that the public would trek out to gamble beyond the neon artery of the Strip. The secret of the Hilton is that it is a city within a city, with an enormous convention business. Once visitors have checked in, they have little motive to move. Thus, the Hilton boasts 220,000 feet of convention, banquet and trade show space. When the ballroom and the pavilion are joined, the floor space is bigger than two football fields: 10,000 people can be seated for dinner. One of modern man's, or businessman's, predelictions is for conferences and conventions. It makes an agreeable break for trade and professional organisations to get together every so often, expenses paid, and twice as nice if it's in a place like Vegas. And after a day of demos and sales talk, these delegates are ready to gamble. Thanks to its Convention Center (currently being expanded to 1.6 million square feet), the city has been stunningly successful in catering to this trend. Hence all those signs like 'Welcome to Ohio Dentists' or 'Free Buffet for Western Bowlers'—even the Baptists, root and branch abjurers of gambling, chose Vegas for their convention in 1989. (I have attended seminars on the dangers of compulsive gambling, no less, on casino premises.)

It was at the Las Vegas Hilton (how long ago it seems) that I saw 'the King'. Elvis Presley was the only performer who sold out every single ticket in the 1,600 seat theatre for 28 straight days, during his annual spring and summer engagements. (One of his glittery high-collared jumpsuits, faded now, and a beat-up guitar, is on display under glass, outside the show room.) John Fitzgerald, president of the Hilton, who took over in 1972, affects a relaxed air about his mammoth enterprise. 'Bigness, if it's done well, works,' he says. There has not been a single day in his presidency when some part of the property was not being renovated or rebuilt. Now there are plans for extensive landscaping, including new roadways and entrances, and, most interestingly (considering various bids for the Hilton properties), a redesign of its logo, the huge elongated H on the side of the hotel. The casino is vast and spread out but despite its broad appeal has relied for a significant slice of its gaming revenue on high roller baccarat, with the Asian market dominant. As president, Fitzgerald carries business cards in Japanese and Chinese as well as English, and a number of employees are fluent in oriental languages. This market has changed dramatically from even a few years ago, when the majority of premium players came from the USA (see Chapter 6). Despite its gargantuan size, the Hilton maintains a one-to-one relationship with these customers; favoured guests may be invited by Barron Hilton himself for a weekend break up at his ski lodge.

In 1990 the Hilton group's total gaming revenue, provided in the main by the Flamingo and the Las Vegas Hilton, was $655m. out of $1,125m. from all of its properties worldwide, an impressive statistic. Despite the challenge from the Mirage and Excalibur, the Las Vegas Hilton had a record year in 1990, increasing operating results by 38 per cent from the year before. The Flamingo, facing the new attraction directly across the street, still showed a small increase in operating income; it plans to strengthen its walk-in business. Vegas remains a dynamic, vibrant market, concludes the Hilton annual report, and its casinos can meet the new competition head-on. So if these two properties are so successful, why should there be talk about a possible sale? A sense, perhaps, that after a twenty-year run since acquiring the properties from Kerkorian, it might be time for a change in the Hilton group.

Looking north up the Strip from the famous crossroads, past the Mirage and its palm trees, the road bends, revealing the Frontier and the Desert Inn left and right, then the Stardust with its cornucopia of stars, out-shining the bell tent of Circus Circus. The disused Landmark tower stands in isolation, far right. They are further apart than they look, all these casinos, because the enormous mass of the buildings foreshortens distance; in the days of summer, anyway, its too hot to cross from one to the other.

The Stardust, now owned by the Boyd group, has also expanded, with a new 32-storey tower, which gives the hotel a total of about 2,500 rooms, enough to put it in the big league. Chuck Ruthe, the president, is an energetic, no-nonsense businessman, who came into the casino industry late in his career. After its notorious decline under the influence of the mob, the Stardust took a long time to hit the come-back trail. Its modernisation is now complete, including revamping of its renowned Lido de Paris show which ran, amazing as it seems, for thirty-two years. ('Showgirls are large, full-breasted women who neither sing nor dance,' novelist Larry McMurtrey explained, introducing Harmony, the heroine of *Desert Rose*. 'They are on stage to wear gorgeous if skimpy costumes and be beautiful.') Paradoxically, the new show chose to feature female imper- sonators under the title of 'Boylesque'. The Stardust is now one of the smarter mass-market places on the Strip, offering the kind of slick, low-budget deals which has put the squeeze on cheap hotels and motels. In the same way, one rung up, the excitement and ballyhoo of the new super-casinos is challenging middle-range places like the Stardust and the Sahara. 'We think Vegas itself will *always* be a draw,' says Ruthe. 'Sure, our customers all want to see the Mirage and the Excalibur. But when they've seen 'em, they come back to us.' The Boyd group also operates the California and Fremont downtown and the western-style local casino Sam's Town on the Boulder Highway towards Hoover Dam.

Here, at the start of the Strip, just past Sahara Avenue which marks the divide from the city downtown, stands another major property, the sleek and glittery Riviera. The Riviera, rising in black glass, opposite Circus Circus, has experienced the ups and downs of gambling in full measure. It became the first high-rise hotel in Vegas back in 1955, when its nine-storey block (which by today's standards would be about as exciting as a youth hostel) rose above the Strip, instead of spreading sideways, ranch-house style, the usual design of those days. In its middle period, the Riviera went bust. It expanded rapidly again through the late '80s. In the 1990s it claimed it would soon be the world's largest casino (these definitions are a bit elastic, depending on the criteria of the measurer) with a floor space of 125,000 square feet.

In 1973 the Riviera was bought by a travel company run by businessman Meshoulam Riklis (who among many other deals once sold Fabergé, the celebrated French perfume producer, for $1.4 billion). Riklis paid close to $60m. for the property, which is now privately owned by him. The money did not come out of his own pocket; Riklis' ability to raise funds, for all manner of projects, made him one of the fastest operators on Wall Street. In those heady days, a lot of young guys in a hurry were re-inventing the game. Riklis, an Israeli immigrant, achieved spectacular success (according to Connie Bruck in *The Predators' Ball*) 'by relying on leverage, invention, keen business acumen and a disdain for the unwritten as well as some of the written rules.' He had started out with a stake of $25,000, buying and merging small companies in the 1950s. By the time he met Michael Milken in 1970, he already controlled a conglomerate which had sales of close to $2 billion. Milken was the originator but it was Riklis who coined the descriptive term 'junk bonds'. It was a sort of bad joke which stuck.

Riklis' technique in acquiring companies was to issue mainly bonds, or debt, in exchange for the company's stock; he would then issue the bonds, as distinct from the cash raised, directly to the shareholders. His method of dealing with the day of reckoning on all this debt was to postpone the date of repayment by offering a slightly more attractive bond, with a longer maturity, to the bondholders. They could not afford to refuse, not because of the improved (postponed) return, but because to call in question such a deal would seriously undermine, if not wipe out, the basic value of the bonds themselves. Milken, as Riklis put it, 'chaperoned' his progress.

The Riviera shows how the wheel of fortune can drive a casino down, like a gambler on a losing streak, as fast as it goes up. After a series of financial and management setbacks in the late '70s and early '80s, exacerbated by the economic downturn, and a decline in tourism due to rising airfares, the Riviera entered chapter 11 debt reorganisation in August 1983. (This is not formal bankruptcy, but a suspension of debt repayment, pending continued trading by an enterprise trying to rescue itself. Resorts International, the first casino in Atlantic City, went the same route in 1989, and Trump has followed suit, see Chapter 1.) Riklis appointed new management, which got the hotel running again in mid-1984. Their prime target was middle-income tourists, with say $2,000–3,000 spending money on a vacation trip, as well as high rollers. Arthur Waltzman, who became chief executive officer, was an accountant who knew the travel and tourism business. Mark Sterbens, a generation younger, once a college football player until he injured his knee, was promoted in-house as president.

'It all starts with getting the customer through the door,' says Waltzman. 'Unless you market your property properly, you can be the greatest accountant in the world but you're not going to make a profit. We knew we *had* to market the hotel. We didn't sell the Riviera particularly, but we sold Vegas . . . the most exciting single resort destination in the country.' A year later the Riviera came out of chapter 11, with new plans for a 24-storey tower, costing $28m., which opened in April 1988, nearly doubling the hotel's size to 2,200 rooms. Eventually, all the creditors were repaid. Sterbens dreamed up a new concept: *mass* entertainment. The Riviera now has four different showrooms (compared with two in most casinos), presenting eleven performances daily. Together these shows bring in 5,000 people a night. 'How do we get new customers through the door? We came up with running inexpensive shows. No matter who you are, we would have something for you. If you were a foreigner you could still see *Splash!* and have a good time. It wasn't like going to see a comedian or an entertainer whose language you didn't understand. You enjoy this show whether you're six or ninety years old.' (My favourite marketing ploy by the Riviera was its extravagant hyping of a chess tournament: anyone acquainted with the royal game knows that chess players *never* have any money.)

When Liberace cut the ribbon at the new Riviera in 1955, he was paid $50,000 a week to appear. In 1981 country singer Dolly Parton got $350,000 a week, almost twice the average for star performers at that time. 'That culminated an escalating headliner price war which eventually forced most hotels to less expensive production shows,' noted a Riviera press release. Today the highest paid performers (leaving aside Sinatra who is in a financial class of his own) can command around $100,000 a night (usually two shows) and make up to $1.5m. for a fortnight's engagement. (Though Trump was so desperate to book a headliner for the opening of the Taj Mahal in April 1990, he reportedly paid Elton John $1m. for two shows.) Riklis has a soft spot for the singing of his wife, cabaret artiste Pia Zadora. She is booked into the show room quite often. The Riviera also stages 300–400 weddings a month in its wedding chapel. Prices range from the number one package, which covers the chapel fee, traditional wedding music, flowers and photos, at $199 plus tax, to the luxury package, which included a video of the ceremony, plus two nights in a hotel suite, for $739 ('price includes bottle of champagne'!).

'We feel confident we can handle the challenge of the Excalibur or anyone else,' says Sterbens. A family man, an economics graduate, who came into casinos through the hotel business, Sterbens is typical of a new breed of college-educated managers who seem as relaxed and sun-tanned as any of their sunbelt customers, yet put in an eighteen-hour day. His confidence in the Riviera was based on the fact that 65 per cent of customers come from California. Millions more people are expected to settle in the golden state this decade. A new 43-storey tower, the tallest in Nevada, was due for completion in 1992, adding another 1,600 rooms. According to Sterbens, the Riviera would then be big enough. But this project never got built. In 1992 the Riviera nose-dived into chapter 11 bankruptcy again. Its basic problem, among others, was lack of a clear identity. Another change in management, though not ownership, was signalled.

For Circus Circus, the flow of customers spills over into super-abundance. Day after day it has had to turn customers away. How has it been so successful? The originality of Circus Circus when it started back in 1968 was that it catered for children as well as their moms and dads. You don't ordinarily see kids in Las Vegas; they exist in the sense that casino employees have families, somewhere out in the new housing tracts. But they are not by law allowed in the casinos. Circus Circus changed all that. A huge circus, built above the main casino floor, offers children all manner of fairground fun and games, like shying coconuts into a bucket or shooting at a line of moving ducks or throwing rings over a clown's head, for cheap prizes. To judge from my own sons' reaction, kids of all ages find the place irresistible. The only snag (for the moms and dads) is that these activities are not free: at fifty cents a go, parents can run through a hundred bucks in next to no time. The billowing circus tent is only for starters. Inside, the place is enormous. It takes some time to thread your way through from end to end, and then there are more walkways and elevators to the pools. So I have to say that Hunter S. Thompson's dismissive comment about the place was unfair – it betrayed a distaste for what the American public wants, which is, in a word, value. Under the direction of William Bennett, Circus became the market leader for family custom. 'Breakfast – 15 hot items $2.29, inc bev', 'Buffet brunch all you c'n eat $2.99', set the style. No matter that the line is sometimes a couple of hundred people long, the buffet claims to serve the most meals of any restaurant in the world. A double room, with two extra beds for children, can cost as little as $19. This is what brings the folks in, and such is the demand that large numbers of visitors – nearly one million room nights a year – have to be turned away and placed in other hotels.

This was what persuaded Bennett to set off in a new direction on a new site, at the far end of the Strip. Circus stands at the beginning of the Strip, as you approach it from downtown. The new property is sited at the other end, a mile south of the Flamingo crossroads, past the Aladdin, past the site of Kerkorian's proposed new MGM theme park, opposite the Tropicana. After a public competition to choose a name for the new place, romance won the day. The Excalibur, a 4,032-room casino-hotel, built like a mediaeval castle – if four 28-storey towers on a square block like Alcatraz can pass muster – rose up on Tropicana Avenue, to open its doors and its drawbridge, in June 1990. What a creation! It went up in only 20 months, at a cost of $290m. (less than half the Mirage cost), the bulk of it paid out of cashflow from Circus' profits. Touring the site, 90 days before the opening date, I felt overwhelmed, under my yellow hard hat, by admiration for the energy and expertise which could take these vast concrete caverns, integrate the tangle of electric lines and conduits and fittings, and conjure out of the whole inchoate jumble the world's largest palace of mass entertainment. Today, jousting knights gallop across the flagstones, under the mock portcullis. The long galleries resound to the merry clamour of minstrels and jugglers and entertainers, cafés and bars pour out thousands of drinks every hour of the day. The mediaeval theme is relentless: the pasta restaurant is named Lance-a-lotta Pasta. In the midst of it all, the slots churn and chunter without cease. 'Our customers,' an enthusiastic executive assured me, 'love it.'

With the launch of the Excalibur, Circus Circus is, essentially, competing with itself, at the lower end of the family travel market. The overflowing bookings at Circus showed the way: but the new venture is really a gamble that the market can support the two properties. Including their expansion in Laughlin, (Vegas' offshoot on the border with Arizona) the company was operating over 11,000 hotel rooms by the end of 1990, with plans to expand much further. The sudden appearance of the Excalibur, like a magic sword rising out of the desert, offering over 4,000 new rooms in a brand new theme-casino, was bound to have a major impact on the southern end of the Strip, notably on the Tropicana opposite. The Tropicana in recent years has not been the bright place it once was, though it has a pool in the shape of a blue lagoon in which there is a floating blackjack table. But assuming people will not stay put in one place for the whole of their 2.3 days at the Excalibur, the neighbouring properties can expect to feel the benefit. Even the ailing Aladdin, a block up from the Tropicana towards Bally's, might be revived. One of the old high-rise casinos feeling the new competition, the Aladdin – though it looks gaudy enough with its magic lamp – had been in trouble for a long time before finally landing in bankruptcy. Various offences against the gaming regulations had brought it to the attention of the Nevada State Gaming Control Board. When its Japanese owner, Ginji Yasuda, who had bought the 1,100 room property in 1986 for $54m., died at the end of 1989, the Nevada Gaming Commission advertised the 1,100 room property for sale on the international market. More than a thousand responses were received leading to about a dozen serious bids. The Aladdin was finally put up for auction in April 1991, but was not sold.

In turn, the Excalibur itself will have to face new competition, when Kerkorian's planned new MGM Grand, one long block before the Tropicana, finally sees the light of day. This project for a 5,000-room hotel and theme park is budgeted at $750m. To make room for the MGM, the Tropicana golf course and 700-room Marina hotel-casino will be demolished. The main theme park, as might be expected from Kerkorian, will be oriented on the movies, with a nine-storey high MGM lion at its entrance.

Picking up on concepts which both Howard Hughes and Kerkorian perceived early on, the Circus' annual report for 1989 offered a sociological analysis of the way casino-entertainment is developing. It took the analogy of the supermarket which, as economist Milton Friedman has noted, may be one of America's greatest contributions to consumers' daily life. The supermarket, introduced in the 1930s, evolved into the shopping centre of the 1950s, which in turn gave way to the suburban shopping mall of the 1970s. The standard supermarket survives, but is generally far larger than in former years. In the 1980s the hypermarket or megastore appeared on the American scene – enormous stores providing a vast selection and variety of goods at bargain prices. Going one step further, 'the modern merchant-shopkeeper tries to give the customer something to see and an interesting place to experience when shopping'.

'The lesson of contemporary retailing is that the customer's loyalty will be related to the merchant's ingenuity. Breadth of selection, rotation of display, original fashions, a sense of recreation . . . Circus is an entertainment merchant. It's just that we happen to merchandise playtime to our customers rather than goods', the report explained. 'Excalibur would, in our formulation, be an entertainment megastore, specialising all the while in dependably low prices – presenting a blend of casino, theatre, festival and shopping mall . . . As merchants of play, we found the theme of a *castle* . . . brimful of play. Tournaments, heraldry, chivalric orders, knighthood, high ceremony and singing . . . a temporary release from the chores of daily life.' On a first impression, Excalibur is as tacky as a travelogue, but ready to joust till you drop.

DOWNTOWN

> Who cares about the decor at the Horseshoe?
> It looks like wall-to-wall people to me.
>
> Teddy Jane Binion

One man who was not rushing in to spend money in competition with Steve Wynn was Jack Binion, whose family owns Binion's Horseshoe downtown. It is about four miles from Caesars and the Mirage to the Horseshoe in Casino Center, but in gambling terms they're a world apart. Downtown Vegas still retains a trace of its old wild west silver mining, rough and ready gambling origins, in the cowboy gear in the stores and swing-door saloons. But the buckskin is overlaid with glitter, glitter which reaches up to the sky, visible as a point of red and yellow light from an airplane over the desert. Fremont Street is only three short blocks long where it really matters: running from the Union Plaza (once the old railway station) up to Binion's Horseshoe and the Golden Nugget, which face each other along an entire block, and then to the Fremont and Four Queens on the next corner. These four casinos at the crossroads of Casino Center Boulevard are the heart of downtown Vegas. By the next block, it's a mixture of catch 'em quick souvenir stores, deadbeat gamblers and drunks scrounging for quarters.

The Horseshoe, measured by money earned on turnover, was consistently the most successful operation in Las Vegas at the end of the '80s. What's more, its formula could hardly have been more different from the Mirage's. The Binions' success was, and is, founded on the principle of not spending money. No shows, no cabaret, no fancy decor, no frills – just gambling. The family racked up a net income of $45m. on revenues of $108m. in 1988, an astounding return, outstripping Caesars, then at the top of the market, which earned $96m. on $390m. The casino average on the Strip at that time was around 15 per cent on revenue, compared with around 10 per cent downtown.

At the end of the year, Jack Binion bought out the Mint, his next-door neighbour in Glitter Gulch. The Mint, 25-stories high, with a spectacular roof-top restaurant, was doing something which, in theory, it is quite difficult for a casino to do – it was actually losing money. Jack Binion tore down the connecting walls and, like a dam breaking, the gamblers poured through. One day the Mint was empty, next day the new Horseshoe was full. The first thing Jack did was throw the music out. 'Ain't no man gonna blow my money out the end of a horn,' as old man Benny Binion once said. Jack's father Benny, then in his eighties, was one of the old-time gamblers, who flaunted his reputation as a hustler, as ready to roll the dice across the bar as sell you a string of horses. In 1931 he was convicted of second-degree murder for a crime which he claims was self-defence. In those feudin' and fightin' days the motto was: 'Kill 'em dead and they won't give you no more trouble.' On another occasion he shot a man for greasing to the cops: 'He was tellin' the truth – he just didn't have no business tellin' it.' When he was accused by a Chicago mobster of putting out a contract on a Las Vegas gambler, Binion retorted that he didn't need any contract: 'I'm capable of doin' my own killin'.' He served three and a half years in Leavenworth, for tax evasion, and in his later years struggled mightily, in vain as it turned out, to obtain a presidential pardon.

Benny was finally called up by the great dealer in the sky on Christmas Day 1989. His obituaries were sentimental. 'Benny was a very fair man,' world poker champion Doyle Brunson remarked, 'he believed in justice. However, he spelled it differently – *just us*.' The Horseshoe's public relations man pointed out that Benny was never tried or convicted for murder. He was sent to prison for non-payment of taxes. 'At that time he was part of a group of Americans who disagreed with how their taxes were being spent by the government and decided to withhold payment. That's why he felt that he should have been pardoned by a conservative president.' Benny's spirit lives on: and his rambunctious face now grins back at you on every gaming chip in the Horseshoe.

'Our success down here,' Jack Binion explained, above the din of the tables all around, 'is 'cos we've followed Dad's formula.' In the old days, Jack confided, Dad was a bit of a bootlegger. 'He brewed the booze in gallon jars and counted up the dollars he got from selling 'em. He had a partner who went around totin' up bits of paper and doin' the accounts. But somehow, at the end of it all, there weren't as many dollars as there ought 'a been.' (Benny could neither read nor write, according to popular report, but he was fluent in the language of the greenback.) 'So one day, Dad had enough. He kicked the guy out. He said: "What counts is gallons and dollars." Gallons 'n dollars was his way, 'n gallons and dollars is my way.' 'Who cares about the decor at the Horseshoe?' says Benny's wife of fifty-four years, Teddy Jane, who lives above the casino and for years handled the coin section of the business. 'It looks like wall-to-wall people to me. When I come down the steps into the casino, if I see any shoulders, I know everybody's not here yet. I like to see all heads.' She was a mite worried about the take-over of the Mint, all that money going into another casino cage she couldn't see for herself. 'It's okay, Mom, it's our cage now,' Jack reassured her.

'It's so simple, I don't know how our competitors can't see it,' Jack elaborated. 'We just give the people better value in their gambling.' Thus, the odds tend to be shaded at the Horseshoe. On the poker machines, nowadays the favourite type of slots, he claims that if they play correctly, players can get a return of 99 per cent. At blackjack, the house plays with a single deck, which makes 'counting' so much easier than with six decks (although every pit boss has eyes like a lynx for professional counters). At dice, the punters are encouraged to press their front line bets, up to ten times the stake, at true odds. At baccarat, the cut on bank hands is only 4 per cent instead of 5 per cent. 'Dealin' high! That's what gamblers want!' Benny maintained all his life. He had founded the Horseshoe way back in 1951 on the premises of a defunct casino he bought out on Fremont Street. 'If you've got a high limit and the dice get hot, a man's got a chance to win a lot of money.' That's the kind of action gamblers crave.

The Horseshoe has taken bets of up to a million dollars at the craps table. 'This guy calls up, wants to bet a million dollars,' recalls Jack. 'I told him, "Come on over." ' There was no great fuss about it. The man walks in off the street and produces the money from a suitcase. In fact he carried two suitcases, the second one empty. He bet $777,000 in hundred dollar bills (the figure seven has magic import to many people). The chips were laid out on the Don't Pass line, the man picks up the dice and throws a 6, then a 9, then sevens-out to win the bet, and walks out carrying his second suitcase jam-packed with hundred dollar bills, just like that. He came back another day, and made the same Don't Pass bet winning $300,000. Perhaps hoping for third time lucky, he came in once again and laid out the whole million. It proved third time unlucky. The bet went down, and the man was later found dead in a downtown hotel room. 'It wasn't losing his money which hurt him. He had a whole bunch of problems with a boyfriend or sumpn',' Jack Binion adds philosophically, crunching an ice cube between his teeth.

'It's a high risk, one million dollars,' said Jackie Gaughan, one of the good ol' boys downtown, and owner of El Cortez. 'Caesars can't afford that kind of a bet.' Gaughan, turned seventy, has known Jack Binion since he was a kid. 'Jack, all he wants is just a little bit the best of it,' he explains, adding half-admiringly, 'he wouldn't give his own mother the best of it! He just wouldn't do it!'

To document fully the sinister deeds of all the socially prominent thugs, panderers, thieves, hopheads and murderers who throng Las Vegas would require a shelf of the Encyclopaedia Britannica, observed Ed Reid and Ovid Demaris, the authors of *The Green Felt Jungle*, by way of introducing Benny Binion. When he arrived in 1946 he was still king of crime in Dallas. His FBI record went back to 1924: his 'yellow sheet', buried in the files of the Dallas police department, listed 'details of crimes that would stagger the imagination of even the most prolific detective writer.' But Benny was never a big man in Vegas, authors Reid and Demaris conclude. His operations were always in Glitter Gulch, he never had juice on the Strip. 'Even in a den of thieves and murderers, Binion lacked class. Instead of the silk suits and Italian loafers, Binion preferred cowboy boots and ten-gallon hats.' Over time, reputations change – in the gaming industry no less than in politics. Benny had for years past been a popular and instantly recognisable figure about town – with his cowboy hat cocked over the right eye and his jaunty sayings – 'He who has the gold *makes* the rules' or 'Tough times make tough people'. He was happiest on his 500,000-acre ranch in Montana, where most of the beef for the casino's restaurants was produced. When in town he held daily court in the Horseshoe coffee shop. By the time he died at the age of eighty-five, Benny enjoyed the affection and admiration usually accorded a folk hero. Only a few weeks after his death, culinary workers and bartenders on strike at Binion's, in support of health and social benefits, picketed the building with a huge banner proclaiming: Nobody Misses Benny Binion More Than We Do. 'We used to call him Papa Binion,' claimed a waitress on the picket line.

Jack, looking ever more worried about the strike, conceded he would never have the charisma of his Dad. He was prepared to make concessions to the union, provided he kept the right to dismiss low-productivity employees. 'As Dad used to say, "If you've got one guy dragging his feet, pretty soon you got a hundred guys dragging their feet." ' Jack could afford to stick it out – he had no debt and no public stockholders. The strike took several months to settle and was a lot of trouble. It also cost the Horseshoe a lot of revenue, judging from its net profit for 1990, which it was estimated fell to only $5m. Jack was already much disturbed by a federal case against his brother Ted (no longer in the business), arising from a notorious incident a year or two back, during Ted's term as manager. Two players accused of cheating were taken into a back-room and severely beaten up. Although the Horseshoe had accepted responsibility and long since paid compensation to the men, the FBI was still on the case.

In his obituary tribute at Benny's memorial service, Steve Wynn said: 'He was a man who never showed one shred of pretence. He was fearless because he was always himself, honest and straightforward. We will never see the likes of Benny Binion in our lifetime again, and that's the sad news.' This was the note struck in all the newspaper obituaries which Benny, in any case, couldn't have read. In 1989, a similar valedictory was paid to another old time gambler and bootlegger, Moe Dalitz, when he died aged eighty-nine. His association with the mob, which dated back to prohibition days in Cleveland, and close friendship with Meyer Lansky, was an open book. But in his old age Dalitz became a philanthropist. He had played a key role in the development of several casino-hotels, starting with the Desert Inn back in 1950. The Desert Inn was one of the first casinos to bring in top cabaret stars to attract gamblers. When Dalitz and his associates acquired the Stardust, the Cleveland and Chicago syndicates were cut in, which was the cue for the biggest skim ever uncovered in Vegas. Over the years numerous investigations were conducted into Moe Dalitz's activities, without ever reaching the point of a criminal case. In 1976 he was named Humanitarian of the Year by the American Cancer Research Center and awarded the Torch of Liberty Award by B'nai Brith.

Comedienne Joan Rivers took it upon herself to present Dalitz with his B'nai Brith award with the following encomium: 'There's one person in this town who represents Las Vegas . . . for his strength, his intelligence, for his toughness and for his wisdom, his gentleness . . . In grateful recognition for decades of commitment to people in need, to bettering our community and to strengthening our democracy . . . The people of Nevada have given you their love and admiration . . .' This was a man who 'was strictly mob, old time mob', according to author Ovid Demaris.

The secret of running a successful casino, according to Jackie Gaughan – who has had points in a myriad different properties in his time – is to play it as close to the line as possible: meaning, as Jack Binion explained, giving the punters the best possible gamble. As one of the old-style owners, a well-esteemed figure downtown, Gaughan has the easy air of a man who has enough money to do what he likes, but now simply enjoys the gambling business for itself. He got into gambling as a teenager, delivering scratch (form) sheets for an uncle out in Omaha. At sixteen he was running a bookmaking business. Learning about odds-making from the inside taught him the crucial lesson of his career. 'Deal it *close*. The closer you deal, the more players you have, the higher your win.'

Gaughan came to Las Vegas during his military service and took a liking to the place. He shook off the dust of Nebraska and got a job at the famous Flamingo in 1954. 'All those old guys were cheaters. They thought you had to cheat. They didn't know about percentages, they probably couldn't figure percentages. So they didn't know the strength of the game.' The partners always won, they celebrated at the end of each month, Gaughan recalled. But the Flamingo did not prosper in the early days. Now, of course, the casino wins more money in a day than they did in a month back then. One day young Gaughan was given a piece of advice he took to heart: 'Any man who comes to Las Vegas with a pair of square dice, he'd win so much money he wouldn't be able to carry it outta the place!' Wise words. Gaughan attributes his long success in the business to his keeping the house percentages lower than anyone else. Like Benny down the street at the Horseshoe, he always gave his customers a better gamble. Gaughan has also had an unusually enlightened role as an employer, paying every employee a 15 per cent bonus on their salaries into a savings plan. That has bound his staff to him. 'Seventy-five per cent of all the people who work in the gamblin' houses in Las Vegas, I broke 'em in, I trained 'em,' he claims. 'In almost every casino there's a boss that started out with me. The head of my slot department, he's got $580,000 piled up. But you know who's gotta wind up with the most money?' He gives a chuckle. 'Guy that winds up with the most money, it's gotta be me! I have $1.1m. in my plan. My son, got $150,000, he owns different places.'

There are still a few old-style gambling operators like Gaughan around town but there's less and less room for them in the sleek corporate-run production-line casinos that now lead the industry. Gaughan has a genial, unselfconscious way of talking, whether it's about his profits or his staff. 'I got a guy started as a dishwasher, he owns 55 per cent of one casino. I got another guy who was a porter, he's one of my partners now, a coloured guy, very capable. I started the first coloured guy in the gamblin' business. Not too long ago, they weren't allowed in, not until about '63. The best customer is the coloured person 'cos he always goes first class. He never has nuthin', but he always spends a lot of money.' Sitting in his office at the El Cortez (a casino a casual tourist might never find, though it's only a block from Glitter Gulch) he rummages through a ledger: 'Look at the handle on my racebook. You can handle a lot of money and still lose. The handle for the whole year was $66m. but I quit loser $320,973. Year before we took $63m. and won $478,000. I played it extremely unlucky. I lost some extremely high bets. You should hold about 4.5 per cent on the racebook.' However, El Cortez' casino made a profit of $6.8m. that same year. 'Here, this is the amount of money I made since I owned this place. $45m. after taxes. Why am I successful? I don't owe any money, I own a lotta things, a lot of other assets. My other income was $3.7m. last year. When the smoke cleared, I only made $4m. after taxes.' Jack Gaughan's lifelong enthusiasm shows that the gambling business can make a man content at any age.

The Golden Nugget, shiny and elegant, runs the length of the block. It makes a flashy contrast with Binion's Horseshoe, which despite its expansion remains what it always was, an old fashioned, come 'n' git it, gambling hall. The Nugget is cool, creamy, dark green up the sides of its 35-storey tower blocks, an upmarket anomaly in the tawdry dazzle of Glitter Gulch,

exploiting its central location. The Nugget reflects Steve
Wynn's creative effort of the mid-'80s. It would have been too
easy, and far too obvious, to try to outshine and out-scream the
neighbouring properties downtown, with a bigger, bolder version
of the old style casinos. It was (see Chapter 1) an inspired move to
take the Nugget upmarket, and turn it, at that time, into the
classiest joint in town. As Wynn got more and more involved with
the Mirage, everyone assumed that the Golden Nugget would
fade away, or at least pale into distant second place. Not so: in the
first quarter of 1990, while the Mirage was pulling in the crowds
and making the news day after day, the Nugget racked up its best
ever figures. It had an operating profit of $13m., a 60 per cent
increase on the previous year.

The man who was appointed to take over as chief executive of
the Nugget was Dennis Gomes. Short, alert, glossy, brimful of
energy, he seemed a replica of Wynn and even sounded like him.
Gomes has a unique record in the casino industry: he has served
on both the Atlantic City and Las Vegas casino control bodies.
His previous job before taking over at the Nugget was trying to
run the Aladdin for its new Japanese owner. He was in no doubt
that he could have turned the place around had the cultural
operating divide not been so wide. Gomes believes that any casino
can be made to pay, provided it is well managed. So how did
Gomes achieve such a strong performance at the Nugget? I found
his answer, which came without any hesitation, an interesting
one. 'People. Friendly people. The casino staff have to be happy.
They must feel good when they come to work. And if they are
happy, it will rub off on the customers.' That is not all there is to
it; clearly, there must be good marketing, to get the public to
come in and gamble in the first place, and good service. The
Mirage is big but the Nugget is not so small either. It covers,
including parking facilities, two and a half square blocks. The
casino floor comprises 63 table games and 1,130 slots, and all the
usual adjuncts like a sports book; the hotel includes over 1,900
rooms and suites.

Gomes believes that running a casino is a job that requires keeping ahead of the game, like guiding a company through its business cycle. Unusually, he has sought to give the Nugget a dual-image, for both high rollers and slot players. The two do not necessarily fit together, but they can both be given star treatment. One of the new marketing devices, which the Nugget was among the first to introduce, is the Slots Club. Regular players are given a card to insert in the machine, like a credit card, whenever they play, which monitors every single pull of the handle – size and frequency of bets and duration of play. According to their action, slot players qualify for comps, which may range from a free hamburger right up to full RFB (complimentary room, food and beverage). These cards give the casinos invaluable information on their customers: if the casino manager knows who his best players are, and can look after them, everything else follows. Such customers will return again and again. At the same time, just two tables of baccarat – pre-eminently the high rollers' game – produced over 10 per cent of the Nugget's revenue.

Gomes' most famous coup, as head of the audit division of the Gaming Control Board in Nevada, came when he broke the skimming operation at the Stardust. After previous sorties on the counting room and cashier's cage had drawn a blank, Gomes led his team of investigators into the Stardust on a raid. They uncovered a secret vault, packed with bags of coins, which had been systematically diverted from the slots, night after night, with the aid of a fake weighing machine. Similar caches were discovered at the Fremont. I asked Gomes if he had ever been threatened during his six years in that job. 'I got a gun in the stomach when we broke up the Stardust scam. That was pretty scary,' he admitted. The skimming at the Stardust and the Fremont casinos, Gomes later reported, amounted to $12m. a year.

Gomes' hard-nosed approach 'had pretty much worn out his welcome in Nevada', according to Demaris' account in *The Boardwalk Jungle*. The authorities, so he suggested, were not

over-scrupulous at that time in examining casino owners' backgrounds or business links. Gomes was hired by the newly-
appointed Director of Gaming Enforcement in New Jersey to set
up a special investigations bureau. But his inquiries into the
dubious operation and background of Resorts International, the
first casino to apply for a licence in Atlantic City, brought him
into continuous conflict, both with the company and the regulators. One day that summer, shortly after Resorts had been
granted a temporary licence, Gomes flew in a team of investigators on a surprise visit to Resorts' casino on Paradise Island in
the Bahamas. They raided the casino and cashier's cage and
seized twenty filing cabinets of documents. Demaris claims that
the documents might have proved very damaging to politicians
and officials involved in casino legislation in New Jersey. In any
case the investigation did not get very far because the special unit
which Gomes had set up was rapidly disbanded. Resorts got its
permanent licence early the next year, February 1979.

Gomes was happy on the regulatory side of the business, and
might never have left it if he'd had political backing from New
Jersey. There are consolations: 'I'm earning a million dollars a
year, and I would never have made more than $38,000 salary as a
regulator,' he explained cheerfully. 'I didn't leave for the money.
I felt frustrated in the job.' Returning to Nevada, Gomes showed
that old hunters make good gamekeepers. He joined the Frontier
Hotel, then part of the Howard Hughes group, increasing profits
four-fold, and was then paid a hefty signing-on fee to manage the
Aladdin, before moving to the Nugget. Running a major casino,
with all the responsibility to employees it entails, is also a way of
making a contribution to society, he feels. But in early 1991,
Gomes fell out with Wynn. Credit to high rollers had got
seriously out of hand, with unpaid debts at the Nugget rising to 13
per cent of turnover, an unacceptably high figure. The row was
hushed up. Whatever the rights and wrongs of the case, Gomes
suddenly left town. He was made a very lucrative offer by Donald
Trump to rescue the Taj Mahal in Atlantic City.

Downtown is never going to be as slick as the Strip, but it is trying to pull itself up by its cowboy bootstraps, taking a lead from the new-look Golden Nugget. Vegas Vic, the 60-foot neon cowboy with his lewd, knowing wink, is the image the public has when it thinks of Las Vegas. Under the slogan 'The Future is Now', the Downtown Progress Association, wants to improve the area, which has been badly neglected over the years. The imaginative plan to construct a people mover over the half dozen blocks to Cashman Field, the convention area and baseball park, has fallen through (see final chapter). A new player on the scene, Bob Snow, tried to revive downtown with his Main Street Station project. This new casino, on the theme of a Victorian railway station, with restaurants and entertainment to match, was based on the model of his extremely successful development at Orlando, Florida. There were objections from some owners downtown to Snow being granted a loan from the city, but it was hoped the project would light up the bleak empty spaces north of Fremont under the concrete span of Interstate 95. Agleam with brass rails and polished wood and high mirrors, the facility was beautifully, even lovingly, finished. But it was a block too far for the customers. They wouldn't walk it. As I mounted the marbled staircase, black beetles scuttled out. In June 1992, Main Street closed its doors and the bankers moved in.

At the intersection of Las Vegas Boulevard and Main, like a hinge in the highways joining uptown and downtown, stands the isolated square block of Vegas World, owned by Bob Stupak. Stupak is a relative newcomer, who barged into the casino game in 1979. Not even his best friends could describe Stupak and his operation as a class act. He is loud, cocky, crude and proud of it. His success has lain in making a small-time joint look like a big-time operation. He also used to entertain political ambitions. He twice ran for mayor of Las Vegas and in 1987 almost made it. Stupak's election campaign (like his career as a casino owner) was coloured by controversy and allegations of unethical conduct. For instance, in the primary, he sent out thousands of letters to householders around town, addressing the fortunate recipients as Dear Stockholder and Voter, handing out free stock in a new company called Vegas World Inc. The issue could be traded for money. He countered charges of trying to bribe voters, by claiming the share offer was part of a promotional campaign for his casino, and nothing to do with the election. In another ploy he sent out thousands of baskets of fruit to senior citizens, with campaign literature tucked into each basket. He had little to say about civic politics, beyond berating the public transport system.

The money Stupak spent on his mayoral campaign gave him and his casino tremendous exposure, which was well worth it – leaving aside any political advantage – from the publicity angle. In the event, the voters chose to elect Ron Lurie, who already had fourteen years' experience as a city councillor. The post of mayor of Las Vegas at the time paid the hardly princely sum of $35,000 a year, perhaps a twentieth of Stupak's campaign costs. His first venture into gambling in Vegas was a slot parlour grandiloquently titled 'Bob Stupak's Historic, World Famous, Million Dollar, Gambling Museum'. (It had 15 machines.) After six weeks it burned down, and he was later accused of complicity in the fire by the insurance company. Stupak vehemently rejected the charge. His claim was eventually settled out of court. His casino-hotel Vegas World was built on the site of the former property, actually a dreadful location, on a no-man's land in mid-town. On his opening day Stupak showed characteristic chutzpah by announcing to the press that the Strip had been extended by a quarter of a mile. The media bought the story.

From the start Vegas World set out to offer gimmicky sorts of bets, to attract new gamblers to its inhospitable location. One such wheeze was 'Double Exposure Blackjack', whereby the dealer exposes his hole card as well as his up-card, so the player can see exactly what he has to beat. For instance if the dealer has a total of 20, the player can go on hitting cards until he goes bust, trying to get to 21 – the only snag being that ties are not a stand-off but won by the house. In practice, this system gave the casino a rather better edge than regular blackjack, but it was such a weird sensation, hitting 18s, 19s or 20s, to try and beat the dealer, that I fell for it. After writing an enthusiastic little magazine article about it I was stunned some months later to find that my piece had been purloined as part of Stupak's publicity material. Another gimmick is 'Crapless Craps' – if the shooter rolls a 2, he does not lose the bet; the 2 then becomes his point. Today Vegas World still contrives to look bigger than it is, taking space travel as its theme: its outside wall displays an astronaut, spread-eagled upside down, connected by a long looping tube to the oxygen of a roulette wheel. No one has yet tried to follow Vegas World into mid-town. It remains a small-time store with a big front. It might get even bigger if his plan to build a 1,012 ft high observation tower (taller than the Eiffel Tower), which ran into trouble with the airlines, ever becomes a reality. Stupak likes to live up to his nickname about town as the Polish maverick.

Finally the 'local' casinos deserve special mention. These places, cleverly sited at the freeway exits of Highway 15 running parallel to the Strip, serve the Vegas community itself, a growing market thanks to all the new workers moving into the casino industry, plus growing numbers of retired folk attracted by the low costs and desert climate. The Gold Coast, and now the Rio, a block behind Caesars, and the Palace Station at the mid-freeway exit, serve the West side of the valley, diverting people who might otherwise have driven on to Glitter Gulch downtown. The Gold Coast, run by Mike Gaughan, has been the most successful. The Rio, dazzlingly lit in Brazilian reds, featuring keno girls and cocktail waitresses in skimpy leotards, is the first all-suite hotel-casino in town. But it has run into financing problems. Sam's Town, a western-style casino, plus bowling alleys, is out of the East side. The Sante Fe (boasting an ice rink) is on the road to Reno – beyond civilisation, but the tract homes are sweeping up from the south-west like a swarm of gnats.

In 1991 (as mentioned in my introduction) nine of the ten largest hotels in the world were listed by the American Hotel and Motel Association as being in Las Vegas. The sole interloper which could claim entry to the top ten was the Hilton Hawaiian Village, Oahu, with 2,522 rooms. The figures vary, as hotels remodel and expand, but the extraordinary dominance of Las Vegas remains constant. What's more, the hotels seem able to absorb the extra capacity: room occupancy, on a total of 73,730 rooms, dropped only fractionally, from 89.8 per cent to 89.1 per cent in 1990. With double occupancy (often more with family accommodation) the total number of beds exceeds 150,000. By way of comparison, the English Tourist Board reported total bed spaces in serviced accommodation in London in 1989 as 138,252. Average room occupancy was 69 per cent. In other words Vegas was offering about the same total accommodation as London, a city of over 12 million people, and with a far higher occupancy.

A pause in hotel building seemed likely, though ambitious new projects still made the news. One was called Carnivaal, a 3,376 room hotel to be built by the Radisson Group, which franchises and manages hotels worldwide. Construction had not yet started in 1991. The Carnivaal, if built, would be another larger-than-life presence on the crossroads of Las Vegas Boulevard and Flamingo, on a site next to the Dunes. The design was described as futuristic and high-tech, shaped like a giant H, with two 30-storey towers and a 26-storey arching sign in front. The biggest project of all, planned to fill 86 acres south of the Excalibur, was called Southstar. It was described as a hotel complex of ten properties, comprising 6,000 rooms, built around a central casino, like the hub of a wheel. Talk of such projects shows how the craze to build was, in its way, as feverish as the craze to gamble.

The pause in construction was only temporary. By 1992 (see my final chapter) more giant projects were on the way.

Way out in the land of the setting sun,
Where the wind blows wild and free,
There's a lovely spot, just the only one
That means home sweet home to me.
If you follow the old Kit Carson trail,
Until desert meets the hills,
Oh, you certainly will agree with me,
It's the place of a thousand thrills.

Nevada State Song

Las Vegas is a city of signs. Signs, almost overwhelming in their size and proliferation, define Las Vegas. At a time when literary critics are obsessed with signs, when semiology has become a science, the innovative character of Las-Vegas-as-a-sign deserves special attention. It begins with the road and the distance: from a long way off, driving in, the signs make the casinos visible. From the air, too, peering down at the bare desert, the lights of the signs glint up, even in the noonday sun. The signs are all different: yet each casino-hotel along the Strip is essentially the same, offering the same deal and the same odds. By their signs shall ye know them: each place focuses its management and marketing effort on *differentiating* its appeal from its rivals.

Could this contribution to the cultural landscape be accredited to Bugsy Siegel, one small entry on the credit side of an otherwise sordid life? It seems so. His Flamingo was the first place, back in 1947, to set the style of hyper-extravagance by its exterior sign: a hotel-casino unlike anything seen before. 'Everybody drove out Route 91 just to gape,' as Tom Wolfe enthused in his seminal tribute to Las Vegas. 'Such shapes! Boomerang Modern supports, Palette Curvilinear bars, Hot Shoppe Cantilevered roofs and a scalloped swimming pool . . . Two cylinders rose at either end of the Flamingo – eight storeys high and covered from top to bottom with neon rings in the shape of bubbles that fizzed all eight stories up into the desert sky all night long like an illuminated whisky-soda tumbler filled to the brim with pink champagne.' Today the Flamingo boasts a huge, yellow-and-orange sunburst, like an orchid opening up in orgasmic explosion. This motif, soaring above the front entrance, is repeated over and over again through the property, on doorways, in rest rooms, on slots and tables, on gaming chips, writing paper, table napkins and book matches.

Route 91 through Las Vegas – the celebrated Strip – reveals what architects term the commercial strip at its purest and most intense. Indeed very large claims have been made for it: 'We believe a careful documentation and analysis of its physical form is as important to architects and urbanists today as were the studies of mediaeval Europe and ancient Rome and Greece to earlier generations.' This provocative comparison with classical tradition was made in a research project on symbolism in architecture, which when it first appeared outraged academic opinion. Take Las Vegas seriously! Whatever next? The initial study, by a group from Yale University back in 1968, was revised as *Learning From Las Vegas* by Robert Venturi, Denise Scott Brown and Steven Izenour, published in 1972. Despite attacks on the authors' lack of social responsibility and so on, the paper has since achieved classic status. (The researchers' enthusiasm for their subject met a typically sceptical reception when it came to seeking local funding. The chairman of the Strip Beautification Committee said that the researchers should pay the city to make the study: the closest they got to financial support was a reduction in the hourly price on the use of Howard Hughes' helicopter.)

The originality of the Las Vegas Strip, the signs and the lay-out, is shown in *Learning From Las Vegas* by contrasting it with other kinds of commercial strip. The Middle Eastern bazaar contains no signs; whereas the Strip is virtually all signs. In the bazaar, communication works through proximity. Along its narrow aisles, buyers feel and smell the merchandise, and the stall-holder bargains directly with the purchaser. In the narrow street of the mediaeval town, although signs occur, persuasion was mainly through the sight and smell – the aroma of hot cakes coming from the doors and windows of the bakery. On Main Street in American towns the sales approach is about equally divided, between shop-window displays for pedestrians and signs over the front for motorists. But on the commercial strip the supermarket windows contain no merchandise. There may be signs announcing the day's bargains, but they are to be read by pedestrians coming in from the parking lot. 'The graphic sign in space has become the architecture of the landscape.'

In Las Vegas, the sign is more important than the architecture. By day, and even more so by night, the Strip is virtually all signs. Downtown, along Fremont Street, the immediacy of the casinos along the sidewalk makes the place more like a bazaar, but the buildings' façades are themselves signs. And, as Wolfe observed, what signs! There is no accepted vocabulary to describe them. He suggested names like McDonald's Hamburger Parabola, Mint Casino Elliptical or Miami Beach Kidney, to which one might add Forked Lightning Zig-Zag, Space Age Tubular and Orgasmic Cloudburst. They're all fun. They all work (except for the signs warning people that it is illegal to gamble under the age of 21 – the minuscule display of these notices must be classified as a counter-sign: the casinos do not want to draw overt attention to them).

And of course signs signal their messages all over the country. The United States is a nation on the road, on the move. It is directed by signs, responds to signs, adores signs. Las Vegas simply took their function furthest. Its signs change year by year, as casinos strive to outdo each other and new places open up, though Caesars' pointy mock-latin script has stayed as it was, instantly recognisable. In the process of change nothing has been more revealing than the design of the Golden Nugget downtown, which in the course of one gambling generation went from a casino with one huge sign on it, a totally sign-covered building, to a building without any signs on it whatever – not even its own name. This refinement, in the mid-'80s, was itself a most imaginative counter-sign, a way of proclaiming that despite being in the middle of Glitter Gulch, the place had class, it could rival the casinos on the Strip. Yet by the end of the '80s, when the Golden Nugget's management changed course to go more down-market again, new signs, like pimples, began to break out on the exterior of the building, small at first but growing into a neon rash.

'Las Vegas is to the Strip what Rome is to the Piazza', claimed the authors of *Learning From Las Vegas*. The comparison with Rome was not just an idle conceit. For Americans, visiting Vegas in the mid '60s was like going to Rome in the late 1940s, the authors argued. It was a revelation to people familiar only with the grid-iron city plan, scaled to the automobile, to discover urban space on a pedestrian scale and the mixtures of styles of the piazzas. Architects in America were perhaps ready for similar lessons about large open space, big scale and high speed. There were other parallels. Vegas is in the desert, Rome in the campagna. Their expansive settings tend to focus and clarify their images. On the other hand, Las Vegas was built in a day, or rather, the Strip was developed in a very short time, not built over an older town plan. Both cities are 'exaggerated examples from which to derive lessons for the typical': each superimposes public edifices on the local scene, causing violent juxtapositions of use and scale: churches in the religious capital, casinos and their signs in the gambling capital. The churches of Rome, situated off streets and piazzas, are open to the public, who can stroll from church to church; the gambler can similarly promenade along a variety of casinos off the Strip. Their entrance lobbies, ornamented and monumental, are the only such places in American cities, apart from a few old banks and railway stations, open to the passing public.

The other place compared with Las Vegas, because it was created in a large empty space, with a lot of money, in an architecturally uniform style, is Versailles. Vegas, because it happened to be built by gangsters, with proletarian tastes, not by the Sun King, never had the recognition it deserved, says Wolfe. A pretty comparison, but more relevant is the lay-out of the two places. In Versailles, the paving, kerbs, borders and flower beds give direction, urns and statues act as points of continuity, in a vast space. Whereas in Vegas the highway signs, through their structures and silhouettes, their images and messages, their positioning, identify and unify the whole. 'They make verbal and symbolic connections through space', say the authors of *Learning From Las Vegas*, 'communicating a complexity of meanings through hundreds of associations in few seconds from far away.' That is what they mean by asserting that the sign is more important than the architecture.

The study identified two types of buildings, 'ducks' and 'decorated sheds'. The duck (named after a roadside stand in the shape of a duck in Long Island) is a building that presents itself as a giant sculpture; its function, structure and material are secondary to its representational form. The building becomes the sign – as in Circus Circus' big top. The decorated shed is a more conventional building that has ornament applied to it, usually a large sign on the front façade – as in the Stardust of those days, which was fronted by a cornucopia of sparkling lights, in red, green, blue and silver.

There is, however, another aspect to the 'architecture of persuasion' which this study, not being concerned with gambling as such, overlooks. And that is that when the motorist sees the sign, turns off the highway into the hotel entrance to park his or her car, and moves into the casino, he or she enters a separate world, on its own. There is no need to leave the hotel-casino complex (while the money lasts out) because every human need is taken care of – gambling first and foremost, but a variety of restaurants, entertainments, indoor and outdoor sports, with abundant sex on call, plus instant telephone or business connections to the outside world. The ambiance is rather like the Pentagon building in Washington, which gives the visitor the same impression of a city-within-a-city, ruled by a hidden power. The power of the casinos is expressed, not in their mass, but obliquely. It is hinted at: by the security guards with their revolvers, their dangling handcuffs, their walkie-talkies; in the solid glint of strong boxes being removed and wheeled away from the tables; in the bars of the cashier's cage; in the heavy-eyed vigilance of the pit bosses (always on the phone, checking out somebody or other's credit); in the constant sense the visitor has of an unseen presence, of surveillance, of 'the eye in the sky'. Big Brother is Watching You. An occasional flurry, as a drunk or other undesirable is pitched outside, reinforces the impression that here, in the too-much-fun club, it does not pay to step out of line. These are also signs, in the margin.

I am rather partial to the backs of casinos. Here, on the reverse side of the glitz and extravaganza is to be seen another kind of sign: service areas, loading bays, refrigerator trucks, a jumble of refuse bins and containers, on a scale which bespeaks profligacy and human carelessness. Only the staff see the rear entrance, while along the side roads, for instance behind the Mirage and Caesars, stand all those bright little shacks with punning, hopeful names like Rocks r Us, Ditch Witch, Totally Clips, the Rose Exterminator company, living off the big corporations like birds on the hide of a rhinoceros.

So what is 'the lesson', architecturally, of Las Vegas? *Vitality*. The vitality that comes from 'an architecture of inclusion' – inclusion of everything in the environment, sacred and profane, past and present; the vitality that comes from easy allusion, to the Roman forum, the oriental harem, to blue lagoons, mediaeval knights, circus clowns, or closer to Nevada, the cowboys and gunslingers of the Wild West. The eye-boggling contrasts that can place a schlock comedian under a classical pediment, site gas stations next to mock-Tudor motels, turn a honky-tonk saloon into a satellite race book. Anything goes! It is a jumble, but it's a jumble which has its own jumbly significance. The 1982 *Guide to U.S. Architecture 1940–1980* dismissed Nevada in a cryptic sentence: 'Las Vegas Strip and downtown by Garish and Greed, architects.' That misses the point entirely. The point is that Las Vegas carries bad taste so far out that it sets a new standard which becomes, in its own context, good taste. It has made bad taste into a science: it works, it pays.

The biggest single structure serving Las Vegas is not a casino-hotel. It is the Hoover Dam. 'Imponderably massive, constructed with exquisite care, our dams will outlast anything else we have built – skyscrapers, cathedrals, bridges, even nuclear power plants. When forests push through the rotting streets of New York and the Empire State Building is a crumbling hulk, Hoover Dam will sit astride the Colorado River much as it does today – intact, formidable, serene.' So says Marc Reisner in his masterly exploration of the water sources and resources of the United States, *Cadillac Desert*. Las Vegas could not run for a day without the water of the Colorado river. The river system illuminates the neon of a city whose annual income is one-fourth the entire gross national product of Egypt – the only other place on earth where so many people are so helplessly dependent on one river's flow.

Hoover Dam was built incredibly quickly. The initial excavations for diversion tunnels were begun in May 1931, but the river was not detoured from its channel until November and the cofferdams not completed until April 1933. Two years later all the blocks in the dam were raised to crest elevation, 726 feet 5 inches high, and a year later everything was finished: spillways, powerplant, penstocks, generators, galleries, even the commemorative plaque in the frieze alongside US Highway 93, which runs across the top. 'The greatest structure on earth, perhaps the most significant structure that has ever been built in the United States, had gone up in under three years', noted Reisner. (It is also, one may respectfully demur, perhaps open to the criticism of being too monumental, redolent of Fascist architecture.) But it is impressive: you feel the pressure, like the heroine of Joan Didion's novel *Play It As It Lays*, visiting the dam. 'All day she was faint with vertigo, sunk in a world where great power grids converged, throbbing lines plunged finally into the shallow canyon below the dam's face, elevators like coffins dropped into the bowels of the earth itself.' The first electrical power was produced in the fall of 1936. The dam is worth a visit (though Vegas gets most of its power from other sources) as a reminder that casinos are not the be-all and end-all of American know-how.

Indeed, there are some good buildings in Vegas, even on Las Vegas Boulevard, for example the Library and Children's Discovery Museum by Antoine Predock, built in 1986. The site is a former baseball field, within walking distance of the downtown casinos. Predock, whose practice is based in Albuquerque, has had extensive experience of building in the south-west. After taking a fresh look at *Learning From Las Vegas*, he decided to do something different from a decorated shed. He made the building more about space than surface. The result was an L-shaped structure, consisting of a library on one side and a museum on the other, linked by a triangle at the centre. The architectural point was that in a desert climate, harsh light flattens subtle distinctions in texture, while throwing the building's simple shapes and profile into sharp relief. The building is also fun: to give it presence, a concrete cone was added to the children's party room in the shape of a party hat, likewise a central tower, leading to a city look-out. In the parking lot, a grove of palm trees suggests an urban oasis. At night, the giant window on the desert fills with dark sky, while airport runway spots cast a red glow on the science tower; fluorescent street lamps add to the other-worldly feel (as the *Architectural Record* described it), by highlighting structural supports for the rapid transit system. This project, which was planned to link the facility with the convention centre and airport, was later cancelled, and all the supports for the monorail had to be pulled out. This side of town, leading out to the wilderness of North Las Vegas – 'a limbo for gunsels, hustlers, drug cripples and losers' as Hunter S. Thompson once put it – remains ripe for development. The Main Street Station project, the casino themed on an old-style railway station described earlier, was intended to fill the gap but failed. This is a desolate part of town.

Behind it all, despite the mix of styles, lies the Wild West. The Strip looks new, but its prime characteristics are firmly based on the frontier settlements which preceded it. It had numerous precursors, in the mining camps and towns of earlier times, notes Hugh Burgess, Professor of Architectural Studies (a new department) at the University of Las Vegas (in 'Las Vegas: Imagery and Mythology of a Frontier Boom Town Restated'). Although only the ghosts of those early settlers linger on, the places where they lived and died still exist in popular imagination, in the main streets and saloons, in the bar-room brawls and poker games and shoot-outs, of western movies. 'A smoke-filled room, men sitting at tables with either wide-brimmed or cowboy hats on, playing cards while painted cats in rustling silk or velvet, their hair adorned with ostrich feathers, are gadding about. To the left the bar with the busy mixologist, to the right the swinging doors. Cowboys resting their spurred, high-heeled boots on brass rails. The blond, blue-eyed hero emerges on the upstairs landing with guns blazing . . .' This is the familiar and well-loved American saloon (a misspelling of the French salon) as recalled in Richard Erdoes' *Saloons of the Old West*.

The dominant feature of the early settlements and mining towns was the line up of buildings along 'Main Street'. The length of this thoroughfare measured the town's status. Every other building was a saloon –

> From the rise of the moon
> Until noon
> Look me up at the Saloon

as a verse in a men's room in Jackson, Wyoming, put it. And every other building was also a 'false front'. 'The false fronts were pasted like sheets of cardboard to one-story log cabins or board shacks to give the impression of splendid two-story saloons. In character with the westerner's proclivity for bragging, for trying to appear a little more than life-size, the false fronts gave the appearance of a stage set . . .' notes Erdoes. As anyone who has been over a film set will know, this same technique is used in western movies, in reverse. The rooms and the furniture are made three-quarters size, so as to make the hero look taller and more manly.

The casinos along the Strip, each separate, competing for custom at street level, with their fantastic façades, can be seen as the modern version of the old frontier settlement main street. Few casinos are off the main street and those that are all have to overcome a location problem. From an architectural point of view, what is missing Dr Burgess feels, is any sense of public values, of a living community, unless you count the palm trees in front of the Mirage and a few flower-beds down the Strip. 'The Strip ought to be developed as the common unique feature of Las Vegas. Now it's just a corridor for running automobiles down. We need to start looking at the Strip as a linear park interspersed with a series of casinos and hotels.' (His own department of architecture, amusingly enough, is housed in the clapboard home of the family which ran the Tropicana; the whole house has been transported from the old casino to a new site on the university campus.)

The façades or false fronts of the frontier settlements communicated meanings – danger and loss as well as gold and success, as do present-day casino fronts. The symbols have a stronger impact for being set against 'the power and eternal qualities of surrounding mountains, the cosmology of the animal kingdom and dream of fortune', as Thomas Graham, Director of Design and Development at City Hall, has said. The façade is the most important element of the building. The transformed western boom town has nowhere achieved such monumental expression as on the Strip. It exemplifies the aggrandisement of every western American main street city, combining hotel-casino, leisure resort, commercial and sports facilities, and latterly amusement or theme parks. In seeking to get away from the old imagery of the Wild West, the Strip casinos have devised all kinds of new signs and wonders, but their frontier origins are still just visible behind the glitz and glamour.

If a casino wants a new sign, the name that first comes to mind is Yesco, the Young Electric Sign Company. The Yesco plant out on the edge of town is a treasure-trove of lights and craft and imagination, a vast undecorated shed in which signs a hundred foot high can be dreamed up and made to measure. Most of the spectacular signs around Vegas can be traced back to a drawing board at Yesco. The Circus Circus sign, in the form of a clown leaning over the top of a huge display board, advertising the casino's wares, was the largest free-standing sign in the world when it was erected in the 1970s. It is still going strong, but was overtaken by the 222-foot long sign at the Sahara, erected in 1985. At another level of information, McCarran airport has 917 signs ranging from elevator call button plaques to 420 square foot roadway signs.

The trend in the 1990s is for electronic message centres of the kind seen outside Caesars and the Mirage. These are huge oblong screens, high in the air, which flash out not just verbal messages – promoting cabaret or buffets or boxing – but also present animated displays, such as a football player charging forward, a roulette wheel spinning round, dolphins sporting in the water, as if on a gigantic outdoor TV screen. They are operated electronic-ally, by TV cassettes, instead of by men on ladder-trucks changing the letters. 'The display,' explains Dave Mead, manager of Yesco in Vegas, 'works equally well in full sunshine as at night.' The screen is filled with electronic modules, each packing 256 three-watt lamps into a sixteen inch square, with a frame rate four times faster than a standard video. The result is a relatively smooth display, without the usual jerkiness of billboard advertising. Considering that thousands of cars use the Strip every hour – often slowed to walking pace – such displays are not wasted on the passing customers.

The creative people at Yesco, a dozen designers, stand at their drawing boards in a warren of offices on the first floor, doodling over ever bigger and brighter signs. Some have come through art school, others have drifted into the business without formal training. 'The idea,' says Shirley Overley, who created the 75-foot high guitar outside the Hard Rock Cafe on Paradise Road, 'is to sit down with the client and work out what he wants to do. Then we try and find the best way of achieving it, technically. I don't follow any particular theory of design.' The guitar is modelled exactly on the famous guitar designed by Les Paul, even to the shiny woodwork effect of the soundbox. 'We don't have a house style,' says senior designer Harold Bradford, who began his career as a professional footballer. *Spectacular* is the catch-all word he favours.

Signs can be expensive: the Les Paul guitar cost $700,000; Caesars' message centre $750,000. The gorgeous cloudburst of red and orange over the new Rio casino, which won a design award, came in at $3m. It displays the name Rio in bold white lettering, against a peacock fantail of colour, shaped like the swaying headdress of a carnival dancer. Below, a message centre gives details of shows and gaming. (In fact the whole of the Rio's exterior wall is coloured, divided in a long S-curve between red and blue, which marks a new idea in structural decoration, also employed by the Stardust for its new tower.) It takes the Yesco people only three days to do a run-of-the-mill design for a shopping centre, but three weeks or more for a major casino project.

Returning to the Strip, some 20 years after *Learning From Las Vegas* was published, what changes may be seen? 'We were pleased to find that the Las Vegas of 1990 is still a brash and lively place, but we also sensed that the Strip may be in danger of losing some of the qualities that make it unique and wonderful', one of the original authors reported in a paper called *Relearning From Las Vegas*. The two biggest changes concern the scale of development and, as a consequence of that, how people move around. 'The Strip seems to be evolving from a pure auto strip into a version of the classic American Main Street depending more equally on cars and pedestrians.' In other words there are more people in town, many of whom like to walk around. This was always true of Fremont Street downtown, where the casinos are part of the sidewalk, like the stores on an American main street. These casinos present open, inviting faces to the street, encouraging pedestrians to wander in and risk a few coins in the slots. Indeed in the block between the Union Plaza at the end of the street and the Nugget and Binion's, a host of young hucksters is on parade, continually accosting passers-by with handbills or cheap come-ons, to entice them inside.

But the Strip, which in the '60s was geared totally to the automobile, *has* changed dramatically. Great numbers of pedestrians stroll along it, by day and night; crowds gather every evening to look at the volcano belching fire outside the Mirage. The Strip casinos have responded to this sidewalk traffic in a variety of ways. For some of the older casinos, which are set back from the street, the pedestrians still have to be drawn in, as along the Caesars Palace walkways. 'Pedestrians enter the walkways from three fantastical architectual confections that are very much in the spirit of excess that gives Las Vegas its unique flavour.' (*Relearning From Las Vegas*) One, for example, carries the visitor through a procession of five triumphal arches, past a classical temple and rows of trumpeting angels perched on columns. Once on the moving walkway, visitors are welcomed by disembodied voices and carried past holographic projections of orgiastic Romans. And of course they cannot get back to the street via the walkways, which run inwards only. Alternatively, some

casinos have moved their fronts directly onto the street. The
Flamingo Hilton, with its little casino-within-a-casino called
O'Shea's, and the Holiday with its iridescent green and red
riverboat, for instance, are flush with the sidewalk. The appeal,
with a lot of neon at street level, is aimed at the pedestrian not the
driver.

In fact, the Strip has become so congested with traffic that
driving is often as slow as in any big city centre; likewise exits
from the freeway get completely blocked in rush-hour periods. So
far, the casinos have failed to agree on any way of breaking the
gridlock, such as a monorail to carry pedestrians along the Strip.
Some new way of relieving the congestion is overdue but
Relearning From Las Vegas warns against any construction (for
example train stations) which blocks the view along the Strip. 'All
of the previous 30 years' investment in signs, façades, volcanoes,
and castles would become irrelevant when covered over by these
structures . . . the most tragic consequence would be the
aesthetic destruction of the Strip.' Far better, it is suggested, to
consider parallel routes, one-way systems, and a re-design of the
sidewalk.

The most impressive change, the report goes on, has been in
the size and development of the Strip. Two decades ago the place
was a rich mix of major casinos like Circus, the Stardust and
Caesars juxtaposed with small-scale stores, motels and souvenir
shops, which now exist only in the central no-man's-land between
the Strip and Downtown – trinket shops, junk food stands, sleazy
motels offering adult movies and waterbeds. Today, development of the Strip parallels the typical American strip with its
ever-larger shopping areas, culminating in regional malls of
multi-million square feet. New casino-hotels like the Mirage and
Excalibur (and the proposed new MGM), with their thousands of
rooms, dominate the street frontage. 'Architecturally, the
buildings are still a mix of ducks and sheds, but it appears the
ducks are winning', notes the author of *Relearning From Las
Vegas*. Excalibur is seen as the biggest duck ever, in the tradition

of Circus and its big top. Excalibur may well represent, in its size and dedication to a single theme, the future trend, though its mass – its teeny-weeny turrets seem ridiculously out of scale – is not consistent. The Mirage, with its expanses of gold glass and sleek, unornamented profile, is described (somewhat mysti-fyingly) as essentially a duck though an abstract one. On the sides of the decorated sheds, neon is making a comeback, reflecting a revival nationwide.

'The main lesson we see in the Strip today (and this lesson hasn't changed in 22 years) is vive la différence,' conclude the authors of *Relearning From Las Vegas*. 'As long as the casinos develop in their own idiosyncratic ways, the result for the Strip and Las Vegas as a culture will be salutary. Conformity and bland "good taste" would be worse for the Strip than an invasion of gamblers with second sight.' It seems safe to assume that good taste on the part of the casinos is about as likely to occur as clairvoyance in the minds of their customers.

II
Sex
&
Money

1. The Mirage: no more neon

2. Steve Wynn: electric smile

3. The Flamingo, 1946

4. The Flamingo Hilton, 1992

5. Bugsy Siegel

6. Jack Binion

7. Benny Binion

8. Binion's Horseshoe, downtown

9. Circus Circus

10. Excalibur

11. An entrance to Caesars Palace

12. Bally's twin slabs

13. Sign for
Circus Circus

14. The Luxor
pyramid (model)

5 SOILED DOVES

The average man would rather behold her nakedness than Ulysses Grant in his full dress uniform.

Mark Twain, on a high-class whore

Gambling and sex go together: or to put it more precisely, one follows the other. Always has done and always will, because the thrill of gambling is bound up, one way or another, with the libido. The images of gambling presented in the movies usually carry a sexual message: eyes flash across the roulette table, as the debonair gambler in his dinner suit joins the femme fatale in slinky silk – a modern version of the cowboy in the bar-room poker game, a painted lady close beside him. And everyone who comes to Las Vegas is aware of the city's reputation. It's part of the mythology of the place – easy money, easy sex – part of the glamour.

The main difference from other gambling resorts is that in Vegas prostitution is given some degree of official approval. Nowadays you seldom see women soliciting on the streets, or trawling for clients from a car, though that doesn't mean it never happens, or that – much more likely – visitors may not be waylaid at the bar in their hotels. Nowhere in Nevada is street prostitution or soliciting legal or accepted. But over the years, local attitudes towards the degree of permissiveness allowed have changed – especially inside the major casinos, where high rollers may require more than tea and sympathy to recover from their losses.

Approval of prostitution in the state of Nevada ranges from simple toleration to ordinances approved by referenda that regard keeping brothels as a regular form of business. So regular, indeed, that an attempt was made to go public recently, by floating a share issue in one of the most famous brothels in the state, the Mustang Ranch near Reno – but the issue flopped. (The owner had tax problems.) So many questions are asked about the status of prostitution that an explanatory note on the subject has been issued by the Nevada State Library in Carson City, written by the research director of the Legislative Counsel Bureau, to provide an official answer. No specific mention of prostitution was made in any Nevada general law until 1911, when certain acts relative to prostitution were made illegal. These included placing a female in a brothel, males habitually resorting in a brothel, and the placing of a brothel near schools, churches or main streets. In 1913 additional provisions were added prohibiting pandering, living off the earnings of a prostitute, or advertising brothels. This is the extent of general law on the subject, except for an important provision of modern times which prohibits the licensing of houses of prostitution in counties with a population over 200,000. Clark County, which includes Las Vegas, was for a time the only one in that category (now joined by Washoe County, Reno).

However, typical of the ambivalent attitudes taken on prostitution, it has also been deemed 'a nuisance'. This ruling was made by the Nevada Supreme Court, under the common law (adopted by the territorial legislature in 1861 from England) in 1949. Accordingly, county District Attorneys are charged with the duty to abate nuisances, wherever they may occur. The court said that the nuisance would merely be aggravated if it occurred near a school or a church, but that to move it away would not change its nuisance character.

Overall, the position is ambiguous. Historically, there has

never been a general law specifically allowing prostitution. Neither has there been a general law (apart from the ban in Clark County) that specifically prohibited it. Since 1949, brothel prostitution has existed in most of Nevada's seventeen counties. The most populous areas of Las Vegas, Reno, Lake Tahoe and Carson City have not tolerated brothels openly for some years, but their location close to areas which do allow brothels means there has been little pressure for change. Politically, there seems to be no desire to press the matter in either direction.

In fact there have always been bars with good-time girls, dancing saloons, brothels in all but name, on the new frontier, especially in the gold and silver mining camps, where women were scarce. What else was there to do apart from gambling and drinking? Money sluiced through men's hands like water in a sieve as they panned for gold. Morals were free and easy. 'The mere mention of the western saloon elicits a cast of glittering "painted ladies" who move about a noisy, crowded bar dispensing earthy fun to a boisterous clientele', says Anne M. Butler in *Daughters of Joy, Sisters of Misery*. The environment and the women, both bawdy and rollicking, complemented each other perfectly, this scholarly study observes. 'So natural was their association that these "soiled doves" of the American West have become standard fixtures in the imagery of the frontier.' 'I think there is somewhere near 4,000 people here – the wickedness is unimaginable and appalling', wrote Reverend Joseph Cook, an Episcopalian missionary, from Laramie, out on the frontier in Wyoming in 1868 (*Diary and Letters*). 'This is the great center for gamblers of all shades, and roughs, and troops of lewd women, and bullwhackers. Almost every other house is a drinking saloon, gambling house, or bawdy . . .' 'The working miners had few pleasures except the unfailing resources of gambling and drinking', noted a report on Virginia City, home of the Comstock Lode, by James Scrugham, an early Governor of Nevada. 'Prostitution flourished, as in all large camps, and courtesans promenaded the streets slowly, decked out in gay dresses and showy jewellery, and drifting about with the restless tide which set to and fro throughout the city.'

One estimate put the number of prostitutes in the trans-Mississippi West at 50,000. They worked in four styles: brothel dweller, saloon and dance-hall worker, crib woman (a crib was a lean-to shack), or streetwalker. Women in brothels enjoyed the best status, both in and out of the profession. The house gave them a place to live as well as work, some measure of protection from law enforcement officials and other busybodies, and – not least – the companionship of their sisters in the game. 'Westerners divided women into two categories – good ones and bad ones', according to Richard Erdoes in *Saloons of the Old West*. For many years only the bad ones could be found in saloons. 'The overwhelming fact that determined the role of women in the West, and their relationship to men, was their almost total absence during the early years.' The sportin' gals, however, were there almost from the start.

> The miners came in forty-nine
> The whores in fifty-one.
> They rolled upon the bar-room floor
> And made the native son.

'The westerner found the women he was most at ease with in the place he was most at ease in – the saloon. He also found them in the cat houses, but to visit those necessitated a trip to a town of some size.' Two types of saloon specialised in providing female companionship for the lonely cowhand or miner. The hurdy-gurdy house or pretty waiter saloon, and the variety saloon disguised as theatre. The hurdy-gurdy house (named after a street accordion) existed to sell drinks. The girls were there to keep the liquor flowing: they were known as hurdy-gurdy girls, honky-tonk gals, beerjerkers, box rustlers or pretty waiter girls. Though considered a cut above the fallen angels, some of them went in for prostitution. Their role was to dance with the men and beguile them into buying drinks, but the point was that they could pick their own clients, or reject them, so far as sexual favours were concerned. Though in some places, it might be hard to draw a clear line between a saloon and a brothel. The term 'red light district' is said to have originated in Dodge from a custom among railroaders of leaving their red brakemen's lanterns hanging outside the door of their girl of the evening, to discourage other visitors. A Babylon of the frontier, one citizen, Robert Wright, termed the town: 'Her virtue is prostitution and her beverage is whiskey. She is a merry town and the only visible support of a great many of her citizens is jocularity. The town is full of prostitutes and every other place is a brothel.' (*Saloons of the Old West*)

'You need one or two hookers in a bar,' a casino manager observed to me recently. 'A bar without girls is nuthin'. But you get a coupla girls around, you sure can sell drinks.'

According to an early Nevada Governor, James Scrugham, the girls of the camps were as basic as food. 'In towns without wives, they substituted. The camps were not for wives. They just couldn't put up with the roughness. Hell, many camps didn't have water. I don't know when it was that Virginia City, for example, first got flush toilets . . . The miners, some coming in from a day in the drifts, some coming in from months of prospecting, hands calloused, boots worn, having smelled only sagebrush and sweat, living like Indians, why, the poor bastards knew the one place they could get a welcome, a smile, a bed with springs, clean sheets, the smell of perfume, was the crib. So the cribs were the place . . . Come evening, the card-sharp and the blacksmith took the same walk down the street of whores. The girls understood; they played the phonograph, and they had pictures on the walls . . .' As soon as a valley numbered a thousand people, a madam would get clearance to bring in some girls, according to a modern account, entitled *The Girls of Nevada* by Gabriel Vogliotti. A typical highway town in 1880 would be three or four streets wide and three or four long. It would have a hotel, whose counter was also the post office, and two small assertive buildings, the Protestant and Catholic churches. Among the bungalows were stores, a school, a volunteer fire department, a doctor, a weekly paper, and saloons. On the edge of town was the house with the girls, with a name like Dolly's or Dora's. 'Most of the women in town might hate Dolly, the pastors might rail against her, there would be arguments about whether Dolly's should be closed or moved further out. But they knew it was the majority will that there be a house. The highway town, like the mining camp, knew it needed a Dolly's.' (*The Girls of Nevada*)

But in *Daughters of Joy, Sisters of Misery*, Anne Butler reaches a bleak conclusion. 'Prostitutes came from among the poorest groups of women on the frontier . . . Such women turned to prostitution at an early age and entered the profession with few skills and only rudimentary education.' The economic rewards proved marginal: the clientele the women served had little money; and what they did earn was pared down by payments to pimps and madams and extortion by officials. Although the women lived intimately with each other, relations were fraught with suspicion and distrust, which frequently led to fights. The West had many names for frontier prostitutes – giddy ladies, painted cats, fair but frail, scarlet ladies, come-on girls, fallen angels, 'boarders' (in quotation marks), ladies of the evening, easy women, fast women, fancy women, fair belles, sportin' gals, owls (for night walkers), crib women. What these women felt about their situation, or what their inner feelings were, we don't know, because the records are so sketchy. Socially, they appeared to accept themselves as lesser people in the community.

Not so, one would imagine, in the contemporary scene. For one thing, there are many semi-professionals, amateurs of the game, working the casinos. Mario Puzo caught the style of this sort of liaison when he noted (*Inside Las Vegas*) how pit or shift bosses have an eye for indulgent girls. Such girls might be working in LA or Salt Lake City in respectable jobs as secretaries, manicurists, dental technicians and so on, and have come in for a weekend of fun with a friend. Pit bosses will chat them up, comp them to a meal and a show, then give the girls their business cards and tell them to call up whenever they're in town and they need something. On a later solo trip, the girl may be introduced to a hotshot gambler – everything to play for, no sordid bargaining about sleeping with the guy. But after dinner and a show and a night scattering chips around the tables (no gentleman lets a lady gamble with her own money, says Puzo) the natural course of events would be to wind up in bed together. Come Monday morning, the girl departs with her 'present'. The gambler has lost, sure, but in more agreeable company (at his advancing age and waistline) than he had any right to expect. Such an arrange-ment has mutual advantages, Puzo suggests.

I don't know if this sort of thing goes on as much as it evidently did when Puzo was writing about it. Certainly if a big loser looks like getting too depressed, raising some doubts about his cheque going through, an attentive host will be there to try to take care of things – and it would hardly be surprising if that should include calling an attractive lady to soothe the customer's fevered brow. (Losing has its consolations.) Alternatively, if a big winner looks like cashing out, which for the casino cage is even more of a disaster, an alert pit boss will be at his side: 'Taking a break, sir? Anything we can do for you? May we send champagne up to your room. . . ? Our pleasure, sir, compliments of the house.' No surprise if a discreet knock on the door reveals a gamesome lady – 'Oops! Have I got the wrong number?' – ready to share the ice-cold bottle. In Vegas sex is just another number on the board.

'Casino bosses have more free sex offered than they could possibly handle,' observed Lee Stolkey, the authoress of a sharp little book about the perils of dealing blackjack, *Dummy Up And Deal*. According to this account, written from the inside by an ex-dealer, the easiest way for a woman to get a job in the blackjack pit – and competition for all good jobs in Vegas is fierce – is to sleep with the floorman. 'Dealers know sex is easy to get in a casino and is generally of a very casual nature . . . Many a floorman has bragged that he has allowed himself to be "seduced" by a dealer with hopes of getting a job where he works.' Usually the bosses get involved with their already-employed female dealers. When the excitement wears off or if the boss feels hampered by her presence, the woman knows the man will either get her a job at another casino, which might be better or worse than the one she has, or switch her shift so they're not working together. Sometimes he will have so much hassle or harassment brought on her that she will quit.

Leaving aside the issue of jobs-for-sexual favours, it is still a very male-dominated milieu. Women did not secure regular employment in casinos, incredible as it sounds, until the 1970s, because in that respect Las Vegas was such a conservative town. Similarly, in those days, black entertainers, no matter how successful they might be with audiences, had to eat and sleep after their shows in their own places off the Strip. It was the Civil Rights Act of 1964 which laid the foundation for the eventual breaking of sex barriers within casinos. Even now, as a recent study, *Resort City in the Sunbelt* by Eugene Moehring, pointed out, there are few women to be seen in supervisory jobs on the casino floor. 'Mirroring the values of postwar America and eager to please their customers, casino executives viewed the smoky, green felt world of gambling as the preserve of white males', says Moehring. 'The pattern finally changed in 1981 when nineteen Strip hotels and four unions signed an out-of-court settlement with a women's group agreeing to end all sexual discrimination in hiring, training and promotion.'

Nowadays, any gambler or conventioneer who checks into his casino-hotel can hardly fail to notice that certain extra-curricular services are on offer, because as soon as he goes out to buy a newspaper, he will see in the rack a sheaf of throwaway magazines or coloured leaflets advertising girls. Anyone can pick up a copy. The one I selected during a recent visit was called *Las Vegas After Dark*, priced at $2 but available for 75c. It contained dozens of saucy ads offering alluring company via a phone number – 'Never a dull moment with me, Kimi' or 'I'm the girl your Mom told you to watch out for, Sunny', and even 'Sexy older woman, Josie', plus several offers of 'Exotic dancers and strippers direct to your room – Speedy service guaranteed'. This was not, however, what I was looking for. What I wanted was information on the brothels servicing Las Vegas. A feature article in *Las Vegas After Dark* provided the answer: 'Since the West was won', it began, 'the cat house has been the greatest Western institution. Today, it's bigger, better and glossier than ever . . . Just 40 miles north of Las Vegas in scenic Nye country, the world's oldest profession is booming. And it's operated more efficiently than ever.' Still better, the report assured readers that 'the girls often display a genuine concern for the male patrons' beyond, that is, 'satisfying their needs and, often, their dreams.' As for the medical side, it was made clear to even the most sceptical tourist that the brothels' employees were paragons of good health, if not clean living. 'The girls who work at the brothels are inspected by a physician weekly for genital disease and it is virtually non-existent' the article claimed. A further assurance was given that the girls also inspected the customers, being 'well trained in this area'. (In support of this claim it is notable that a University of Los Angeles medical survey of 246 prostitutes who worked at the Chicken Ranch between 1982–89 found not a single case of HIV infection.)

The Cherry Patch and Mabel's Whorehouse were recommended as the closest brothels to Las Vegas, 21 miles over the county line. Cherry Patch 2 in Armagosa Valley was a particular favourite, the review added, because it was the only brothel with a gas station, truck stop and restaurant-bar on the premises. Madame Butterfly's, out beyond the township of Crystal, advertised a Japanese-type bath, available 24 hours. Would-be customers, soothed by warm, scented oils, were invited to enjoy exquisite relaxation in the 'love tub'. And so on. Until recently there was even a fly-in brothel, with its own landing strip. I decided to make a field trip.

*

One cloudy evening I drove out to take a look at the brothels in Nye County. As the light faded, the road levelled out to reveal, like a pin-ball table in the dusk, a long line of ghostly blue lights marking the runway at McCarran, and at the end a round disc of pale green. The translucent green of the light was quite unearthly, as if signalling that here all the accepted values of living had been inverted. Driving out (with plenty of money in my wallet), I remembered that I had a snapshot of the Cherry Patch Ranch from nearly twenty years ago. In the course of a magazine article on Las Vegas, I had paid a brief visit to the Cherry Patch.

The name Cherry Patch had a homely ring to it, but I had found the place defended like a mediaeval fortress. The land was completely inhospitable, with not a sign of any living thing in the dark, not even a friendly light in the distance. An old style bordello was what I had expected, as in a Western, with a long bar, a honky-tonk piano, and lacily-clad girls sidling up to greet the gen'lemen in a lazy southern drawl. Instead, the Cherry Patch of those days was a low, squat bungalow, surrounded by a trench and a high wire stockade. The place looked as if it had been barricaded by the last paleface family against a horde of blood-thirsty Indians. The gate was operated by a buzzer from inside. When I asked for a beer I was given the incongruous answer, for a brothel: 'Sorry, no liquor licence in this county!' The line of girls who marched in, in single file, turned and faced me without a sound being uttered. The girls, all young and attractive, stood there, not quite smiling, silent. The one I picked looked cute in a baby-doll dress. She led me to a small room, actually the back of a trailer, with a large bed looming out of the half-darkness, and brought me instead of a beer a cherryade. Simply to talk to her, she explained very sweetly, was going to cost me $100.

She explained that there were house rules, strictly enforced as they had to be with fifteen girls living together. They had three weeks on the go, working round the clock, and then a week off. One of the rules was that the girls were forbidden to speak when they lined up for the customers – talking was considered 'dirty pool'. If a girl did speak, she got fined $25. It was evident from the respectful tone of her remarks that the trailer was wired too. I got a sense of tight control just behind the curtains of the Cherry Patch, force you didn't mess with. At the time I assumed that the place was fortified like a blockhouse because of the danger of rowdy customers beating the place up. Not so. The defences were against rival brothel owners. In the mid-1980s a little local war developed in this underground tributary of the American dream, a real-life tale of skulduggery in the desert.

It began when an ex-Marine, owner of a trucking company in Denver, turned nightclub owner, Walter Plankinton, decided at the age of nearly fifty that what he really wanted to do for the rest of his life was run a brothel. During his years as a trucker he had whiled away many long hours driving up and down the bare Nevada highways, fantasising about this ambition. He had spent enough time in the brothels out there to know that you could buy a plot of desert land for $10,000, spend another $50,000 on half a dozen old house trailers and some used furniture, and soon be spending your days and nights surrounded by 'working girls', meanwhile raking in half a million dollars a year for your time and trouble. There was no problem finding girls, either. Once Plankinton built his place, which he named the Chicken Ranch, phone calls came in almost every day from working girls all over the country – from New York, California, Idaho, Michigan, Texas – all of them wanting to know if he had a bedroom for them. It was a 'national whore's grapevine', according to Plankinton; word was out that the new whorehouse, only 60 miles from Vegas, was open for business. 'We've got Chinese girls, black girls, Mexican girls, white girls, redheads, blondes, brunettes, big-titted ones, fat ones, skinny ones,' he boasted, 'we got 'em all.'

The girls worked fifteen hours a day and cleared over $1,000 a week, after having split their takings fifty-fifty with the house. This kind of money helps to explain why some girls might prefer

such employment to dealing blackjack. What Plankinton did not
realise was that the owners of other brothels in the area might take
exception to his muscling in on their territory; at any rate he did
not hesitate in taking them on. The 'war' that ensued, in which
the Chicken Ranch brothel got burned down in a night attack,
aroused fiercer passions than anything that went on in the beds
inside the trailers. This episode (as recounted in *The Nye County
Brothel Wars* by Jeanie Kasindorf) shows how savage life out in the
west can be, even now. The arch rival and objector to
Plankinton's operation turned out to be the owner of the
Shamrock brothel, situated eighty miles north on a desert
crossroads (renamed Cherry Patch 2 after the war was ended).

The fire completely destroyed the Chicken Ranch. It was just a
lucky chance that none of the girls was burned to death in what
was an act of criminal violence. Plankinton was not a man to give
up. Perhaps he relished the fight. He had his own version of the
American dream, and immediately set about re-building his
brothel. So it was no wonder the place was so heavily fortified. It
needed to be.

My latest field trip was on a Thanksgiving weekend, so I expected
to see a crowd of celebrants. The roads were empty and the
landscape out there, fifty or sixty miles north of Las Vegas, not far
from Death Valley, is as bleak as the surface of the moon. The
report in *Las Vegas After Dark* had claimed that Armagosa Valley
was one of the loveliest areas of Nye County and one of the fastest
growing communities in the United States. Soon to be constructed was an MX missile site and a big investment was going into
mining molybdenum – so the number of prospective customers
for the brothels in the county would increase and multiply. The
map of the area included in the magazine proved wildly out of
scale, and turning off the main highway the road seemed to go on
for ever. I came to a place called Crystal. Sure enough a painted
sign, sticking out like a relic of some previous civilisation,
advertised Mabel's Whorehouse. It pointed away towards a long

narrow landing strip, strewn with boulders and sagebrush. Somewhere in the back of beyond was the Cherry Patch. Down the track was a corrugated tin barn called the Crystal Bar.

To fortify myself, I went in for a drink. It seemed unlikely anyone would ever stop at such a desolate spot, but two weatherbeaten ol' boys in overalls were sitting up at the bar, drinking beer, served by a dumpy woman with grey hair. I asked if she had any wine. She poured it out from a flagon, filling a half pint tumbler to the brim. Shamed to be judged a weakling in such a godforsaken place, I felt obliged to gulp it all down. Outside, the overgrown track leading past the landing strip to Mabel's Whorehouse looked so wild and remote, my courage failed me. I turned the car around and headed back to the main road. Cherry Patch 2, the brothel situated on highway 95, seemed a safer bet. As I mentioned earlier, this was originally the Shamrock, the rival brothel to the Chicken Ranch. The owner had been found guilty of instigating the fire at the Chicken Ranch, and in a separate incident had later been gunned down. His widow sold the place for $900,000.

Armagosa Valley was hardly a township, just a couple of buildings on either side of the road, and despite its name, quite flat. A sign by the gas station proudly proclaimed: 'Million Dollar Sunsets, Air Like Champagne.' The brothel, a single-storey structure, like a white Nissen hut, surrounded by a stout wire fence, stood next door. Two young men in peaked caps were filling up a truck at the gas station. One of them grinned at the attendant: 'Hey, these girls at the brothel – are they as good lookin' as they say?' 'Never seen 'em,' said the man dourly without looking up from the pump. A large wooden board outside the brothel advertised Cherry Patch T-shirts, posters, coffee mugs, bumper stickers and other souvenirs, like a tourist spot. It also offered prospective clients the benefit of American Express, Master Card or Diner's Club, in payment for services rendered. I pressed the buzzer, waited while someone inside took a look, and was admitted into the stockade.

A heavy door swung open and a youngish woman in a yellow dress came forward and said, 'Hi.' The room was low and dim, shabbily furnished with a couple of sofas. Above a curtained doorway, a row of pictures of bosomy western gals, as displayed in casino bars downtown, smiled archly down in welcome. 'Siddown, the gals'll be right along.' The front door had clanged shut behind me. No way of backing out now. There was the sound of footsteps, the swish of a curtain, but instead of the seductive chorus line I was expecting, just two girls appeared. One looked as if she might be Mexican, the other was tall and black. They wheeled to face me, in tight skirts and off-the-shoulder blouses, not quite smiling, ready to go to work. The scene was about as sexually stimulating as cold turkey after Thanksgiving.

'I'm waiting for a friend,' I improvised.

'I've heard that before,' said the woman. The girls stood there silently.

'Can I get a drink?'

'We got beer, five dollars. Or orange juice.' I took the orange juice.

The Mexican girl smiled and came over. 'What you like?'

'I'm sort of waiting right now.'

'You wanna come my room? I tell you what we do. You have good time.'

'Maybe later.'

'We got beeg bath here. You have nice bath, massage, you relax? I make you relax. Maybe two girls is good! Yes?'

I took a swig of orange juice.

'We have good time. No hurry.'

I began to feel guilty about letting down what was expected of me on the male side of such transactions. After all, who goes to a brothel just to take an orange juice. 'What does all this cost?'

'We don' talk here, you come my room. You tell me what you like. Is good, OK?' I stood up to follow her when the outside buzzer sounded. The woman in the yellow dress peered through a peephole. I sat back on the sofa, suddenly alone.

The door was buzzed open and in waddled one of those massively overweight young fellows you so often see in Vegas, a really huge guy, about twenty-two years old, weighing three hundred pounds if he was an ounce. He wore, as such heavy-weights seem to do, crimson satin shorts from which his massive thighs and legs descended like the pillars of Hercules. He planted his feet apart and stood there grinning broadly. Here he wasn't going to have to apologise to anyone about his size, here he was just gonna have a *good* time. The two girls wheeled back in and paraded in front of him. He gazed amiably down at them. 'You choose which one you like,' the madame told him. I saw from their expressions that each of the girls was really desperately eager to be picked, never mind the guy's girth, they just wanted to go to work. The young man relished the moment of choice for about two and a half seconds, then pointed to the Mexican girl who half a minute ago had been propositioning me for her services. She smiled up at him and without a backward glance seized him by the hand and led him off through the dim hallway.

 ' I finished my orange juice on my own. Then a surreal moment occurred. From the darkened end of the hallway, a bright blonde girl emerged pushing an invalid's frame, like a hospital bed, on which lay a gaunt, pale young man with wispy hair. She was leaning down, chatting and laughing to him as she pushed his bed along, and he, half propped up – though it seemed he could not properly speak – was responding with animated signs, nodding his head as if on a stalk and flapping one arm in the air. They reached the door, she gave a broad smile of farewell, pushed the bed frame and the young man, still waving, to someone waiting outside, waved again and then came back in. She was still smiling.

The black girl decided to try her luck with me. She was pretty enough but had a surly look about her. 'C'mon, honey. You wanna come on now?'

'Listen, how late do you girls work?' I enquired, stalling.

'Alla time. We don' stop. Any time.'

'Are you very busy out here?'

'You bet. Oh yeah. Buncha guys come in four inna mornin', ya never know. That's how it is here. Any time. You wanna do business now?'

I got the message. A man's gotta do what a man's gotta do. I followed her past the curtain and turned into a little space, no more than an alcove, in a pinkish light, presumably the back of a trailer. There was a mirror facing the bed, and a basin. Rock and roll from a cassette player.

'OK, honey, what's it gonna be?'

'What've you got?'

'Depends what you wanna spend, honey. Whyn't you take a love tub?' She ran through a catalogue of sexual indulences, sizing up my reaction, gauging how much I might spend. 'Or we got videos.'

'Listen, can I buy you a drink?'

She accepted a twenty dollar bill, slipped out and returned with a glass. We talked for a few minutes. The airstrip was no longer in operation, she explained, but when it was – oh boy, people flew in from all over. Her hand strayed along my thigh towards my crotch. 'You wanna party with me now, honey?'

'No I don't, but let me give you something.' Digging into my pocket, I came up with a fistful of greenbacks and dropped them on the bed. She collected the money briskly.

'Okay,' she said, in a tone which implied we get all sorts of weird guys out here. On the way out, she picked up a little basket filled with book matches. 'Here, take some. Case you wanna come see us again.' I thanked her. 'Sure, any time.' The matches pictured a girl in a floppy hat and a suspender belt. Under the heading 'Las Vegas closest brothel' it offered Japanese baths, photography, dominance, largest selection of girls, outcalls, adding on the striker: 'Best little whorehouse in Nevada! Only minutes away.'

It was dark outside now and rounding a bend, a few miles down the empty highway, a red light suddenly hove into view, out of the blackness, a round disc flashing on and off, far away on the right.

It came from Mabel's Whorehouse, signalling its age-old message. In the desolate Nevada night the winking red light was hypnotic. It proclaimed an elemental message: S-E-X! Here it is! Come 'n git it! In this vast silent range, the red light seemed perverse. Granted the brothel was handy for construction workers or airforce personnel stuck in the middle of nowhere. But why would anyone drive out all this way, to this point of light in the void, when sexual life was so throbbingly in abundance in Vegas itself? An hour further on, round another bend in the road, the distant lights of the city came into view in long diamond clusters. These cosmic reflections were brought down to earth by an unexpected conclusion to my brief visit. That same evening, as I stood waiting for the elevator in my hotel, the doors slid open to reveal a young man lying on a hospital bed, pushed forward by a nurse. The poor man was spastic, seriously handicapped: his head nodded to and fro, his eyes rolled, and his right arm was strapped to his side to prevent it flapping out. I recognised him at once from my visit to the brothel. I lowered my gaze in tribute to his will to live.

In the Gambler's Book Club, that haven of Las Vegas punters, I came across a little guidebook entitled *The Best Cat Houses in Nevada* ($5.95), and checked my impressions against the entry for Cherry Patch 2. 'The interior is plush and nicely appointed, with a dozen or so women working in the rooms, ready, willing and able to satisfy most of the requests presented to them by the visiting men. What you have here is an oasis in the middle of a desert . . . more than just an ordinary cathouse . . . the only one with its own gas station, full bar and restaurant, and one of the most unique museums of brothel memorabilia around.' (I passed on that one.) The guide, which lists thirty-two brothels in Nevada, says that a working girl's shift is usually three weeks on duty, working twelve to sixteen hours non-stop, *partying* anywhere from zero to twelve times a night, although anywhere between two and five parties a night might be standard. They are 'independent contractors', which means they set their own prices. Successful girls are said to earn $75,000 a year.

In hyperbolic vein, the authors of *The Green Felt Jungle* gave a 'conservative estimate' that 10 per cent of the 64,400 population in Vegas back in the early 1960s was engaged, one way or another, in prostitution. 'Where there's gambling there's easy money, where there's easy money, there's whores, where there's whores there's extortion and narcotics, and where there's narcotics there's everything else.' Among those lumped together in this blanket condemnation were cabbies, bartenders, bellhops, newsboys, proprietors of liquor stores and motels, gamblers and casino security men, as well as professional pimps. Casino managers today, when asked if providing girls for gamblers is part of their service, blush at the mention of such an impious thought. Soliciting is illegal! They would never dream of such a thing (not when talking to a journalist, anyway). They have a point, though, which is that it would be foolish to run such a risk with a good customer – he might be rolled for his wallet or beaten up, anything could go wrong; and then he could hold the casino liable for damages. No, high rollers must find their own ladies, or better yet, bring their own. On the other hand, if a man has lost a six figure sum at the tables, is the pit boss going to turn around and say: 'I am sorry, Sir, but as a loyal citizen of the State of Nevada I must uphold the laws against soliciting in every respect'? One manager in North Las Vegas was more forthright when he told me: 'Listen, if a guy lost half a million in my place, I would personally drive the limo to his bedroom door!'

How many 'working girls' are there in Las Vegas? Bell captains maintain a list of prostitutes. Such lists range from about 20 names to more than 70 in the larger hotels, according to a sociological study done in 1985, 'The Organisation of Bell Desk Prostitution' by Reichert and Frey. Methods of getting on these lists vary. Some girls enter through personal contacts or recommendatons from friends already on the list, or from hotel employees. Coercion was also a means of recruitment. Bell captains and bellmen are key personnel in hotel-casinos, because they are usually both the first and the last employees to be in contact with guests. Such jobs are among the lowest paid, but are much sought after; through tips a bellman probably earns three to five times as much as other service employees. So far as procurement is concerned, the bellman gets a substantial cut on each trick, up to 50 per cent of the girl's fee. If she doesn't pay, she risks getting beaten up. This study concludes that working via the bell desk, a girl gets a high degree of protection, both from the police and, on the customer side, from weirdos.

The risks are not all taken on the female side, as is shown by this cautionary tale, which happened to a fellow I know, a professional blackjack player. The psychological strains involved in counting down the blackjack deck are severe, because the casinos are always on the look-out for counters to give them heat. But my friend Tony was disciplined. So much so that when he found himself next to an unusually pretty girl at the table, and kept running into her at odd moments during a three or four day stay at one of the big hotels, he paid her no particular attention. Once or twice they had a drink or a coffee together, but this was not love at first sight. Late one night, when, as it happened, he had enjoyed a good run and was a few thousand dollars richer, he ran into her again, apparently by chance, on the casino floor. They had a drink, then supper. This young woman was a college girl, cool, ironic, not your usual Vegas type. Tony was impressed. A more amorous relationship seemed entirely natural as Tony escorted her, she a shade reluctantly, up to his room. He poured out a couple of drinks, they raised their glasses, she smiled a knowing smile, and the next thing Tony remembers was waking up in hospital 36 hours later after having had his stomach pumped. A friend, worried by his absence had asked hotel security to enter his room. His wallet, needless to say, and his credit cards were all gone. He had been hit with a very dangerous drug, analysed as Scalapomine. Tony had swallowed an almost lethal dose. Forget the lost cash, the police told him: he was lucky to get away with his life. The story has a twist in the tail. A while later, the police apprehended the girl and brought her to court. Tony looked across at her in the dock; he was convinced that she probably was the smart cookie who had knocked him out, but he could not absolutely swear to it. She was acquitted – probably to deliver a sucker punch to another unsuspecting gambler.

In addition to his notable contribution to hotel-casino design, Bugsy Siegel could also be credited as the man who 'pioneered' the sexual market in Vegas. When the Flamingo opened in 1946, sexual mores were a lot stricter. According to Vogliotti (*The Girls of Nevada*), it was not so easy as it now seems for a man to walk into a hotel lobby and ask for his room key, when accompanied by a lady who was (quite obviously) not his wife. At that time the big hotels in New York had 'grim, grey-haired ladies' facing the elevators, to stop any hanky-panky (like the concierges in Moscow hotels in the Brezhnev era). Or a house detective was liable to rap on a man's door demanding to know if there was a woman in there. The Flamingo was different. 'Siegel saw the whole sensual fun package in a single flash – gambling, shows, excitement, girls.' The hotel was built out in wings, so no one would ever see, let alone care, if a man took a woman in. The formula devised by Siegel (recounted by Vogliotti) seems strikingly modern: There must be girls, as many as the men demand. But you must not be so vulgar as to offend middle-class America which fills your hotels. It must not become so open, so raw, that it hurts the real business, which is gambling. But the town, the State itself, must accept the fact that it is in the sex business.

It remains true of Las Vegas today that the rampant sexuality of the place is overlaid by a thin layer of respectability, like the chiffon on a showgirl. The brothels are not allowed to advertise publicly, soliciting is against the law, prostitution has been swept off the streets by the sheriff. Overall, the Mormon ethic which condemns illicit sex but tolerates gambling, remains strong in the community. Mormons are well to the fore in civic administration and banking. And casino managers and their minions do not (openly, at any rate) procure for customers. Instead, Vegas has something different: the Yellow Pages.

No less than 40 half-page ads in the Yellow Pages list entertainment services under saucy names like Desert Foxes or Sophisticated Ladies, with a more or less overt sexual thrust to them. Most of them offer 'dancers' or 'entertainers', ready to fly to the caller's hotel room at any hour of the day or night. I chose Companions, which had a slightly more sociable sound to it. 'Do you have a young lady I can talk to?' I enquired of the agency. I admitted that my interest was journalistic, as distinct from seeking a 'companion'. There was a pause at the other end of the line. Evidently they got calls from all kinds of freaks but this was something new. The woman's voice, metallic and practical, said she would call back. And inside of five minutes, Normandie came on the line (they go in for fancy names, these ladies).

Normandie began questioning me: what did I want? Where was I from? She sounded extremely wary about giving me an interview. 'There's only one thing I *can* do,' she said candidly. But when I offered to meet her anywhere in town, instead of her coming out to my hotel, Normandie relented. It turned out that she could make use of me as a taxi, for an engagement she already had that night at a Strip casino. 'I could be persuaded,' Normandie conceded, adding in the same breath, 'So what's your budget here?' We agreed a fee and arranged to meet at a French restaurant of note. How would I recognise her? 'I'll be wearing a thigh-length dress spangled with gold and silver sequins,' she told me.

First thing Normandie did, arriving punctually at the bar, was to ask me for the money. She looked like a gift-wrapped version of a football cheerleader: shiny, pretty, pliant, immaculately made-up, with long silver earrings dangling over her bare shoulders, aged about twenty-four. Normandie turned out to be very self-aware and motivated. 'I am not an escort,' she began. 'That word's taboo. We're hostesses now.' What's more, so Normandie claimed, she had recently given up the quick-call-to-a-hotel-room style of entertaining. She worked now only on 'straight dating' to accompany, as she put it, a gentleman to a dinner or a show. 'What happens,' she explained, 'is that a guy like you comes into town. You look in the yellow pages and ring the agency. They ask what kind of girl you're looking for. You know – short, tall, blonde, dark, busty, the variations are endless. Everyone's got their own type. I pass for twenty to thirty-five. There's a very large turnover of young ladies. They're not the most stable young ladies. Some are only working to make enough money to pay their bills or something, you know.'

Normandie blew in from Florida two years ago. She was running a little business down there, which got into trouble. 'So I came up here for a month and I saw how easy it was, this life. The money, there's so much money. All this money, it just boggles your mind.' She sounded as if it was a fact of life which no longer surprised her. 'So the agency bleeps me or calls me on my car phone. I'm always on call. So I ring your hotel room. I say, "Hello John, I hear you might be needing some company." First thing, I try and find out what sort of man you are. What you're doing in town, what you want. I check for speech patterns or innuendoes. I don't want to run into any trouble, or get involved with anyone who's into drugs or intoxicated. So I get an idea what you're like. I explain the agency fee is $125, but that doesn't include something for myself. This will bring it up to $400 or $500, depending how you spend the time. Up to an hour. Then I get a reaction from you, find out if money's a problem, find out how much you're willing to spend.' Normandie took a sip of her Perrier. 'And I offer to describe myself.'

Some girls deal in quantity, Normandie explained, depending how badly they needed the money. She went for quality. She prefers to pick and choose. One client a day is her usual rate. The 'agency' – in reality no more than a woman with a phone line and a long list of girls – takes a cut of about a third. The fee which the gentleman pays is negotiable. Earning a minimum of $500 for a five-hour evening date and usually substantially more – 'Oh, you want to take coffee up in your suite, after we finish dinner?' – she could easily earn $1,000 a day.

'When I get to your hotel room, I listen at the door, to see if anything's going on. Police may have rented the room, posing as clients. They've got several means of entrapment, they'll use any way they can. Usually I get an escort to take me through the hotel. It's dangerous for a girl to walk on her own in some of these places. Security will detain you. Take you away and look in your purse. All they find is a credit card stapler and a bleeper, and a packet of you know what, they got you.' The secret of cruising, according to the black hooker who befriended John Gregory Dunne in his *A Memoir of a Dark Season*, is to keep moving: 'Caesars first, then the Tropicana, then the Sands. No luck. No more than two drinks in any casino. Stay for more than two drinks without making a connection and hotel security begins to get nervous. The hotels draw a very fine line. They like the girls available for the roller who wants a pop, but then they don't want the casino to look like a lamppost.' Or to take it from the opposite viewpoint. One of the things Maria, the heroine of Didion's *Play It As It Lays*, would never do: walk through the Sands or Caesars alone after midnight.

Normandie sounded aggrieved: 'They don't want working girls in the hotel who may roll a client. They figure a guy spends $1,000 on me, he might've spent the money in the casino.' Sometimes a man gives her money to play with while he gambles; she bets as little as she can get away with and pockets the chips. 'When I go into the hotel with an escort, I'm safe. I came here with an escort tonight.' She gave me a narrow look. 'I don't know who you are, you might be playing some kinda game. I was remiss, actually, in not asking to see your driver's licence.' She was a very careful lady, I suggested. 'Yeah, when you're dealing with life and death, right.'

Normandie continued: 'I knock on the door. That's the

moment of truth. The guy sees you for the first time. I sit down,
we size each other up. I say – Gee, I could recite this in my sleep –
"Would you like to exercise your option to ask me to leave?" They
usually say, "Oh no! Do stay!" That gives the guy a hook, he can
say he doesn't want me to stay, this isn't going to work. Okay, no
hassle, just give me the taxi fare back home.' (Only once was
Normandie turned down.) 'So I say, "We need to take care of the
financial arrangements that we discussed on the telephone." I go
into the bathroom and take a look around for any sign of drugs.'
When the money has been exchanged, or the credit card slip
signed, and she feels comfortable, she rings the agency. 'I tell
them I'm with Mr – at his hotel room, and I'll ring back in one
hour. Or five hours if it's an escort job. It's a ridiculous game,'
Normandie added in an ironic, self-deprecating aside, shrugging
her bare shoulders, 'dealing with a total stranger. It can turn you
crazy. You don't think about it. You think of something else. I
think of it as "dating", deliberately, to rationalise the idea of
prostitution. I don't think anyone is in this game because they like
the work. You're someone else. I can be whatever they want me to
be. I'm a chameleon. Some clients are romantic types, they order
up champagne and roses. Some people know exactly what they
want. We move along swiftly. They pay for my time and my
company, for up to an hour. It's "one conversation" in the time.
Half an hour is usually enough, and I'm on my way.'

Normandie's clients range between young and old, eighteen to
seventy-five, rich and poor. 'A man might have saved up for four
months, just to get $500. And for some men money has no
meaning. It's a fantasy. Away from home, having a total stranger
come to your room. Knowing you are going to make some sort of
contact. It's dark and mysterious. What do they want? The scope
is incredible. Some men just want to have company. A lot of my
job is full of tenderness. We might just take a bubble bath
together, it might not lead to anything. I'm more of a therapist. A
man will tell me things he can't tell his wife. Pillow talk can be
very profitable. I've had a couple of stock deals. It's so easy,

sometimes, so easy. I make my exit, I do it graciously. "Here's a hot towel." But after some men . . . I need to go home, and fall in the jacuzzi with a glass of white wine, I need to go to bed for a week.'

When you are accustomed to her kind of money, it's hard to let it go, Normandie said. She sounded not entirely content with her life. She had given up, so she said, these quick calls because it was too risky. The police were always trying to bust you for prostitution. Normandie found it hard to convey the awfulness, the abject humiliation, of being busted. 'There's a knock on the door, the cops come in. Sometimes they'll go and call up the agency to trap another girl. They take you down to the station and book you, and you're thrown into a cell. You're in there with the absolute dregs of society, drug addicts, criminals, penned in. You may be there a couple of hours or twenty hours. They won't let you get to a phone. And you can't get released until you make bail. I'm just lying on the concrete floor, it's horrible, all I'm looking for is a piece of tissue to lay my head on the floor, off the filth. When do they let you go? Not until . . . not until you've not got one shred of dignity left.' If a working girl is busted three times she faces thirty days in gaol, which may be why Normandie, so she said, was giving up Vegas. She was working now mainly with repeat customers, people she knew, which was safe, and sticking to escort service work. She saw herself as a smart businesswoman. She planned to return to Florida soon, she confided, to run a resort.

The agencies are no more than little store-front operations. Their biggest expense is taking a half-page ad in the yellow pages, which costs $2,500 a month. An agency might have 100 girls on file and get at least 20 to 30 calls a day. It will make $100 to $150 a call from these girls, who are mostly glorified hookers off the street, supporting a habit or with some kind of personal problem, Normandie said. Agencies became very rich. Normandie, from a white middle-class, mid-Western background, was troubled, too, by the big secret in her life. 'If you rang my sisters and told them what I was doing, they wouldn't believe you. Just couldn't believe it. When I started two years ago, I tried to talk to the other girls. To try and share this secret in my life. But I couldn't associate with them. They're so flaky.'

As I drove Normandie over for her evening engagement, she sounded pensive. 'I know a girl, making $150,000 a year. Money means nothing.' She gestured across the gleaming Vegas Strip. 'I can go in there to the Shopping Mall and buy a dress for $500, make-up for $200. It's just a lunch. Yeah, but what does five hundred bucks mean, if you're gonna feel sick afterwards? You know what? I'm thinking of writing a book about my life.' We drew up outside the casino. Normandie swung open the door, slithered out of the passenger seat in her glittery sequinned dress and sashayed up the steps, without a backward glance.

My account of the sexual market in Las Vegas would be unfair and one-sided if it was confined to the masculine side of the bargain alone; there are, after all, two sexes involved in the process. The question was, how could one discover something of the female side of the pursuit of pleasure? There is no *Good Brothel Guide* for the woman visitor in search of a good time. The ads in the throwaway brochures, it appeared, didn't cater for female tastes, or consider them at all. The whole schtick was aimed at men. So I did what anyone needing help is advised to do, I went back to the Yellow Pages. Only two agencies listed male 'companions' available for women – which probably indicates the division of services in Vegas between the sexes.

The ad I chose seemed to have it all. Under a line drawing of a clean-cut man in a fedora and a girl with long hair, it proffered Convention Hosts and Hostesses, Models, Party Strippers, Tennis, Masseuse, Tour Guides and Translators, 24 hours direct to you, with the helpful addendum that these services could be charged to a credit card. Rather than spin out some cock and bull story about seeking to engage a suitable companion on behalf of a woman friend, I told the agency exactly what I wanted, and asked if I could invite one of their guys to lunch. No problem: a couple of minutes later Tony called my hotel room. His price wasn't cheap: $125 fee for the agency, plus a tip, which we settled at a further $125, for himself. But I have to admit, Tony gave good value.

He was instantly identifiable in the line at the restaurant: a slim, lithe, sun-tanned young guy, more of a boy than a man, dark haired and dark-eyed, slightly Italian looking, average height, dressed in open-necked silk shirt and designer jeans. Gold good-luck charm dangling at the chest. Easy smile. A lick of long hair over the back of his collar. He confirmed the meeting on the message bleeper on his belt before we sat down, asked if he might smoke and ordered a brand-name whisky on the rocks. This occasion was, evidently, a new and slightly unsettling experience for Tony.

'I take 'em out, show 'em a good time,' he began circumspectly enough, describing his role as a companion. 'Go to dinner or a show, just talk about things, to and fro.' And then? 'Sometimes they want a companion in a different way. Mostly ladies, but we get a lot of guy calls too.' He worked, he indicated, both sides of the fence. The job was a busy one, three or four calls a day, especially over holidays like the Fourth of July. Tony was not fazed by having to provide his services pretty often, on the contrary, he welcomed it. The ladies concerned paid varying amounts for his company, depending how much time they wanted to spend with him; around $1,000 (his tip plus the agency fee) seemed to be the going rate. For this purpose, he carried a pocket credit card printer, making out the charges to 'convention catering'.

Tony was not a fluent talker, but observing me taking notes, he warmed to his theme. It became clear that in nearly every call he received, actually in every single one, Tony was required to make love to the woman. Forget the 'dancing' to the portable radio he carried, forget the dinner date, *that* was what they wanted. And

Tony was happy to perform. 'Yeah, it sends my blood pumpin',
it's like an addiction. Knowin' they want me. They make the call.
I make the transaction. It's exhilarating.' Tony would normally
go straight up to the lady's hotel room (to avoid any possible
misunderstanding that my call might be taken as a 'guy call', I had
arranged to meet him in the restaurant). He would grab hold of
the lady right away, kiss her, and start embracing her. With
ardour. She would kiss him back, but then, before one thing led
on to another, Tony would pull back.

'Hey, wait a minute! Baby, you're terrific! Wow! But we gotta
discuss things, right, see how long you wanna spend with
me . . .' This is the intricate part, because he can never say what
he is going to do, straight out. That would be soliciting and
against the law (which is one reason why some men prefer
brothels, they are legal). But if consenting adults want to do their
own thing . . . And out comes his credit card dispenser. Aids? No
problem if you take precautions. These ladies were mostly aged in
their thirties to mid forties, occasionally a fifty year old.
Sometimes a young girl showed up, once a mother and daughter.
But regardless of age, every woman he met wanted, as he put it, to
be romanced, to feel romantic, to be turned on. If he did not act as
if he himself was turned on by the lady, she would be disillu-
sioned, the idea of their spending time together, up in her room,
would not work. She had to be made to feel, so Tony explained,
like she had never felt in her whole life, to feel that he did not do
this with everybody.

Once in a while a woman might try to talk him out of his job – as
if he was following a university course, Social Studies 101 or
Moral Studies 102, and he was free to make a switch. I told Tony
that with his empathy for women he could become a writer. He
preened. 'Yeah? I wanna be an actor. Life's a big act, right?' Tony
could apparently rely on himself to perform well, every time, no
matter what the client might be like physically. (Only once, when
the lady was six feet tall and weighed 300 lbs, could Tony recall
ducking out.) But as he described his job, it became clear that

Tony was indeed a sort of actor, an actor who simply loved his role, making women feel wanted. In the warmth of their reaction to him, their pleasure in him, he loved himself. 'You'd be surprised what mind and money can do. I been with women not exactly the most beautiful, okay. But it's the thrill of tryin' to excite them that turns me on. I really like to make people happy. What I do, it makes 'em feel better about themselves.'

In Tony's line of work, all this might be taken for granted. What depressed me, as he continued his story, was something he revealed about the nature of his clients. They all of them, so he claimed, women on a business trip, women without their husbands, lonely women, girls wanting to boast to their girl friends when they got back home from Vegas, all of them wanted to feel wooed and made to feel attractive and loved for themselves – and they always said, all of them, that it was their first time with a companion like him. So his greatest pitch, which he used every time, was: 'Baby, you're fantastic! Normally this is work for me, but with you, it's a pleasure. I mean that sincerely.' He said it every time, it was his downright duty to say it, and every time it worked. Many a client, weakened or won over by his flattery, would suggest they prolong their meeting, but without money. 'Baby, I'd love to stay with you. But I'd get into trouble with my boss.' (His boss was a very nice lady, he assured me.)

Tony was less sure about his own life. Everyone wanted a young guy as an escort, he said, which meant twenty to twenty-five years old, maybe twenty-six, or at the very outside twenty-seven, if he was young looking. Tony was already twenty-four, so what did his career hold in store for him? 'Yeah, well, I look younger, don't I? I'm okay for a coupla years.' He smiled at himself: he could assume whatever age a lady wanted – he could be twenty-one, he could be older, he could be artistic, he could act macho. But for all his jaunty confidence, Tony's prospects looked a bit uncertain. When he had a girlfriend of his own, as happened sometimes, he could never reveal to her what he did for a living. He liked to call himself, grandly, a financial exchange consultant.

When he confessed to one girl, whom he loved a lot, what he really did, she threw him over. 'No one ever understands personal relationships, right? She couldn't deal with it.'

Tony was a womaniser, he confessed, quite apart from his employment as a companion. The trouble was the girls he had met outside of his work did not appreciate him. He was giving it away with them, and all they did was give him 'attitude', you know, which he didn't need. He'd tried the love thing and it didn't work. Yet for all his endless string of professional successes, girls still drove him crazy. Through lunch, whenever an attractive woman passed by the table, Tony couldn't resist raising his glance to flash her a quick look. For himself, he liked working out in the gym, he liked horseback riding, but most of the time, it seemed, he sat around waiting for his next call. My hour was up. As we left the restaurant, Tony threw a fast look at a chic woman in a swimsuit on her way to the pool, but it slipped right past her. 'What you're missin', baby!' his glance said. I felt distinctly queasy after spending an hour with Tony though I didn't doubt that, in his own way, he brought much happiness to Las Vegas.

For a typical Vegas thrill, some friends took me to the Palomino Club, in downtrodden North Las Vegas. Advertised as the 'largest total nude show in America, hottest live show in town, ladies are welcome', the Palomino turned out to be a big strip-tease joint, but of bizarre style. A $10 dollar entry ticket leads the visitor into a deep cavernous room, dominated by a long narrow cat-walk. It is dark and noisy but the atmosphere is attentive. For along this runway parade a succession of girls with no clothes on, introduced night after night by Artie Brooks, a knowing old comedian, practised at sassy one-liners and put-downs. 'Here's Lisa . . . Ya wanna know where Lisa comes from, hunh? . . . Lisa's from . . . (whispers to the artiste on stage) . . . Boise, Idaho!' (Applause.) 'You're lovely . . . I want you for my wife . . . She'd like you.' Along either side of the runway, rows of seats go back ten or twelve deep, filled with an assortment of rugged customers, all male. Two beers cost twelve bucks. A sort of friendly club atmosphere prevails, with a lot of back-chat to the comedian. 'Get off the stage,' the men shout at Brooks. 'Bring on the broads.'

First come the 'amateurs', girls who simply walk out on stage and stand there with their backs to the audience, drop their clothes on the floor, and parade up and down the runway for the duration of a pop song. The routine of each act was brief and identical. The music ends, then – 'Okay, shall we see another girrrl?' (Catcalls and shouts of encouragement.) After the amateurs come the 'pros', who take off their clothes more slowly and elegantly and sometimes do a bit of 'dancing' with a veil. All the girls without exception were extremely good to look at, but as one 'act' followed another, it was hard to distinguish between them. The performers hustled for tips from the men at the end of the runway, by flashing the customers a good view of their vaginas; they make $100 a night with tips. Through it all the men talked and joshed and drank, until the girl marched backstage to pick up her clothes and the next one came out. It seemed innocent to a degree.

The Palomino offers another attraction, however. For $30 a half hour or $60 an hour, customers may dance or chat with the girls in a room next door. To the side of the dance space, this room contains half a dozen little booths with tables. In each booth sat a man with one of the girls, for whom he had of course to buy a bottle of champagne, chatting or canoodling side by side. It looked a frustrating experience, flirt but don't touch. On the other hand this was a not too expensive way of meeting an attractive strip-tease artiste, and perhaps making an assignment for later. An acquaintance of mine became friendly with one of the girls and took her on a vacation to Europe. Now he was incensed because she had found a new admirer, who was contriving to pay his alimony out of her earnings as a dancer. The thing about the Palomino which I really did find offensive was another service, offered upstairs. Here, in a little space above the show room, a man prepared to pay for it can engage a dancer he likes to do a private strip-tease in a booth, for him alone, staring very close-up. 'The girls in this town are like everyone else,' another habitué complained, 'after they finish working they go right back to their homes and children.'

The Palomino sums up the Vegas attitude to sex pretty well – pay for play.

> *rich person*, wealthy p., well-to-do p., man or woman
> of means; baron, tycoon, oil magnate, nabob,
> moneybags, millionaire, multi-m., millionairess;
> Croesus, Midas, Dives, Plutus; moneymaker,
> money-spinner, fat cat, capitalist, plutocrat,
> bloated p.
>
> *Roget's Thesaurus*

Money is how you keep the score in the casino game. The casinos which make the most profit on capital invested are, by definition, the most successful. The casinos that lose money are playing the game the wrong way: either they tighten up their act or they go out of business.

It should be easy enough, making money in a casino, when you consider that every single gambling game has a percentage edge built into it, working for the house. And that this edge applies in exactly the same way whether a player is making a one dollar bet at the craps table, or laying out a million at baccarat. The house gets its little slice off the salami. What's more all the separate one dollar bets at all the different tables accumulate; they soon add up to a million when they are lumped together at the end of the shift, or the end of the week. So how much *do* the casinos win? In Vegas the official figures are published as collective totals, for the Strip and for Downtown, not under individual names, as in Atlantic City. But it is possible to work out pretty well how individual casinos are doing. According to the specialist casino publication *Rouge et Noir*, the top performers for the fiscal year July 1989 to June 1990 were the Mirage, which racked up gross gaming revenues of

$232m. in the 33 weeks after it opened in November, Caesars Palace with $301m., and the Las Vegas Hilton with $160m.

It's no coincidence that these three casinos run big baccarat games. Baccarat is the most interesting and least known of casino games. It is also the most dramatic and stylised. Its importance to the top casinos can hardly be overstated. It's a paradoxical game, baccarat, because from the outside it looks so utterly boring; yet it produces by far the biggest action, in relation to floor-space, of all modern casino gambling. The three or four leading casinos in Las Vegas rely on baccarat for their income to an extraordinary degree. The new Mirage, for example, for all its 2,250 slots and 118 table games earns around one third of its gaming revenue from just 10 baccarat tables. From its opening day, the baccarat took off: the Mirage now has the biggest continuous action in the world – players with a $50,000 dollar a hand betting limit are always in house, players with $100,000 limit are fairly common. The mighty Las Vegas Hilton, whose baccarat pit is no more than a red plush alcove in its vast casino floor, was used to earning 30 per cent of its net win from baccarat, before the Mirage started. The same sort of reliance on baccarat applies to Caesars. Conversely, when a big player hits a streak at a table, it puts a crimp in the bottom line of the whole casino operation. The Desert Inn, which as a smaller casino had built up a reputation for its high-rolling baccarat game, also felt the competition. Rival establishments, big and small, could not but be badly hurt: the Mirage had projected a baccarat win of $75m. in its first year. The outcome was $115m., 28 per cent of total gaming revenue.

The first thing which strikes one about baccarat in Vegas is that it is not really an *American* game any more. It is primarily run for the Asian market – for gamblers from Japan, Taiwan, Malaysia, Singapore and Hong Kong, for rich Mexicans and other Latin Americans, for any foreign player with big bucks to gamble. Only around 10 per cent of the players are American. It follows that the supervisors and dealers who work in the baccarat pit are special employees. They bring an unmistakeable air of service, if not servility, discreet and polite as they are, to this Asian market. It is almost as if the United States, having been plundered so long by Japan and the countries of the Pacific rim by their fast-growing exports of cheap consumer goods, had found a way to claw some of the money back, via baccarat.

And how they gamble, the orientals! The Japanese in Mario Puzo's novel *Fools Die* are a frightening sight, marching ten-strong into a casino, 'looking like undertakers come to collect the corpse of the casino's bankroll'. They all wear black business suits, badly tailored by western standards, with white shirts and black ties. Arriving at the airport, they look like a band of very earnest clerks instead of the ruling board of Japan's richest and most powerful business conglomerate. 'The band of ten Japanese terrorised the casinos of Vegas. They would travel together and gamble together at the same baccarat table. When Fummiro [the leader] had the shoe, they all bet the limit with him on the bank . . . they played with a joie de vivre more Italian than Oriental. Fummiro would whip the sides of the shoe and bang on the table when he dealt himself a natural eight or nine.' He is depicted as a passionate gambler who would gloat over winning a two-thousand-dollar bet, despite being worth over half a billion dollars.

On the face of it, the game is flat, without any variation or indeed any skill on the part of the players. 'It seems to me to be about the most unintelligent mode of losing your own money, or getting somebody else's, I ever heard of,' observed the famous advocate Sir Edward Clarke, Solicitor-General of England, in his opening address to the jury in the Tranby Croft trial of 1891. This was the notorious accusation of cheating, which scandalised English high society, at a private baccarat party in which the Prince of Wales himself was acting as Banker. To play baccarat all you need is plenty of money. Four cards are dealt out from an oblong plastic box, known as the 'shoe', two to the Player and two to the Bank, the object of each side being to get closer to a total of 9 (court cards and tens count zero). The hands are then turned over

face upward, so the total on each side can be seen and called out by
the dealer. Each side, Player and Bank, may then draw a third
card or stand pat, according to certain fixed rules, to try to beat
the other. No variation or choice is allowed in the matter. And
that is all there is to it. An early edition of Hoyle comments on
baccarat: 'Although from a bare description it may sound stupid
and uninteresting, it needs but a single experiment in actual play
to prove its charm and fascination – that is of course from a
gambling point of view.'

This is the game which attracts such tremendous action that
the major casinos maintain offices and run agents throughout the
Far East in order to trawl for new players. This is the game for
which the casinos employ highly paid hosts and hostesses whose
sole job is to keep in touch with individual high rollers, and to take
care of their every wish and whim while they are in town. (One
successful host was paid a $500,000 'signing on' fee, so valuable
was the list of players he brought with him when he was poached
from a rival casino. He earned it back for his new employers in his
first weekend at work.) This is the game which, virtually on its
own, finances the luxury end of the casino business: staging a
contest to see which of two hands adds up closer to nine. Seems a
tad easier than exporting cassette players and colour TVs, doesn't
it?

The American version of the game came to Las Vegas in the
1950s, some 450 years after the original Italian baccara found
favour at the royal court in France. *Baccara* originally meant
zero. There is one important difference between the American
game and baccarat as played in Monte Carlo and other European
resorts, or in London where it is known as Punto Banco. In
America, like so many other things which originated in the old
world, baccarat has been made simpler and faster, streamlined.
Thus, in American casinos, one player on his own can sit down
and play, without waiting for others to arrive and make up the
table. (Though there are always 'starters', as shills are known,
coiffed and manicured ladies with bored expressions, in evening

gowns, ready to take a seat and get the game going.) The action is continuous, apart from the period of the shuffle. To speed the betting, the 5 per cent commission due on winning Bank bets is paid by the players only after the shoe comes to an end (not as the game goes along).

The house, which bankrolls the game, has an edge of about 1.2 per cent – which seems low, but is more than enough to make its fortune.* The point is that each player is giving up a notional 1.2 per cent on every hand he plays. Cumulatively, the casino expects to hold upwards of 20 per cent of the drop, depending on how long players remain at the table. What this means is that if $100m. is wagered across the table in the course of a month, which with players betting up to $100,000 a hand is not so improbable as it sounds, the house's theoretical expectation of gain would be $20m. In practice, the figure can be far higher, because baccarat players do not play just one session and then walk away. They live and die for the game. So what about the downside? What are the casino's operating expenses? It might employ twelve dealers (croupiers) per table, four per eight-hour shift, on three shifts a day, and half a dozen managers, whose combined salaries over a month would probably total less than $1m. Then agents have to

---

*The house edge comes in this way: in a game of 8 decks, the Bank hand will win 50.68 per cent of hands (leaving aside stand-offs when both sides are equal) against 49.32 per cent for the Player.

So in a series of 100 one dollar bets the Bank hand wins $48.15 ($50.68, less the 5 per cent commission) and loses $49.32, leaving a net loss of $1.17, or an edge of 1.17 per cent against the Player. On the other side, the Player hand will win $49.32 and lose $50.68, a net loss of $1.36, or a 1.36 per cent disadvantage. The overall house advantage is simply the average edge between the Banker and Player hands, which is about 1.26 per cent. It may be noted that these percentages against the punter are the most favourable odds of all casino games in Nevada.

In actual play 9.55 per cent of hands will be tied. Most casinos pay '9 for 1' on a tie, which means odds of only 8 to 1. As the true odds are 9.47 to 1, this gives the house the horrendous edge of 14 per cent – just about the worst bet on the whole casino floor. But that doesn't stop many baccarat players trying it: the usual rule is that a player may bet up to 10 per cent of his normal stake on a tie.

be paid, out in the field, there are the usual overheads and comps, and let's not forget that the casino has to pay for several thousand decks of new cards each week – they are changed, religiously, after every shoe. Oriental players love to bend and squeeze the cards, in order to prolong the suspense.

The only *risk* is that one or two high rollers get lucky. What they are actually doing, these very rich men, is gambling against the casino one-to-one, eyeball to eyeball. In all the little games across the casino floor, the gamblers cancel each other out, two thousand people, say, bet on red, two thousand bet on black, and the house grinds out its percentage. At baccarat, some of the players are richer than the casino, they can break the place! And that, in a sense, is their aim – a mighty act of self-assertion given expression at the gaming table. Certainly when a baccarat player walks away with a few million dollars of casino money, it hurts. The casino expects to get it back of course. But only if the player remains faithful to that establishment, and doesn't go and blow his money in Atlantic City or Australia or some place else. Such losses are a necessary part of the operation, and the best possible advertisement for baccarat: if the players never won, the casinos would have no customers.

One of the curious features of the game is how ritual takes precedence over action. Typically, the room is hushed (but not when the Latin-Americans are in town) separated by a rope barrier or partition from the rest of the casino. One or two management figures are always hovering close to the table, like attentive courtiers. They are sleek, well-groomed, ready to serve, smiling as they dance forward to approve credit or give a ruling. They monitor closely the rate and size of each gambler's bet, ensuring that the record of his action is kept up to date. The computer screen is lit, discreetly, at a desk to the side. The computer tells the baccarat management everything about the player – his past play, his credit rating, his habits, his present position. Then the supervisor on duty, even if he does not know the player, can step forward and say: 'I hope you had a good trip,

Mr Teriyaki. How is the weather in Yokohama?' It is flattering, though the oriental players, partly through language difficulties, deal almost exclusively with their hosts, who are normally close to hand.

The baccarat table is a big kidney-shaped table with twelve seats, numbered counter-clockwise. Before play can begin the cards must be made ready. This is the most elaborate ritual of all. The dealer takes the first pack of cards, breaks it open, and fans the cards in a wide semicircle over the table, to check that they are complete, repeating the process with all eight decks. How pretty they look and what whirligigs of fortune they hold in their shining sequences! The shuffling is extensive. The cards are stacked into handy sections, shuffled, cut, reshuffled. All three dealers at the table are involved in the shuffle for security reasons. The different sections are re-assembled, cut into new sections, reshuffled, re-mixed. And again. The process is not yet complete, though. Now comes the most important point of the ritual. One of the players at the table is invited to insert a blank card into the long stack of eight decks, to make the final cut. Who shall it be? With so many oriental players deeply superstitious, this is a fraught moment. Some players shrink from the decision, others seize the yellow card like a samurai sword, sometimes the honour is accorded to one of the ladies in the party. (In reality, the cut has no significance – it is just another chance event.) The dealer re-inserts the blank card 20 cards from the front of the oblong row; this is to prevent anyone counting down the shoe as it is dealt, to try to predict exactly which cards might be left before the last coup. Unlike blackjack, however, there would be no advantage anyway (except in astronomically rare cases such as all the remaining cards being ten-cards, when you could happily bet your life savings on the hands being tied!).

At last the shoe is ready to go. It passes to the first player, sitting in number 1 seat, to the right of the baccarat dealer who stands at the indented part of the kidney-shape, directing the game. Nowadays the dealer is often a young woman, friendly but impersonal. The first player taking the Bank deals out four cards from the shoe, two to the Player and two to himself. All the players round the table meanwhile have pushed out, just in front of them, in squares marked 'Bank' and 'Player', the stake they want to bet – (including the person acting as Banker who may back whichever side he prefers). The two cards are slid over the table to the player who has made the highest bet on 'Player' winning. He (or she) turns his cards over first. The Banker turns his hand. And in obedience to the rules, which dictate precisely the order of play – the players have no choice whatever – a third card may be dealt out to one or both parties.

What suspense! What excitement! As the dealer announces 'The Bank wins', 'The Player wins', or a tie, little shrieks, groans and grimaces, exultant whoops of triumph, run round the table. The baccarat dealer at each end of the table collects the losers' stakes and pays out the winners. If the Bank wins, the player dealing the hands keeps the shoe and deals again, until a Player hand wins; the shoe then passes to the next person on his right, and the process is repeated. It makes no difference if everyone bets on the same side, or if only one player is at the table, because despite the use of the word Banker, it is the *House* which bankrolls all bets. This is the ingenious part of the American version of the game compared with the old-style European chemin de fer or classical *baccarat á deux tableaux* (double-table baccarat) where a full complement of players is required before the game can start. A fast moving shoe with a single player may be dealt out in 15 minutes, with a full table 40 minutes. Although there is no skill as such, there is a lot of 'money management' in baccarat, which is life or death in gambling. Money management means keeping control of your bankroll, judging bets in proportion to your luck, picking up the good swings and minimising the bad runs. This is a matter of experience which all gamblers have to learn the hard way. Though I am bound to add that mathematicians deny that 'money management' is a meaningful term. You might just as well say of someone 'He's an expert smoker', according to Professor Peter Griffin, of California State University at Sacramento, who has written extensively on the mathematics of gambling.

Can a player ever cheat at baccarat? Well, players can cheat at any game under the sun. Always have and always will. At baccarat, the most obvious way is by palming a perfect hand of 9 to replace the hand as dealt. The gambling writer John Scarne (*Scarne's Guide to Casino Gambling*) claims he performed this feat at a casino in Havana in a private bet with a sceptical casino manager. At the chosen moment, he bet $10,000 on the Player side (the money was just for show). 'After the player's two cards and the banker's two cards had been dealt, the croupier scooped up the player's two face-down cards with his palette and slid them directly in front of me. My left hand reached for the two cards and I held them face down for a split second, then rapidly turned them face up and called, "Nine", dropping them face up on the layout.' A jack and a nine of spades. The croupier scooped up the four cards dealt and dropped them through the slot in to the discard cylinder. The stunned casino manager's first thought was that Scarne had simply hit a lucky shot. But when he went through the discards, he found that the house cards had been switched for a jack and a nine from a different deck. This trick required a very high degree of skill, and one may also suppose that the supervision of gaming back in the bad old days in Havana was not what it is now in modern casinos. Casinos are always on the alert for 'a slug', a sequence of stacked cards inserted by a dealer, working in collusion with a player. Scarne says that the commonest way for the house to cheat is with a crooked shoe which contains a hidden pocket by the opening, holding about eight cards, which can be released singly by the dealer by squeezing the box with his left hand when dealing with his right. When a big hand comes up, the dealer passes his accomplice two cards from the hidden pocket to give him a 'natural'. The elaborate ritual of shuffling and cutting and stacking the cards in modern baccarat evidently serves a purpose.

After accumulating all this lore I felt in honour bound – it was more than a duty, it was a pleasure – to put myself to the test. So I sat down at a high rollers' table. Players on either side of me were stacking up glistening coloured chips marked $5,000 and $10,000, like children's counters. No one paid me the slightest attention as I changed a modest ten $100 bills into chips. I bet $50 on Bank on the first hand and it lost – the price of dinner for two. I switched sides, marking my score card, and won. And then? Then I made the discovery which none of the theoretical accounts of the game had prepared me for. Hoyle had got it right. Baccarat is fantastically exciting! The excitement is not choosing whether Bank or Player is going to win, which is just blind chance. It is that having backed one side or the other, the suspense of waiting for the result, as the cards are turned and counted, is so thrilling. The tension comes from the fact that each hand, as it is played, can see-saw either way in the course of the same deal: you may look like winning on the first two cards, and then get outdrawn on the third card, or start with a dismal hand and then dramatically leap ahead. You can win with 1 and lose with 8 – no hand is too good or too bad to provide a certain result until the play is over. Even when the Player hand turns an 8 or a 9, the Bank still has a faint hope of saving the bet. This suspense is what gives baccarat its excitement. Behind their calm oriental smiles, all the Japanese and Asian punters are writhing in internal agony and pleasure. It may not be a sexual thrill, directly, but it is certainly physical. No wonder the players squeeze the cards.

Unlike the player to my left, I knew enough about baccarat to follow the side in form. This Japanese gentleman, holding the Bank, started doubling up on the Player – $5,000, $10,000, $20,000, $40,000 – and lost each coup, smiling ever more faintly. After his next loss, he withdrew to raise more money. I had won five times in a row on the Bank, and decided to break the habit inculcated over a lifetime, by bucking the bad odds to bet the tie. It lost. I stayed through the shoe, paying nearly $80 in commission on winning bank bets, and still left a small winner.

The supervisor at the table, unfazed by my feeble little bets, asked if I wanted my play to be 'rated', for comps purposes. I declined because I had no intention of becoming a baccarat freak, even at low stakes.

The word has got out, these days, about casino comps (meaning complimentary services). Every gambler, even the little old ladies in sneakers, is looking for a pay-off somewhere along the line, even if it's only a voucher for a free hamburger. Although the casinos appear open-handed, they are alert to every customer's worth in hospitality and entertainment. It is so open to abuse, for example by players setting up a $50,000 line of credit and then making one or two ostentatious bets, without giving the house any action in return. Though with computer tracking and total video recall, this is far less likely than in the old days, when executives with 'the power of the pen' could comp their friends. If a player is flown in on a private plane, and given a suite for the weekend, and signs away all his restaurant bills, the casino makes damn sure it gets value – which means the guest must play for high enough stakes, for a long enough time, to give the house a chance to earn its expected return.

When the Malaysians play baccarat, they all back the same side to win, but with the nice distinction that the highest ranking personage makes the biggest wager, with the other members of his entourage following suit down the line in diminishing amounts. The Chinese really enjoy their gambling: they shout and scream in Cantonese and squeeze the cards out, to prolong the suspense. The huge stakes heighten the sensation. But this whole family of foreign players, known on first name terms to a few top-line casinos, totals only about a thousand people. One problem, from the casino point of view, is to stop the dealers in the baccarat pit from becoming desensitised to money. 'You see so many people playing off a million dollars that watching players dropping two or three or four million gets to be routine. So when someone is playing off $50,000 it seems nothing at all, like small change,' a casino executive explained. 'And then the restaurant's full and the guy can't even get dinner, because other players, who've been losing even more money than he has, have taken all the reservations.' Such are the social problems of taking care of high rollers. 'We only win one bet an hour. That's all our edge is. We have to pay all our expenses out of that. We try to make our baccarat staff realise that every player counts.'

A rather endearing nickname is bestowed on the highest of high rollers by the crews who run the baccarat games – not a *fish*, as in an easy mark at cards, but a *whale*. A whale takes some landing, but is worth the effort. The biggest of all whales was a Japanese businessman named Akio Kashiwagi. He won $19m. at baccarat in Darwin in Australia early in 1989, which sent the casino there (partly owned by British gambler John Aspinall) into a tailspin, wiping out a year's profit. (Kashiwagi had lost $10m. and was down to his last $200,000 bet before he hit his streak.) From there he went to Atlantic City to take on Trump Plaza. He won $6m., but the casino kept its nerve and he was lured back in May. Kashiwagi began his working life carrying rucksacks for climbers on Mount Fuji, and is reportedly now worth $100m. The Plaza set up a baccarat table for Kashiwagi and two friends in a discreet corner of the room. A whole clutch of casino executives hovered in attendance, including Trump. Over four days of play he dropped $9.4m. Trump, sweating the action, then shut down the game. Kashiwagi, who still had $2m. in credit, left in a rage. Caesars sent a white limo to pick him up.

Playing up to $200,000 a hand, it does not take long to run through a million. At one point, Mr Kashiwagi lost eleven straight hands without flinching, it was reported. Such players represent a high risk for the casino. As I explained, they are gambling against the house one-to-one, which gives the management the jitters. The house hates to put its whole bankroll on the line but it can't resist the action. It knows that if the whale plays long enough, he will be beached. The deal set up by the baccarat analyst advising the Plaza on how to structure the game for Kashiwagi (casinos never hesitate to call in academic experts to back up their calculations) was as follows. With a maximum bet of $200,000 a hand, play would continue until either the player or the house won $12m. – which at $200,000 a hand meant 60 coups ahead (or behind). According to calculations done for me by Professor Peter Griffin (whose views on money management I mentioned above) this gave the house approximately an 82 per cent to 83 per cent probability of winning, depending on whether the gambler bet the Player or the Bank. Conversely the gambler had a 17 to 18 per cent chance of doubling his money. The game, including ties, would be expected to last 60 × 60 coups, Griffin adds. Kashiwagi was found murdered at his home in 1992, apparently in a squalid dispute over minor debts.

In gambling there comes a point, however rich you are, when you are betting high enough to really feel the excitement – baccarat is like a live wire which transmits that current. The high rollers do not need the money, in the sense that you or I need the money. They are playing for a variety of motives, of which financial gain is one of the least important. They want the thrill, as all gamblers do; they take for granted the attention they receive from the casinos, which in the real world people cannot command in quite the same way, even if these favoured players understand, as they surely must, that it is no more than the pay-off for their hyper-extravagant play. They relish, some of them, the pleasure of beating the house. The profligacy of the super-rich seems repugnant, but they have the right to spend their money as they wish, like lesser gamblers. The turn of the cards is probably the *only* thing in their lives which they do not control.

The casinos know how to please. One Asian ship-owner, who could buy or sell any casino he visits, flies in to Las Vegas regularly twice a year. The casino director has visited him in his home in his own country, played golf with him, knows all about his hope for his sons, his anxiety over his daughters. As this man sets out from his home and his office, thousands of miles away, where he already has everything that money can buy and is venerated practically as a god, his anticipation of his long-awaited trip quickens, rising all through the journey, until by the time the flight is over he is in a frenzy to hit the tables. Everything is ready for him: his host is waiting at the airport, his penthouse is filled with orchids, an oriental chef is posted to the private kitchen adjoining his suite. This man normally plays for ten days. The action he generates is tremendous. Does he ever win? How could he win? One Christmas, the casino presented a lady for whom he had a certain *tendresse*, with a new Mercedes sports car. Some executives feel a moral twinge sometimes, torn by a sense that they are cultivating friendships with players in order to betray them, by encouraging them to gamble. Something like a spy-master deceiving his contacts – except of course in the casino world it is all open. It is a complex relationship, host and guest: but it is also true that casino managers sometimes act to protect gamblers from themselves, by preventing them – of course in the casino's own best interest – from going too far.

Another player at a big baccarat game in Las Vegas decided, after winning two or three million or so, to give his interpreter-hostess (a stolid oriental lady) a little present. He instructed one of the hosts to call up the local Rolls-Royce dealer and send over a car. The word came back that the firm could indeed offer him a car, if he would be so kind as to step over to the showroom. The high roller waved his hand impatiently. No, no! Please drive the car over. How much was this model? $245,000? Please bring it over at once. The car duly arrived at the porte-cochère outside the casino. The high roller produced the money in cash and the salesman counted it out. There was $5,000 too much. 'Please keep the change!'

Credit is very important in the casino business. The judgement of the credit manager is what underwrites the casino's risk. Players, even rich players, can get into trouble. If a premium player, whom the casino knows, loses heavily and prefers to leave town without writing out a cheque – they don't worry. He will be sent an invoice in a couple of weeks, then a polite reminder. The casino is unconcerned by payments delayed up to say 30 days. After that, a more formal request might be made, perhaps a personal call by a casino representative at the player's office. Terms will be worked out, repayment spread over a period, if necessary. In some cases, undoubtedly, deals are cut which reduce the debt: very high limit players, with $1,000,000-plus credit lines, try to arrange a discount on losses – of anywhere from 5 to 15 per cent. Naturally the casinos do not talk about such matters. There is a saying in casinos, 'The house always loses the last bet' – meaning that a player will go on losing and paying, losing and paying, but finally the moment is reached when he resolves, during a dark night of the soul: 'That's it! I quit! And I'm not paying this last one – they've won enough off me.'

As for strong-arm tactics – threats, violence, loan-sharking – in this milieu of corporate-executive gambling (so one is assured) all that is a thing of the past. The fountain pen is mightier than the sword. The rate of bad debts in casinos is estimated at somewhat less than 5 per cent in recent years, which compares well with the record of credit card companies. Gambling debts have been enforceable by law in Nevada since 1983. But players always pay up, if they can, for the same reason. They want to get back in the game. Even if a player defaults, he will probably be allowed back eventually, on condition he plays with cash. But credit can get out of hand. As mentioned earlier, when bad debts at the Mirage totalled $23m. in early 1991 and $15.7m. at the Golden Nugget (in the latter case an unacceptably high proportion of revenue) Steve Wynn reacted sharply. Dennis Gomes, president of the Nugget, suddenly quit his job – presumably in a row over this issue – and a clamp was ordered on all high roller credit at both casinos. As Wynn told the *Casino Journal*, in times of economic turmoil 'a certain level of diligence is needed' on credit. 'There is tremendous wealth from the Persian Gulf to the Pacific Rim . . . Our market keeps getting bigger; our list of guests and customers from all parts of the world keep getting bigger; but, with that, there is an additional burden to deal with credit intelligently.' His point was that if casinos used credit as a marketing tool, simply to attract new business, they were dead ducks. Credit for casinos should be merely an instrument: people do not carry large amounts of currency. The casinos can facilitate such players by granting them credit. But he was absolutely opposed to attracting customers simply by giving them more and more leeway – that way, he warned, lay disaster.

How far should a casino go in checking up on a client's credit? The whole way, as far as possible. A host, or the credit manager, has to assess how much a player is good for – what's the point of beating the daylights out of him at the table if the casino can't collect afterwards? Which raises the moral question: should the casino take a view, one way or the other, on the colour of a player's money? Should it be concerned if, say, it suspects a player is gambling with illicit funds? (Under current banking regulations, all cash transactions over $10,000 have to be reported to the tax authorities; this rule, which is a terrible nuisance to the casinos, was introduced to help combat the laundering of drug money.)

A classic case of *not* asking a player where his money came from happened a few years ago. It proved highly embarrassing to the casino (and of course the bank) concerned. Over a period of months in 1982, a twenty-five-year-old Canadian assistant bank manager, Brian Molony, dropped ten million dollars or so at the tables, over a third of it at Caesars Palace in Atlantic City. He had devised an ingenious way of embezzling funds, by juggling false entries in loan accounts, in order to fuel his compulsive gambling. Week after week, while flying him down from Toronto on their private jet, Caesars studiously failed to enquire where all Molony's gambling cash was coming from. Instead, the casino management contrived to get round legal and financial restrictions –'Anything we can do for you, Brian? Just say the word, Brian' – by flying a couple of junior employees up to Toronto to get his signature on a blank form, and then wiring the money out via its Las Vegas casino. 'Caesars had to know that something was wrong', noted William Thompson, Professor of Public Administration at the University of Nevada-Las Vegas (quoted in a review of *No Way Out*, an account of the affair by Gary Ross).

'But they wanted his money so badly that they helped . . . dodge international money transfer rules as well as New Jersey Gaming regulations.'

Molony himself was an uninspired gambler, throwing his money away week after week. It wasn't that he ignored the laws of probability, rather that he had got himself into such a hole, cheating the bank, he was like a man who has to bet on a 50–1 shot simply to get even. When Molony was finally rumbled (as a result of a routine wire-tap in Toronto), Caesars was severely punished. The Atlantic City casino was shut down for 24 hours, on 30 November 1985, which probably cost it a million dollars. Or was the punishment so severe? The casino employees responsible for organising the transfer of Molony's funds escaped virtually unscathed. The company eventually settled with the Canadian bank out of court – rumour had it that it paid back half of Molony's losses – but the details were never revealed. Neither side wanted publicity. Molony, who emerges as a rather colour-less figure, spurning all the juicy comps on offer in preference for ribs and Coca-Cola, got six years. In due course he was paroled.

The Caesars' executive who waved the magic wand to turn Molony's credit into gaming chips was a clever fellow named Larry Woolf. In rendering unto Caesars, he had acted like a hero; in not asking questions about where the money had come from, he had been super-tactful. 'A casino responds to action the way a teenage boy responds to sexual instinct. The moment drives everything', was the summing up given by Ross in *No Way Out*. 'If someone's betting big money, keep him in action . . . face the consequences later.' By way of 'censure' Woolf was exiled to run Caesars' hotel-casino on the shores of Lake Tahoe, on the border of northern Nevada and California. Though in comparison a small-time operation, Tahoe is one of the loveliest places in all America. Woolf did not stay too long to enjoy the scenery, however. A couple of years later he was hired by Kirk Kerkorian, to take on his giant new MGM Grand Project (see Chapter 8).

*

Besides being big gamblers the Japanese are the only foreigners to try their hand on the other side of the tables, by buying casinos in Vegas. The experience, so far, has been discouraging. Japanese owners have signally failed to make a success of the properties they have taken over. On the contrary, three years after Japanese investors began buying up failed casinos, they were all losing money. A basic problem, it seems, is the slow Japanese style of decision making. Their instinctive sense of reserve in dealing with people, the collective approach, inhibits quick action. Such an approach (which may work very well in gigantic manufacturing companies geared to mass-production of consumer goods) is completely at odds with the fast buck style of casino management in Vegas.

Michael Rumbolz (the then chairman of the Gaming Control Board who was later hired by Donald Trump to plan his own foray into Vegas) commented that cultural differences underlay the Japaneses' problems. 'They do not trust Americans enough to give them latitude. It makes it impossible for the management to run the casino.' One of the most experienced people in the industry, Bill Friedman, author of *Casino Management*, told me succinctly: 'The Japanese lost money because they had a contempt for the casino industry. They thought all you had to do was to sit back and let the money roll in.' A bit like the Japanese's idea of winning at baccarat, I couldn't help thinking.

Blackjack is a different story, because at a certain level of expertise it is a game of skill – the only casino game, in fact, at which a player of skill can have a positive expectation against the house, as Professor Edward Thorp first showed in *Beat the Dealer*. Players who have the ability to count the cards as they are dealt from the deck can secure an advantage over the house: this is because they can estimate, from knowing what proportion of high cards and low cards at any given point are left in the deck or the shoe, whether the hands coming up may be in the player's or the dealer's favour. If favourable to the player, they immediately increase their bet. The percentage swing can be substantial, from as much as plus to minus 3 per cent. Casino attitudes have relaxed somewhat from the fear and loathing they used to display towards 'counters'. They still dislike counters, however, and are always on the look-out for them. Almost every player at blackjack counts to some degree, at least to check broadly how the deal is moving or how many aces are left. Provided a player's variation in stakes is not too extreme, say from one to two units rather than suddenly jumping to five times his basic stake, the major casinos are now inclined to take a reasonably tolerant view of counters, instead of barring them completely. The game, even with counters, is such a good earner.

High roller blackjack, played at specially reserved tables, is not nearly as big as baccarat. But with a player able to play seven spots at once, with a maximum stake of $10,000 a hand, it can still be a big game. (Recently the Australian multimillionaire Kerry Packer asked a number of casinos for very high limits, specifically six spot blackjack at $100,000 a spot; this was deemed too risky even for Las Vegas – though he was offered terms which got close.) Blackjack dealers and pit bosses have a closer rapport with players than at other games, because it is slower than craps and more intimately one-to-one than baccarat. Here is an amateur player, out of his depth, who got lucky in a blackjack game thanks to his being mistaken for a regular customer. It comes from *Keno Runner*, my favourite novel on Las Vegas, by David Kranes, and catches exactly the intimate-yet-exploitative relationship between pit boss and player.

He sat down at an empty blackjack table. The dealer nodded. A smiling man in a pewter-colored suit moved forward from the pit to the table. He stuck his hand out to Kohlman. 'Mr B!' he said. 'Finally back! How's the war?'

Kohlman shook the man's hand. *Mr B?* '. . . Fine,' he said.

'We haven't seen you!' the pit boss said.

'No,' Kohlman said.

'You've been away.'

'Yes.'

The pit boss put a hand on the dealer's shoulder. 'Start Mr B with a mark of two, Lonnie.' Then he looked up at Kohlman: 'Two – Mr B? Am I on target? Did I remember?'

'Fine,' Kohlman said. He had no idea of what was being transacted.

'Standard fare,' the pit boss said to Lonnie, the dealer. 'Whenever you see Mr B – start him off with a mark of two.'

Things were happening; Kohlman was watching. Something was being filled out on a voucher pad. The dealer was gathering stacks of chips from his tray, lining them up, counting them, restacking them, lining them up again, counting. The pit boss pushed the voucher pad to Kohlman, handed over his pen. Kohlman hesitated, then scratched a signature where the man had indicated on the pad . . .

In fifteen minutes, Kohlman keeps hitting hands and more than triples his original chips. The dealer asks if he wants to cash in his mark. Kohlman is given thirteen gold chips worth a hundred each and a black one for twenty-five, which he hands back to the dealer as a toke. The pit boss returns as Kohlman is leaving the table.

'God, you did it to us *again*, Mr B,' he said to Kohlman.

'Well . . .'

'What can we get you? What can we do? How can we be there for you? It's ten minutes past nine: Breakfast?'

A friend of mine who plays professional blackjack reports that it is hard to show a profit. Professional players form a small, tough, anonymous group, working the casino tables, looking for good games where they can apply their technique. Some players prefer tournaments, where the aim is to beat the other players rather than the house. Counters may be figure-perfect from a mathematical point of view but still find themselves unable to withstand the psychological pressures of a losing run; or they may crack under continuous hostility from casino dealers, who shuffle up the deck or take other preventive measures. 'The casinos know more about the game then they used to,' this player told me, 'but not as much as the counters, who live and die for blackjack.' One of the counters' new techniques is 'shuffle tracking', which means keeping an eye on the dealer's shuffle to track sequences of cards which may stick together. The adroit player then tries to cut the deck, to place the sequence of cards he knows about where he wants – an extraordinarily tricky feat but one which experts can perform. Even at roulette, I was informed, there are players working on tracking the spin of the wheel and trajectory of the ball, to predict the outcome on a mathematical basis – a visual version of the elaborate technique with a concealed computer first tried by Professor Thorp. Use of computers is banned in Nevada casinos. But some new trick or technique is always coming up.

Blackjack, like baccarat, makes a lot of money for the casinos. But craps has the fastest action. It is the one game which can set the whole table on a roar of excitement, with all the players packed in around the rail gambling as one. But important as they are, it is not these games which fuel Las Vegas' mighty profits. The biggest money earner is everywhere, ever-ready.

Slot machines, which are to Las Vegas as cherry blossom to Yokohama, used to be *infra dig*. Slots were low class, slots were for little old ladies in white sneakers, carrying plastic cups brimful of nickels and dimes; or moving a couple of notches up the social register, slots were for high rollers' wives, to give the ladies a way of passing a couple of hours after dinner while their husbands played for high stakes. Slots were not about serious money.

Nowadays Las Vegas runs on slots. Slots are very, very, big. They account for about 50 per cent of most casinos' revenue, and more like 62 per cent statewide. At around $2,500m. a year, that is a lot of slot play. By far the most popular machines are the quarter slots. On 1 January 1990 there were nearly 50,000 quarter slots, out of a total of over 85,000 machines, ranging from penny slots up to one-hundred dollar and five-hundred dollar slots. On these big money machines, where players cannot physically stuff such large sums down the chute, casinos issue special tokens. (It seems slightly obscene, sticking $100 into a slot machine: but when you come to think about it, it's no different from sticking down a hundred dollar chip at craps or roulette. The difference is that slots are played with money or its close equivalent, tokens, whereas table games are played with chips.) The net effect of this surging proliferation of slots, one could say, has been to turn the whole casino industry into one gigantic slot parlour. Considering that slots operate twenty-four hours a day, never stopping, and that it takes only about five seconds for a pull of the handle, this is almost perpetual motion in gambling. If half the machines are in action half of the time, visitors to Las Vegas are making (roughly) something on the order of 370 million pulls a day.

There have been four distinct stages in the technology of slots which mark the evolution of these games. The original slot machines, which now look like museum pieces, and do in fact have value as antiques, were operated by a handle which pulled three reels, operated on a spring. The configuration limited these reels to 22 stops. Wear and tear skewed the distribution, so they were not too reliable. On a three reel machine in which each reel (to keep it simple) has 20 symbols there are $20 \times 20 \times 20$ possible outcomes = 8,000. The symbols and pay-offs can be distributed in any number of ways. A typical configuration might be one jackpot of 200, 16 pay-offs of 100 and several hundred pay-offs of lesser amounts, such that in 8,000 plays the machine would pay out a total of 7,360 coins. In this case, the net loss to the players – or gain to the house – would be 640 coins, or 8 per cent.

The first innovation came in the mid-1960s, with the electro-mechanical device. This was electrically driven, which meant that the handle was no longer the driving force. The machine could be run far more efficiently. Bally's, then the leading slot machine manufacturer, introduced light and sound effects, multiple coin betting and triple-pay lines. Still, slots accounted for only around 30 per cent of gaming revenue in Vegas up till 1975. Then dollar slots appeared. Because of the higher action, the house could reduce its hold percentage, from 10 per cent or higher to a very low margin, even, on some machines, down to 1 per cent. Players got more play for their money, better value.

The big breakthrough came with the invention of the video poker machine in the late '70s. Here was a slot machine which offered the player, with every single pull of the handle, a *choice* of how to play the hand. What a great idea! Every American worth his birthright learns the ranking of poker hands, from a pair up to a straight flush, practically at his mother's knee. By putting a hand of five cards on the screen of a slot machine, people were given a decision to make, just as in draw poker. With a regular slot machine, the only decision a player makes which can influence the pay-off is the number of coins he plays. On the poker machines a line of five buttons, placed below each card, enables the player to hold the card as dealt, or change it by drawing another. But the play is made without the hassle, as in a real poker game, of a dealer or intimidation by other players.

The man credited with this imaginative achievement is Logan Pease, now senior engineer with slot manufacturers International Game Technology. 'No,' he explained to me, 'all I did was make the first successful one. They had "pokers" back in 1897. What I did was more of a technical breakthrough. It was just lucky. A matter of timing. Like a lot of people built airplanes, but the Wright brothers got the credit for it.' Pease began his career in aviation with Boeing, then switched to the Apollo program and the moonshot with NASA. 'The space program was running down. I saw an ad in the paper for designing gaming machines. So I went along there and took a look inside a slot machine. It was very crude.' Pease went through several jobs before joining IGT and moving up to Reno. 'They had a video slot machine which was a technical curiosity to me. It wasn't designed with a microprocessor. I went and designed one that was very programmable.'

But it was not very reliable. The challenge of designing games,

Pease found, is that they have to be more accurate even than the space program. 'These things have to really work, because you are dealing with money. Slots have to be 10 or 100 times more reliable than the military. We never had a moonshot yet that was 100 per cent perfect.' He started over again in January 1980. At that time slot revenue had risen to 42 per cent of total gaming revenue. The first game he designed was a video game simulating blackjack. It was very successful. It could be played with quarters or dollars. The poker machine which followed was the first one on the street, the first one in colour and the first one which hit the public. Everyone caught on at the same time, but IGT was there first. The company leaped into production with 15–20,000 machines a year. For the public, as for the industry, video poker was one of those instances of the right idea at the right time.

A certain degree of skill is required by the player to get the best return from these machines. The pay-off for each hand – from a pair all the way up to the jackpot of a royal straight flush – is displayed above the screen. For example, a player faced with four cards in suit and a pair of aces, can go for the 'correct' play and hold his aces, or play his hunch, and go for the flush, just as in real poker. Either way, the player sees the next cards, which adds to the excitement of the game. With a conventional slot machine, spinning oranges and lemons and cherries around when you pull the handle, the hold percentage established by the manufacturer is fixed. With the video-poker machines, the manufacturer sets a hold percentage, given a certain play logic, but the empirical result will depend on the quality of the players. The choice in a sense is artificial, because (unlike a live game) the slot player can never beat the machine. It is programmed to hold a certain fixed percentage of the total coins bet, regardless. But with the hold and draw buttons under his fingers, the player does have a real choice.*

*Let me advise anyone tempted to play video poker to choose the machines which offer 9–1 for a full house and 6–1 for a flush, and avoid machines which pay only 8–1 and 5–1. At best, the coins not paid out simply increment the ever-elusive jackpot. The lower odds machines would only be advantageous if the progressive amount is very high.

This in turn led to the decisive breakthrough, which was the computer-driven slot machine. The number of stops on the reels could be increased, more reels could be added to produce bigger pay-offs, a huge variety of combinations could be set. Indeed the reel, which in the old days was limited to 22 symbols, could be more or less infinite – with, if you like, just one jackpot symbol on it. Finally, the computer chip meant that slots could be run simply and economically, on an entirely random basis, and programmed to produce all kinds of interesting combinations – notably the near-miss. This was a diabolical twist, dreamed up by the Japanese manufacturers. Its main popularity was with the normal three-reel slot. Because the game is played with a computer chip, the reels could be 'instructed' to stop in such a way that the player could see the symbols of a big pay-out, just above or just below the central line, which gave the impression that he was getting very close to the jackpot, only missing it by one line. 'Quick, get me some change, honey, I'm hot!' – as if the machine had some sort of personal rapport with the player. But despite being so close, the player never got there. There was a moral issue raised here, of misleading punters by giving the false impression they were about to hit a jackpot. The gaming authorities became involved and stopped it.

The challenge from the California lottery and other states' lotteries around the country posed a direct threat, and potentially a very serious one, to gambling in Las Vegas, certainly at the cheaper end of the market. After all, why should a casual player bother to drive all the way in from LA for a night out at a casino, when he could simply buy lottery tickets, as many as he liked, promising huge prizes, at an electronic machine (rather like a slot machine) at every street-corner grocery store? Quicker, easier and in a way more exciting to go for the lottery ticket. The challenge was solved by IGT, with the concept of 'Megabucks'. Megabucks, introduced around 1984, was a way of linking slot machines throughout the whole of Nevada into a single grid, so that anyone playing on a Megabucks machine was, in effect, playing one gigantic slot (like a lottery) with a jackpot of a million dollars or more. As every dollar coin entered one of the machines, so the total of the collective jackpot was flashed overhead like an electronic ticker-tape, giving the running, ever rising, total.

IGT ran the whole operation, which proved a fantastic draw. It took a great deal of research and testing before the system was judged reliable – it was not the kind of operation which could afford mistakes. 'When you are dealing with money it has to be right,' Pease told me. 'Money is almost more precious than human life in this business.' There are still a lot of technical problems, he adds, in making the system operate reliably in a hostile environment – heat, dust, electricity, interference of one sort or another. One out of four Nevada gamblers now spends 10 per cent of his or her gambling budget on Megabucks, the company's research shows. What's more, despite earning a return on every machine installed, IGT does not pay out the million dollar jackpot (or whatever the jackpot total is) in one go – it pays out $100,000 a year for ten years, meanwhile retaining the balance for its other operations. In the first three years ten lucky winners scooped jackpots totalling just under $30m. Hence the slogan: 'One pull can change your life.' Whenever a big jackpot was won (as luck would have it, a $4m. jackpot was hit at the Mirage on its opening day), the publicity gave the game another boost. Megabucks proved so popular, even though multimillion-dollar pay-outs occur only intermittently every few months, that IGT introduced Quartermania on the same principle in 1989, following this up with Nevada Nickels in 1990.

Why does one slot machine attract a player over another? All sorts of factors come into play including light, colour, animation in the machine, music and sound-effects. Walk along any aisle of slots and one is dazzled by the array of ingenious designs and visual come-ons. Casino managers are forever shunting their machines around, putting slots which seem to attract a high drop into new positions, tempting customers to move to different areas of the floor, monitoring each machine's take. If a new machine is not paying its way in two or three days the operators are on the line to the manufacturer, kicking and screaming. In the fall of 1990 a machine called Red, White and Blue took the punters' fancy: it had red sevens, red bars, blue sevens, blue bars, white sevens and white bars. Why did this machine do so well? Could it be that patriotic colour scheme carried a subliminal appeal at the time of the Gulf crisis? No one knows what turns gamblers on to particular slots. 'You might change around a whole bank of machines,' a downtown manager explained, 'and then find the reason you was doin' such good business was 'cause you got a good lookin' blonde on change in that section.'

The appeal of slots is that they are quick, simple, colourful, sociable, offering a new hope and a new decision every pull, in short user-friendly. One may approve or disapprove of slots, but no one can doubt that Americans like them. In Britain, the Gaming Board with its patrician disdain for public taste has always turned its face against slots. Believe it or not, casinos in London are restricted to two machines each; a move to allow clubs four machines failed at the committee stage in the House of Commons.

Many scams and cheats have been tried over the years on slots, from primitive devices like attaching a coin to a piece of string or fiddling inside the machine with wires, to moving the symbols round with magnets or monitoring the rhythm of the reels, to hitting the works with huge electromagnetic discharges in an attempt to create a false jackpot. Even in these days of sophisticated technology and eye-in-the-sky cameras, there is always someone on the look-out for a short cut to the jackpot. The biggest fraud in slots ever uncovered in Nevada was the Vaccaro case in 1984. The team won an estimated $3.25m. before getting caught.

It is not difficult to tamper with a machine, if you know what you are doing and have a key to open it up. The tricky part, you might say, consists in managing to do this without being detected – considering the fraud must be done in a public place. The Vaccaro team got around this problem by using a number of people as blockers and look-outs, who kept a watch on casino personnel and prevented anyone seeing what was going on. The mechanic drilled into the side of the machine or opened it up with a key, in order to line up the reels to hit a jackpot. The gang's second original twist was to employ a stooge to hit the jackpot, a John Q Public sort of guy who would never be suspected of a con. While the gang melted into the crowd, he collected the jackpot and was paid off a small percentage for his trouble.

As usually happens in such conspiracies, the gang got too greedy. By the time one Gus Econopolous hit a then world record jackpot of $1.7m. at Harrah's in Lake Tahoe, the authorities had got suspicious. The gang was indicted on 19 charges of rigging jackpots in Las Vegas and elsewhere. One gang member later testified that the group had rigged as many as 1,500 jackpots and stolen as much as $10m. Eventually the leaders were convicted. Vaccaro, who received nine years, achieved the distinction of being the first cheat, as opposed to organised crime figure, to get his name in the Black Book, the List of Excluded Persons, banned from casinos; his wife Sandra followed suit. (The hapless programmer who blew the whistle on this scam was later gunned down in front of his home in Vegas.)

Big prizes have also lured people to try to beat the system legitimately, by operating in teams. On a progressive machine, the jackpot – displayed in lights above the carousel – rises as the devices are played; which means that the hold percentage of the machine decreases as the jackpot grows. If a player knows the number of reels and the number of stops and symbols, it is possible to calculate the hold percentage. Team players have done this on the theory that when the progressive meter has risen to a level that gives them a positive expectation, they can play the machine until they hit – in effect changing roles with the house. In one case which got into the papers, members of a team were paid $9 an hour, like foot soldiers, to sit and pull the handles on a progressive slot carousel. Starting on a Monday morning, playing 12-hour shifts 24 hours a day, the team jammed more than

$160,000 into the machines, losing money at the rate of $200 an hour, before one woman hit a big backpot. But it was worth only $145,650. When the total amount of money the team has left runs low, it has to decide whether to cut its losses. All slot players are prone to that fraught feeling that the moment they give up, the very next player who walks in may hit the big one. But the fact that a machine has not paid off in a long while does not mean that it is then more likely to pay: the probability of any outcome is the same for each pull of the handle, as it is for each spin of the wheel at roulette.

Cheating has not always been on the player's side of the machine. Both manufacturers and operators have sought to tilt the balance in their favour, relates Nik Costa in *Automatic Pleasures*, a history of the coin machine. Some operators of the prewar three reel gambling machines ensured that a good proportion of winning combinations were unobtainable, leading to a pay-out of less than 50 per cent. Other operators used a device called a 'bug' (so-called because of its shape) which when screwed over a particular cog inside the machine prevented one of the jackpot symbols from ever appearing on the win line. An interesting case came up in Vegas recently, where a supplier of slots to certain bars was found to have put 'bad' chips in the machine, effectively eliminating some results. The casinos make tremendous publicity about how many jackpots they pay out per day or per week. A bell rings out across the casino floor and a light on the machine goes berserk every time a jackpot is hit. For the big winners, there is a family photo and crowds of envious well-wishers. But the casinos never say what proportion of the players enjoy success, or how many coins they have poured down the chute on average to win a jackpot.

How much do casinos hold? The average return in Nevada is probably around 6 per cent (in Atlantic City around 11 per cent, perhaps another reason for its failure). The cost to the player is higher on the nickel and dime slots, 7 per cent or more, because these low denominations are more trouble to operate. On dollar slots, where the handling of coin is easier, the house would normally be satisfied with a 5 per cent edge. The high-roller slots of $100 or $500 might perhaps have a house edge of only 0.5 or 1 per cent. Another key reason for the growth in popularity of slots among operators is their profitability. Pits are very labour intensive, whereas a slot machine does not call in sick, go on strike or suffer emotional problems. It shows up every day and does its job. The latest technological advance is for machines themselves to make change or accept cash, which may eventually eliminate the need for change people. The day of the totally automated money-eating operation is not far off.

A lot depends on location. If the casino is catering to a rapidly passing trade – like a crowd on its way out after a dinner show – slots might well be set disproportionately high. The casino's attitude towards players is hit 'em while you can. But in a local casino, full of regular punters who come in day after day, the slots would be set correspondingly low, perhaps at an average of 2.5 per cent. People do learn from experience, even in slot play. Thanks to continuous monitoring of each machine's performance – its take, pay-out, percentage hold and historical record – the management knows exactly how it's doing, all the time.

The first full-scale, computer-driven, player tracking system was introduced at the Frontier. Before then casinos had made some attempt to identify players, such as jackpot winners. But the realisation that slots players were becoming the heart and soul of casino gaming, and that this low grade business was the high road to profitability, led to a new interest in slot players. Tracking devices, on the same principle as frequent flyers on airlines, are now standard in the industry. The player inserts a little electronic card in the machine when he begins playing, and every pull he makes is automatically recorded. For the player, the reward is comps and other services in return for the action he gives the casino. For the management, tracking allows precise evaluation of its customer base. Repeat business is the name of the game.

7 NOBLE ART

Life is like boxing in many unsettling
respects. But boxing is only like boxing.

Joyce Carol Oates, 'On Boxing'

Americans prefer active sports. 'In the red corner. From New
York City. At 223 pounds. The undisputed *HEAV*-yweight
champion of the world . . .' Before the master of ceremonies can
exhale another breath into his hand-held mike, an exultant roar
surges up under the stars. The ring, diamond-bright in the blue
dusk, sits low down in the centre of a crowded square, hemmed
in. The sky is darkening by the minute. Row upon row of seats on
metal scaffolding rise high on each side of the square. The desert
night, carrying faint shouts and the roar of traffic from beyond the
arena, is fused by the sense of impending combat, of blood-ritual,
of a moment of decision which will affect the whole gathering, like
witnesses at an execution.

Of all the sports which Las Vegas has to offer, the biggest draw
is boxing. In the 1980s Vegas became, in effect, the world capital
of boxing. The leading casinos were in ever fiercer competition,
out of the ring, to promote the big fights. What has boxing got to
do with casino gambling? It was not because the managements of
Caesars and the Las Vegas Hilton and the Mirage were suddenly
seized by an altruistic concern to patronise the noble art that they
decided to get in on the act. The crowds who went to these

matches were hardly devotees, or even particularly knowledge-
able about championship boxing. After all, fights could have been
staged in New York or Chicago or any other big city, far more
conveniently. No, the audience was made up of gamblers. There
is something direct and elemental about two fighters slugging it
out under the night sky that really gets to gamblers. It's action in
the raw. Often the fights were an anti-climax. On the other hand,
you never know when emotion is going to hit. When Sammy
Davis, Jr. died there was a ten-count to mark his passing – ten
clear, plangent strikes of the boxing gong ringing out over the
arena – which stilled the crowd to silence with its fleeting echo of
eternity. The major casinos bid for the fights because it is a
wonderful way of bringing in high rollers and injecting high-
octane excitement straight into their bloodstreams. With all the
advance hype surrounding the fights, and the betting on the event
itself, the spectators get wound up to a frenzy of anticipation
before the gloves ever touch. Nevada is the only state where such
wagers are legal, a further plus for the sports books.

How sweet it is, for the gambler, to get an invitation from his
favourite casino to a title fight. A suite for the weekend, with all
the trimmings, second ticket if you like for wife or girlfriend, limo
at the airport, and all of it for free. It's irresistible. Only one little
catch: the pampered guest, in return, has to gamble off a
sufficiently large credit line to justify the casino's hospitality.
Typically on such big nights the stakes are raised across the casino
floor. All the talk of millions of dollars makes the players' own
wagering seem like chocolate money by comparison. What's a
twenty-five chip? Small change. What's a hundred dollar bill? A
minimum bet. What's a thousand? The numbers melt. Under the
stars, the fight may be good, may be bad. One of the sluggers
usually finishes stretched out on the canvas. But the moment it's
over, and the referee in his white shirt and bow-tie has moved to
the middle of the ring to announce, over the uproar, the official
verdict, the real challenge of the night begins. The crowd streams
out past the debris of plastic beer cups and crumpled hot-dog

cartons straight into the casino. The blood spilt in the ring is as nothing compared with the gore at the tables after the event.

The money paid out to stage these fights is indeed enormous. Sugar Ray Leonard, the champion who captured the public's imagination in a series of fights against Duran, Hearns and Hagler, earned up to $30m. a fight, thanks to TV rights. Mike Tyson and other heavyweights enjoyed comparable pay-outs. Even an obvious loser, roped in as a punch-bag for a world champion, could earn a million bucks for a couple of rounds' humiliation. The casino's contribution in these bouts is the 'live gate'. Heavyweight Larry Holmes attracted the two largest live gates in boxing history in the early '80s in bouts at the outdoor stadium at Caesars Palace. His fight against Cooney in 1982 drew a crowd of 30,000, paying over $6m. Leonard v. Hearns in 1989 was again over $6m. even though Caesars had scaled down its ring and the crowd was only 12,000. Prices for a half-way decent ticket on these occasions start at $200 and go up to $1,000 for a ringside seat – for all those ordinary patrons of the fight game who are not the beneficiaries of casino largesse. Yet the fight is just as likely to end inside a couple of rounds, or even a couple of minutes, as go the distance. With Donald Trump getting into the act in Atlantic City, the rival bidding to stage fights threatened to go through the roof. Leonard and Duran were paid around $30m. and $17m. respectively for their third fight together, in December 1989, shortly after the Mirage opened. The way it was going, a single fight could gross $50 or $60m.; the figure is likely to hit $100m. in the '90s. Which goes to show just how much the American public is prepared to pay for its entertainment.

If there was one man who stood out even larger than the boxers themselves, it was promoter Don King. An ex-con, streetwise, his real gift was for hyping himself. In a sport previously run by white promoters, King made great play of emphasising his bond of brotherhood with fellow blacks. His first coup was matching George Foreman and Muhammad Ali in Zaire, the 'rumble in the jungle' of 1975. Dispatched by Ali, Foreman dropped out of the big fight scene, only to emerge fifteen years later, at the age of forty-two, as a new challenger. It looked like a desperate throw by the promoters to find any half-way credible figure to stand up for a couple of rounds against Mike Tyson. In the event, Foreman surprised everybody by going the distance against the new world champion Evander Holyfield.

At the end of the '80s, the dividing line between promoters, managers and matchmakers in putting on title fights had become blurred. At that time King was impresario of the whole show. He had the backing of Tyson, which meant that the leading contenders in the game knew that if they wanted a crack at the heavyweight title, they had to work through him. With his jive talk and showman style, King was phenomenally successful in upping the ante from Las Vegas promoters. Dressed in a white suit, his orange-tinted hair standing on end like a candelabra, King was always ready with a quote or a put-down. 'This is the most excitin', stimulatin', pro-vocative event to be held in the home of championship boxing for a long, long time,' King would declare as he hyped up another evening of mediocre sluggers at Caesars Palace. 'This is one of the o-ccasions when a pro-moter can be unbiased, impartial and ob-jective . . . This is open warfare in the middle of the desert, like in the African jungle. My man is fightin' lions with a switch. He's eatin' red meat.' The boxing press, who had heard it all before, groaned aloud, but I loved it. No doubt about it, King had whatever counts for chutzpah in fisticuffs.

Then along came James 'Buster' Douglas, a journeyman fighter from Ohio, to knock the hitherto indestructible Mike 'Iron Man' Tyson flat out. It wasn't just a lucky punch. Tyson was whupped, out on his ass. It happened not in Vegas but Tokyo, in February 1990, and was the biggest sporting upset in modern times (Douglas had been a 42–1 shot in the Mirage's sportsbook). It was terrible news for King. Tyson, the man he had locked up every which way under contract, had been the most rock-solid money earner in the history of the fight game: all of a sudden he was the former champion. Events outside the ring were even more bizarre. Douglas at first was denied the title. The argument which King peddled volubly to camera was that the Mexican referee had been too slow in making the count of ten when Tyson had floored Douglas two rounds earlier. The replay confirmed that the referee had indeed been wrong. Two of the regulatory bodies in boxing immediately said that they upheld King's verdict. None of this did anything to rescue the good name of boxing. The decision taken in the ring, right or wrong, was the only one which counted. But the heroic knock-out by the unknown Douglas, and the controversy over his victory, was like oxygen to a sport at its last gasp. In an orgy of TV re-runs, Douglas' victory was belatedly accepted by all the boxing authorities concerned; the abject referee apologised for mistaking the count; and King, only winded, was quickly back on his feet. He had the rights to Tyson, and sooner or later a re-match was going to be held. Everybody wanted to see if Douglas' knock-out was a fluke or the real thing.

Enter Steve Wynn in the new champion's corner. In a significant but little reported event, Wynn flew Douglas back from Tokyo in his private jet. Buster, at that stage, was the greatest possible draw that any Las Vegas casino could dream up, and Wynn saw his chance. Donald Trump had already booked Tyson to defend his title against the next challenger in line, Evander Holyfield, at Atlantic City in June. But Tyson was no longer the holder. Trump had paid Tyson $11m. to fight Spinks for the undisputed heavyweight championship in 1988, boosting the drop at Trump Plaza by a reported $30m. After the about turn in Tokyo, the rivalry between Trump in Atlantic City and Wynn in Las Vegas broke all bounds. Each was desperate to stage the Douglas-Tyson match. Wynn tempted Douglas with an offer of $24m. to defend his title against Holyfield, twenty times the amount Douglas earned when he beat Tyson. (In fact it was a two-fight contract, worth $60m., if Douglas won the first fight.) The financing of these matches came in the main from television rights. The casinos were promoters, bidding for the right to stage the match on behalf of King, who controlled the event. Wynn decided to handle the whole thing himself. First, though, there was the legal dispute to be settled: there was no doubt that King had Holyfield under contract, so any future deal would have to be negotiated through him. It was settled in court in New York, Wynn having to pay Don King $2.4m. in compensation and getting rather the worst of the deal. But Wynn is never a man to count the odd million or two when he wants something. The Douglas-Holyfield fight was booked at the Mirage in October 1990. For days beforehand Wynn did practically nothing else but direct operations. Elaine Wynn strove to gratify the rival egos of movie stars and assorted celebrities who wanted ringside seats. It was as big an event as Vegas can stage. Everyone wanted to see the fight. 1,000 journalists flew in from around the world. The square of scaffolding set up in the car-park rose beneath my hotel window on the 22nd floor like a fretwork toy. It seated 16,100. The crush was so great that on the day of the fight, the entire casino and its restaurants had to be barred to anyone not a registered hotel guest or ticket holder. The name Mirage, as site of the fight, was beamed across America in a series of sharp TV ads, and all round the world via the media.

Wynn put a brave face on his costs. He projected an income of $36 to $37 million for the fight as against $37 to $39 million in costs. The fighters were being paid $32m. On top of that, a further $5 to $7 million went in advertising and legal fees, including the out of court settlement with Don King. Income from the fight was estimated at $16 to $19m., including the live gate, plus a further $19m. in the Mirage's share of pay-per-view television revenue. Wynn quoted a comment by Henry Gluck, chairman of Caesars, that if you came within two or three million of meeting expenses in putting on a fight, it was like hitting a home run. In fact Wynn turned a profit because the fight proved the largest pay-per-view event ever. Over 1,000 local cable TV companies signed up to carry the fight, which meant it was available to 16.5 million households, at a cost of about $34.95 per home. During the week of the Sugar Ray Leonard v. Roberto Duran fight, a fortnight after the opening, $15m. a day had been wagered at the Mirage. The Douglas v. Holyfield fight was almost as good, with an estimated $40m. wagered in the casino over the long weekend. The baccarat pit had a drop of $25m. In addition, the sports book wrote over $4m. in bets on the fight. 'How do I lose?' Wynn demanded.

And what of the fight itself? Douglas, all his life a palooka, was dazed by the sudden rise in his fortunes. Flabby and overweight, he had swollen up like a balloon. Word was that he had spent much of his training, in his special quarters at the Mirage, ordering up juicy snacks from room service. He was certainly in no shape to box and after the huge pay-out he had secured, he probably lacked any motivation to fight. He was hit by a good right in round three, fell back, half looked up, and collapsed in a heap. Wynn did not provide his private jet to fly Douglas back home to Columbus.

How can such excessive expenditure be justified? The casinos, who buy up blocks of tickets as soon as they go on sale, have done their sums. Their calculations are based on the well-established equation that they will hold close to 20 per cent of the drop: so if a man buys in for say, $50,000, the casino's expected win, on average, will be $10,000 over the weekend; for a $100,000 player, the expected win would be $20,000, depending again on the player's action. How long does it take in a regular business to clear $10,000 or $20,000 per customer? This is a pretty nice return, even allowing for the comps – how many meals can a hotel guest, even a hungry boxing fan, eat in 72 hours? If a casino buys a hundred tickets and brings in a hundred good players, it is going to wind up well ahead of the game. Naturally the welcome varies according to the style of the casino. A salesman from Seattle or a doctor from Des Moines with, say, up to $10,000 to gamble, might not rate too highly at the top end of the market, whereas at middle-American places like the Flamingo or Tropicana, or in the

grind joints downtown, such punters would be pampered like
golden geese. When a big fight is on, the whole town buzzes as if it
were New Year's Eve.

Calculation of a gambler's 'expected loss' (which is the
technical term for what happens when the odds are against you) is
quite complicated. Casinos have become very sophisticated these
days in assessing the real worth of a player's action. This is not
merely good business: it was a necessary defence to the spread of
comps and junkets (group travel), at all types of casinos, as the
easiest way of bringing in new customers. A contest between the
casino and the customers, like a tug of war, is going on just under
the glossy surface all the time. It's a battle of wits – the casino
requires the customers to play long enough and high enough to
justify the money they are giving away; and the players on their
side are trying to get the maximum amount in comps in return –
ideally, a completely free vacation. It is *so* gratifying to have
everything paid for, to be treated like a sultan: it's a return to
childhood self-indulgence, with all the sweets in the corner shop
yours for the asking. The casinos can afford it, provided that a
sufficient number of players do gamble. But the expected win of
20 per cent of total money staked is only a guideline. Each player's
individual action has to be 'rated', as accurately as possible.
That is why so many keen-eyed staff are floating around the big
baccarat and blackjack tables with their little note-pads.*

---

*Take a popular high roller game like craps. The basic house edge as everyone
knows is (only) 1.41 per cent playing front line bets. But what does this mean
in actual play? It doesn't automatically follow, as you might suppose, that a
player making $100 bets will, in theory, lose $1.41 a time, and that
cumulatively over a hundred bets he will therefore lose $141.

It takes an average of 3.38 rolls of the dice to determine the outcome of a
front line bet. Thus, the true theoretical cost to the player making these line
bets works out at 0.42 cents per dollar wagered per individual roll (1.41 per
cent of $100 divided by 3.38). Assuming 75 rolls an hour (a minimum rate,
which could be twice as high in a fast moving table) his expected loss on $100
bets is 75 × .41 × 100 = $31.50. How long would such a player have to play
(leaving out of account all the other bets at craps) for the casino to win $1,000?
Answer: he would have to play this way for nearly 32 hours. This example,

In the 1980s, according to a detailed analysis of comps in the casino journal *Rouge et Noir*, there was a trend towards professionally trained managers replacing streetwise casino operators who had come up the hard way. These operators had an instinctive feel for the game and the players, probably acquired in illegal joints or off-shore gambling in the good old days. By contrast, the new breed of managers was college educated, many with business degrees but little first-hand experience of gambling. They differed in style and they differed in judgement, nowhere more sharply than on the value of comps. The new men put their trust in cost analysis; this works very well in periods when demand, in the shape of eager gamblers, exceeds supply, as offered by casinos. But in time of economic recession, as in the early 1980s, they were liable to make the same sort of mistakes as the others. A similar situation may recur now in the 1990s, when the huge expansion of casinos, and a decline in travel caused partly by the recession, partly by international tensions, was hitting profits. Dealing with individual players, which is what high roller gambling is all about, a nose for a good risk is probably worth more than a degree in economics.

The higher the gaming revenue, the higher the comp-and-junket ratio. On average over the year, one-sixth of total room and food sales at the Strip casinos is comped and over one-third of the drinks. Smart gamblers, knowing how the casinos think, try to

obviously, is a bit abstruse: the other bets, mostly at horrendously unfavourable odds, radically change the equation in the casino's favour. If such a player, for example, makes $100 hardway bets the house would win on average $208.5 in an hour.

The point is that these kind of calculations provide a very accurate management tool: if a highly comped player is not at the tables at least three hours a day over the weekend, making substantial bets, he is not going to be invited back – indeed he probably won't even get his airfare reimbursed on his present trip. The practical effect of granting regular players a slice of their expected loss in comps is very neat. It has extended the range, in terms of cultivating customer loyalty, right across the market, because it can also be applied at the bottom end. A customer at the slots, with a gaming budget as low as $500, could qualify for comps with a retail value as high as $50, says *Rouge et Noir*. So why not take it?

generate a lot of markers at the tables: 'Hey, Jack, gimme another coupla thousand, will ya –' Doing this every half hour or so, meanwhile betting quite sparingly, makes a pretty pattern at the cashier's cage. Even legitimate high rollers may try to claim airfares and other expenses from two or three casinos at the same time. And the casinos will not argue, if the players are the right sort of customers. But such practice may also be criminal. At Caesars a hotel guest was arrested on charges of obtaining money under false pretences. The scam, operated over a number of years, was to obtain reimbursement for airfares and enjoy elaborate comps through the use of a fake rating card, which showed him to be a high roller. In reality the man (an associate as it transpired of one of the east coast mob families) was simply using Caesars for free vacations. Such a fraud could work only with the connivance of someone on the gaming staff, deliberately over-rating his action.

However, the casinos are prepared to 'give back' a fair slice of a player's expected loss in comps (up to one-third is probably the outside limit). All the suites and complimentary services are priced retail, but in practice are provided at cost. So comps are not quite as expensive as they look. If a premium player gets lucky and beats the casino out of fifty thousand, on top of all his comps, so what? It's even more likely he'll be right back. The golden rule which casino managements live by, as Mario Puzo (himself a gambler) observed in *Fools Die*, is *percentages*. 'Percentages never lie. We built all these hotels on percentages. We stay rich on the percentage . . . You can lose faith in everything, religion and God, women and love, good and evil, war and peace, you name it. But the percentage will always stand fast.'

To return to the boxing: in round figures, a major casino might budget the expense of a long weekend for one of their best players roughly as follows:

Suite . . .	$3,000
Meals and service . . .	$1,000

Ticket to the fight . . .	$1,000
Airfare Dallas – Las Vegas . . .	$1,400
TOTAL:	$6,400

A fairly modest investment (even throwing in a second ticket), one might say, for a customer who's prepared to risk losing forty or fifty thousand bucks or more. For a regular high roller, living in less luxurious style, the cost might be only a quarter of this figure. So at the end of the long weekend, when the big fight is only a fifteen second bite on breakfast TV, who is left prostrate on the canvas? 'Sure hope we see you again real soon, sir! The limo is waiting for you.'

Boxing, along with other sports, attracts tremendous betting. Sports and race books (as betting shops are called) are becoming ever more popular, especially with a younger generation new to casino gambling. At the Stardust (first to open at eight a.m. with the morning line), the Las Vegas Hilton (with 14 satellite dishes), Caesars, the Mirage and other casinos, the sports books represent gambling in the space-age. Light years removed from the old back-street bookies, these new arenas, flickering with electronic light, combine two American passions: betting on anything that moves on field or track and wizardry in communications.

On the far wall, in a wide curve, flash lists of runners, riders and teams, displayed in coloured lights. Alongside, huge TV monitors screen the games and the races, live. On a Sunday afternoon there might be a dozen football games across the nation, or half a dozen race meetings; baseball or college basketball, ice hockey, tennis, TV chat and trivia, according to the season. All of it live, immediate, magnified in close-up, with instant re-plays, and all of it – this is the sublime point – available to bet on. At floor level below the TV screens is a line of betting windows where staff are ready to take the fans' money, print out their tickets, and compute the whole thing into a single, vibrating circuit of odds and prices, profit and loss. Plus drinks on the house! It's almost too good to be true. The crowds who throng the sports books evidently believe so. These Sunday afternoon fans are not the collection of sweaty horse-players who used to hang around the off-track betting parlours, which have all but disappeared and which were hardly the place for a woman. These are boisterous white-collar folk, with a median income of $38,000 a year, brunch parties, university kids out on a spree, tourists living it up, as well as regular sports fans. The sports books have become big business for all the casinos, though the profit margins are tight.

The first sports book in a hotel-casino opened in 1976 at the Union Plaza downtown. Until the mid-'70s, there were less than a dozen in Vegas, with a total handle (money bet) in the low millions. Through the second half of the '70s, when the federal tax was reduced from 10 per cent to 2 per cent, the number of sports books tripled, and the handle rose to $290m. in 1980. The profit on this huge turnover was $12m. or just over 4 per cent (a good year). As the idea, and the style of the thing, caught on, casinos came to feel they had to have a sports book, or risk losing customers to rival stores. The automatic processing of bets by computer led to a far better audit, allowing bigger bets. It also prevented cheating. What's more the sports book crowd had the right economic profile – high earning twenty-five to forty-four year olds – just the kind of new players casinos wanted to attract. With satellite transmission bringing in more and more games, and a broader cross-section of people drawn in, the market exploded. People like to bet on what they can see. Federal tax was reduced again in 1983 to 0.25 per cent. By 1989, the number of sports books had risen to 67 with a handle of $1,356m. But increasing competition and costs of marketing had reduced the net profit to 2.79 per cent or just under $38m. The race and sports books are now situated cheek by jowl with the gaming tables which lie in wait to tempt and divert sports fans on their way out: in other words, the sports books have themselves become centres for entertainment.

A tidal wave of sports betting, legal and above board, is about to sweep the United States: by the mid '90s, there will be advertisements for sports books linked to horse race tele-theatres, sports betting by mail, betting by telephone, and state and charitable lotteries selling sports cards, according to Professor I. Nelson Rose, author of *Gambling and the Law*. 'Sports in America is America's mirror on ourselves. It is everything we wish we were and hope to be. It is our children.' In other words, nearly everyone loves sport and the only major block on legal sports betting has been the concerted opposition of professional sporting bodies. Betting on sports is as common as drinking beer. Nationally, illegal betting is enormous – one estimate puts the total at $20 billion a year – all of which is more or less 'lost' to the economy, because it goes through underground channels. In other parts of the world, as in Britain with football pools, sports betting is taken for granted (and the government takes a fat cut out of it). As legal gambling becomes more and more acceptable, the sports organisations will have to give in, says Rose. There is simply too much money at stake. In this process, the Vegas sports and race books obviously stand to be big winners.

Among a small group of professional betters, who rely on an inside knowledge of sports and wagering to give them an edge, the best known is the aptly named Lem Banker. He has become almost a public figure in Vegas, through his newspaper column and TV spots and his *Book of Sports Betting*. Banker is an amiable man who works as hard at his 'profession' as a stockbroker studying the market: 'Women, booze, and late hours knock off a lot of gamblers, but bad money management remains number one on the hit parade.' Money management is the key to successful sports betting, he says. His advice to fans is to gather their own information, sift and refine it, and make their own decisions, instead of taking other people's tips. He spends five hours a day on research, rarely bets less than five figures and often bets $50,000 on a game or fight. He likes underdogs and when handicapping a

game looks for emotional factors – revenge, letdowns – as well as
form. His technique is to make a lot of plays, trying to grind out a
winning margin (as the casinos do) rather than going for a big kill.
The biggest mistake a gambler can make is to try to get even fast,
by increasing his bets when he falls behind – it's like being caught
in quicksand, he says. Like all sports betters, Banker has had his
lean times: his worst moment was a series of losses in 1966 when
he was down to his last bet. He put it all on the outsider in a
national football game. It won – since then he has not looked
back. As an aid to thinking about odds, he works out every day in
his gym.

The official prices on sports games are made by the odds-
makers, experts who assess the form and all the other factors in a
sporting event, and then set the price in such a way as to attract
money for both sides. In football games this is achieved by
handicapping one side as favourite by a given margin.* The
professional gamblers are in essence betting their judgement
against that of the line makers. That is why they like to get to the
sports book first thing in the morning, to check out the line and
see what's on offer, before the prices change under the weight of
money flowing in. Sometimes the odds makers are right and
sometimes they are wrong – one of the best known in Vegas,
Michael 'Roxy' Roxborough, a former gambler himself, finds it
necessary to change his telephone number from time to time, to
avoid irate punters. Sports via satellite and cable is modern
society's alternative both to playing games for recreation and to
actual physical combat. It is a serious business, even though, as
social psychologist Erwin Goffman observed in his essay 'Where
the Action Is', commercialised sport is staged for an audience and

---

*Suppose the odds makers give the San Francisco Giants as minus 5 against
the Chicago Bears; then the Giants must win by a margin of more than 5 points
for a winning bet; a bet on the Bears will win if they win the game or do not lose
by more than 4 points. (5 would be a stand-off). The sports book pays 10 for 11
on these bets, which is a margin of 4.5 per cent (money paid out on winning bet
10 + original stake 11 = 21, money staked on each team 11 + 11 = 22).

watched for fun. The screen shows conflict and combat without the blood and suffering involved in real warfare. The point was vividly brought home in the Gulf War when the American bombing raids on Iraq coincided on screen with the Super Bowl. The commentary in the sports books cut from one to the other, but the language was the same – hitting and zapping and crunching the opponent. 'From News Four War in the Gulf, it's now back to the Game.'

8 UNWISE GUYS

My kind of town, Chicago is . . . My kind of people, too.

'Chicago', sung by Frank Sinatra

Where did the Mafia go? Las Vegas is supposed to be a mob town. Stories of Mafia involvement, of skimming and fraud, of gangster rivalry, of torture and murder, are part of the stock in trade of the place. Yet nowadays, everyone, from the regulatory authorities and casino managers right down the line, protests that Las Vegas is clear of the Mafia. In the '90s, they claim, Las Vegas has entered a new era, squeaky clean. Can it really be true that the wise guys have been driven out of town? Does human nature, in this case human greed, ever change?

Some things do change. Foremost among which is the licensing procedure for running a casino. In the old days, – 'Hard times make hard people,' as people like Moe Dalitz liked to say – anyone could get into the business, because out there, in the West, you didn't ask a man a whole bunch of questions. Now it is very, very tough. The process is lengthy and thorough and almost unforgivably intrusive into applicants' private lives. The process of investigation, in fact, is said to be more rigorous than security clearance for politically sensitive posts in Washington. Everything the investigators can uncover in an applicant's past – bank statements, income tax returns, private correspondence, down to the smallest detail, comes under scrutiny. No scrap of paper is too insignificant to attract official attention, even – to cite a recent instance – an applicant's wife's Christmas card list. One man who was subjected to this kind of inquisition recently, himself the author of a standard text on casino management, told me that his interrogation, which lasted nearly six months, was the worst and most humiliating experience of his life.

The licensing authorities' motivation is clear and simple. It is to eliminate applicants who have had any kind of association with the Mafia, however light or indirect it might have been. A worthy aim, and a necessary one given Las Vegas' past.

It was the Kefauver hearings of 1950–51 which first focused national attention on organised crime. Kefauver and his team spent only a couple of days in Vegas, a place which the Senator obviously disliked on principle before he ever got there. Kefauver was widely thought to be furthering his presidential ambitions by the root and branch condemnation of illicit gambling in his report. But that didn't diminish the impact it had. 'Gambling profits are the principle support of big-time racketeering and gangsterism', he reported.

The bad reputation of Las Vegas was further highlighted by the lurid exposure of mob operations reported in *The Green Felt Jungle* by Ovid Demaris and Ed Reid, which had a major impact on public opinion in Nevada, and beyond. The book named all the bad guys, listing in gruesome detail their criminal activities in the leading casinos – at that time, around 1963, there were eleven casino-hotels on the Strip, each one of them, so it seemed, more corrupt than the next.

The current licensing system was introduced by a reforming State Governor, Grant Sawyer, in 1959–67, and was elaborated under his successors. Sawyer's instructions to his team were: 'Get tough and stay tough'. In those days, recalls Sawyer (now a partner in a law firm), the corruption in the industry was rank. There was widespread alarm in Nevada that as things stood the Federal Government, in the person of Attorney-General Robert

Kennedy, intended to introduce legislation to prohibit states' gambling altogether. This would have done more than clean up Nevada, it would have wrecked the state's economy. Sawyer campaigned to bring the industry under state control and won election somewhat against the odds. But while the new licensing rules might screen new applicants very effectively, the authorities couldn't get rid of the good ol' boys like Moe Dalitz, who were already in the woodwork (see Chapter 3).

The stoutest friend of the gaming industry in former years had been Senator Pat McCarran. He played the role of line-blocker in the Senate. Every time (and there were many) the anti-gambling lobby made a rush, he got in the way. His argument was that every state had a constitutional right to run commercial gambling if it chose to do so. 'Nothing of any consequence happened in the state without his knowledge or consent,' noted the celebrated editor of the Las Vegas *Sun*, Hank Greenspun (who had a running feud with McCarran over the latter's association with Senator Joe McCarthy). He never admitted acquaintance with the major crime-syndicate figures involved in casino gambling, though he had close dealings with all of them. McCarran cherished many old-fashioned ideas, as Greenspun put it: Nevada came first, then the country and finally – though he never quite accepted it – the world. He liked to consider himself a benevolent despot, ruling a realm which he often called 'my empire'. But he died in 1954 and his influence was spent.

After setting up the new system of licensing, Sawyer went to Washington to see Kennedy and convinced him there was no longer a case for federal action against gambling. The anxieties of Senator McCarran and his friends were allayed.

Yet in a funny way, Las Vegas' reputation as a haven for the mob has been part of its attraction, its glamour. Nevada's dangerous image, as a recent chairman of the Gaming Commission, John O'Reilly, observed, has probably attracted tourism. When people gamble – particularly in American society, where everyone has been raised to believe in thrift and hard work – they want to feel an edge of excitement, of transgression, of living on the edge. I have heard local people say, only half in jest, that day-to-day life in town was a lot safer when the mob was in charge – that the wise guys ran things their way and kept the muggers and sneak thieves off the streets. Nowadays, you would think twice before walking into an unlit car park. In the classless equality of the gaming tables, the Mafia-types were regarded as dudes of the game.

It is still hard to believe, whatever officials may claim, that the Mafia has left town and lost its influence. After all, where is it *not* found in American city life? Anyone browsing in the Gambler's Book Club, that treasure trove of gaming lore, will find a whole shelf of books detailing Mafia connections with gambling, including not one, but two, full length biographies of John Gotti, the man reputed to be the boss of organised crime in New York City. Such figures are written up in the media like movie stars. The shiny image of the Mafia, the way its members are fêted and looked up to in restaurants and night clubs and on the showbiz fringe was brilliantly depicted in Martin Scorsese's movie *GoodFellas* (1990). What seems to be true in Las Vegas is that the Mafia – or Cosa Nostra as its members refer to their fraternity – is no longer *directly* involved in running gambling. Beyond the new licensing procedures, the change from personal to corporate ownership of most of the major casinos has created a completely different business structure. The Mafia has been driven to the fringes of the gambling business, first of all at street level in drug trafficking. Las Vegas is notorious as a lucrative outlet for the drug gangs operating in Los Angeles. Indeed it has the second highest drugs abuse record of any place in the United States, obviously a reflection on the transient population.

Secondly, there is probably a mob connection with prostitution in Vegas. All the services masquerading under entertainment, listed in the Yellow Pages (see Chapter 5), which send exotic dancers and escorts direct to the caller's hotel room, imply a degree of pimping or behind the scenes organisation, even though the licensed brothels themselves seem to be private enterprises. And thirdly, it has been suggested that the Mafia or their associates may have tried to penetrate middle management, at some weak points, after licensing and ownership regulations were tightened up. There are going to be some dishonest people in any kind of business, and especially in a business with a gigantic cash flow like casino gambling. But to suggest that the Mafia might have succeeded in planting contacts here and there – like spies engaged in espionage in a foreign country – shows how far Vegas has changed from the days when major casinos were seen, literally, as 'Our Thing', Cosa Nostra.

The most vivid account of the rise and fall of organised crime in Las Vegas that I have seen, was a documentary called 'Mob on the Run' by a television reporter named Ned Day. It was made for a programme called *Eyewitness News* on the local station KLAS TV, screened in the spring of 1987. Not long after his programme was shown, Ned Day – still in his early '40s – drowned while on vacation in Hawaii. Was Ned Day's untimely death, after his exposé of organised crime on a popular TV programme, an act of petty vengeance, to be taken as a warning to prying journalists? Apparently not. According to the evidence, there was no suspicion of foul play. (The Mafia do not operate outside their own territory, so one is assured.) What Day's programme did was to present, *visually*, the progress of Chicago's operations in Las Vegas, in context. It conveyed, in a matter of fact but dramatic way, the chain of corruption and how it all worked.

Day began with Lansky and Siegel coming into town in 1941, 'our founding fathers'. A shifty, brutal-looking pair; but nothing compared with former mob killer turned informant, 'Jimmy the Weasel' Fratianno, who resentfully explained to camera how the Jews among these early gangsters got so big at the expense of the Italians. 'The Jews showed money. They had money. You give an Italian a million dollars he puts it under the cellar . . . That's where the Italians made a mistake. They shoulda done it themselves.' The Mafia preferred to work through surrogates, partners like Bugsy Siegel, or front men like Wilbur Clark, vague as a will o' the wisp about business matters, at the Desert Inn.

Behind every success story, there is usually one good idea. The real trick of the mob, in getting hidden control of casinos, lay in using its bankroll for investment. (In the late '50s and '60s banks and insurance companies did not dream of investing in the casino business: this was long before junk bonds). The jackpot in terms of cash was the Teamsters' Central States Pension Fund in Chicago. The Chicago crime family, led by Sam Giancana from 1956 to the late 1960s, (later shot in the basement of his Chicago home), achieved extraordinary influence in controlling this fund. Their link man was Allen Dorfman (son of an old Al Capone gunslinger), who built up a very close relationship with the Teamsters' leadership. Working hand in glove with corrupt officials, in particular one Roy Lee Williams, he was able to manipulate the Pension Fund's huge resources to obtain 'loans' for front men, to buy up or finance casinos in Vegas. The Fund became, in effect, a private bank for the Chicago syndicate.

In 1973 Allen Glick, a thirty-two-year-old businessman from San Diego, suddenly popped up. He bought up all the shares and became owner of the Stardust. How did a young man, with no money of his own and no experience of casinos, pick such a plum? Glick happened to go to college with the son of the mob boss of Milwaukee; the son recommended Glick to his father, who recommended him to Chicago – 'and presto', reported William Roemer, the distinguished FBI agent, in his memoirs *Man Against the Mob*, 'this young kid with no background in gaming gets a $62.75m. loan from the Central States Pension Fund.' A few months later he got further loans totalling $30m.

The chain of corruption extended. Caesars, Circus Circus, the Aladdin, the Stardust, the Fremont, the Dunes, were all funded with the aid of Chicago mob money. As the casinos prospered, the 'points', or percentage shares of ownership, held by mob leaders grew ten or even a hundred-fold in value. It was Lansky's role, living in Miami, far away from the action, to keep track of everyone's interests: he had the financial acumen and, most important, was trusted by his partners in crime to keep the record straight, according to *Little Man*, a biography of Lansky by Robert Lacey.

The Mafia loved the casino business. Not only did it gush cash like an oil well – it also had glamour. From the earliest days there had been a mutual attraction between Hollywood and Vegas, with the razzmatazz of opening nights, flying visits by stars, gossip column tattle. Bugsy Siegel knew all the movie stars (and was himself a sort of star). Many came as guests to the Flamingo. The showbiz connexion with Vegas, always close, was personified by Frank Sinatra, noblest Roman of them all, as Caesars Palace once put it. It was not all sparkly good times but from the mob's point of view the star names shimmering down from a hundred signs and billboards along the Strip were a guarantee of success.

The master-image in the cast of villains assembled by Ned Day in his TV report was Tony 'Big Tuna' Accardo. A former bodyguard of Al Capone, suspected as one of the gunmen in the St Valentine's Day Massacre, he had been a long time consigliere of the Chicago family. Big Tuna was caught on camera, by the time of his trial a fierce, bent, old man, one leg half-twisted under him, shuttling rapidly forward like a crab. He grasped a walking stick, displaying on the handle the superb golden-scaled head of a fish, like the symbol of authority of a renaissance prince. His presence exuded evil and power.

Big Tuna's great coup was to consolidate Chicago's grip on Vegas to the virtual exclusion of all the other crime families. He secured this prize by an astute piece of diplomacy, in negotiating a division of spoils a year ahead of the opening of casino gambling in Atlantic City in the summer of 1978. According to Roemer's account, at a meeting of 'the Commission', the ruling body of the national mob, Chicago advanced a proposition: 'You guys in the East take Atlantic City. Chicago will take Nevada.' At first the eastern mobsters protested. Joey Aiuppa, representing Accardo, who had coached him in his lines, told them: 'We will grandfather you guys in' – i.e. protect their interests for them. The argument made sense: the eastern mob families would be given the run of the Boardwalk in return for Chicago retaining undisputed sway on the Strip.

Through the 1970s and most of the '80s, the Chicago mob's interests came under the control of one of the nastiest gangsters ever blown out of the windy city, a cold, cruel killer named Tony Spilotro. Short and stocky, nicknamed Tony the Ant or Little Tony because of his baby-faced look, he had arrived in America, uneducated and alone, at the age of fourteen. His vicious streak showed early on, in petty crime. He became a 'soldier', climbing up the organisation over the corpses of his victims. His brutality had commended him to a gangster named DeStefano, who dominated loan-sharking in Chicago: on one occasion DeStefano had hoisted a rival on a meat hook, to torture–murder him. When, in his turn, DeStefano was gunned down, Spilotro was the suspected killer. By that time he had risen to the lower levels of 'the Outfit', as the crime syndicate in Chicago (founder Al Capone) was known. In 1971 Little Tony was sent to Vegas as an enforcer, to ensure the cash funnelled from the mob casinos flowed back to the bosses in Chicago. He had a swaggering, ruthless style, at odds with his baby features, and a reputation which sent the chill of death into everyone he encountered. Even in his own milieu he was despised: 'this guy's an animal, a punk, with no class, no finesse,' one old mobster, Johnny Roselli, who worked as a coordinator in Las Vegas, described him. Since 1960 he had been arrested, questioned or listed as a suspect – but never convicted – in at least 25 mob-style killings. Many were marked by the same trademark: shots fired at close range into the eardrum, mouth and forehead from a small-calibre pistol fitted with a silencer, according to a series of articles in the Los Angeles *Times* by Michael J. Goodman.

Spilotro began by securing the lease (under his wife's name) of the jewellery-gift counter at Circus Circus. This was a valuable concession in itself, which could not be obtained without 'juice'.

It so happened that the major owner of the casino at that time had borrowed nearly $20m. from the Chicago-based Teamsters' pension fund. The jewellery store became the centre of Spilotro's rapidly expanding operations, until he moved to the Sands, and then – after heavy pressure on its members by his partner, Frank 'Lefty' Rosenthal – the swanky Las Vegas Country Club. One of the Club's founders was none other than Moe Dalitz.

In the first three years after Spilotro's arrival, more Mafia-type murders occurred in Vegas than in the previous 25 years. He soon overtook Rosenthal, who as a Jew could never be inducted into the highest levels of the Outfit. Under Spilotro's rule an enormous range of crimes, big and small, were perpetrated all over town. (He even organised burglaries at the homes of his neighbours – which refutes any fond idea that Vegas was a safer place under Mafia control.)

In contrast with Tony the Ant, his old pal Frank 'Lefty' Rosenthal, whom he teamed up with in Vegas, was unthreatening. Operator of a sports book and reputedly the sharpest odds maker in the country, he had a long record of misdeeds (including a run-in with the law for fixing a college basket ball game in Carolina). Now he was working on the inside track, as a senior executive at the Stardust, though without ever obtaining a licence. When Spilotro came to town, Rosenthal's role was organiser and link-man, reporting directly to the mob bosses in Chicago. 'All the skimming, and believe me . . . they're skimming the shit out of these joints, is Lefty's responsibility', Roselli confided to hitman 'Jimmy the Weasel' Fratianno (in *The Last Mafioso* by Ovid Demaris). The partnership between Rosenthal and Spilotro – Mr Inside and Mr Outside – was the axle around which all Mafia activity in Vegas turned.

The mob's favourite method of making money out of casinos was by skimming. This means lifting money illicitly, either between the tables and the counting room or in the counting room before the daily tally is taken, explains William Roemer. Skimming can only be accomplished with the connivance of casino employees and by evading security cameras. According to Roemer, the money skimmed in Vegas was Chicago's number one source of income for more than two decades.

Probably the greatest coup which Rosenthal master-minded for the Chicago outfit was the skimming operation at the Stardust. Under his direction, the Stardust had been completely penetrated. A separate counting room was set up for the slots, with false scales for weighing the money. Thanks to this scam, the mob was skimming up to $40,000 a week in coins and another $40,000 in hundred dollar notes. A parallel scam was practised on the drop boxes from the tables. The FBI eventually broke the Stardust racket, thanks to a wire-tap of a 'business meeting' between gangsters of various families who had assembled in Kansas City. The main purpose of their meeting was to discuss how to emulate the Stardust scam at the Tropicana (reported at length in *The Boardwalk Jungle* by Ovid Demaris). Spilotro's activities were certainly aided and abetted by police corruption and informants in the Sheriff's organised crime unit. Many agents were getting their meals, drinks and show reservations comped: it was so flagrant that when a special investigation team was dispatched by the FBI in Washington to take a closer look, it got comped too. In addition to penetrating the police force, Spilotro had influence, through bribery or intimidation, at political level.

The popular image of Las Vegas' corruption was spread by fiction, films and TV drama. 'Look,' one of the leading characters remarks in the novel *Fools Die* by Mario Puzo, 'we can always handle trouble with the federal government with our lawyers and the courts; we have judges and we have politicians. One way or another we can fix things with the governor and the gambling control commissions. The deputy's office runs the town the way we want it. I can pick up the phone and get almost anybody run out of town. We are building an image of Vegas as an absolute safe place for gamblers.' This was overstated, no doubt, but as the stories of corruption over the years bore out, not so wide of the mark for that time. For three or four years Spilotro seemed 'untouchable'.

On TV, Spilotro came over not as a baby-faced little guy, attractive to women, as so many accounts present him, but as squat and puffy-eyed, a brawler with a hangover. Rosenthal was merely oily and obsequious. 'I serve at Mr Glick's pleasure,' he claimed. He was, for a time, very adept at his job.

Dazzled by all the glitzy cabaret artists winging in from LA, however, Rosenthal conceived his own ambitions in show business. While running the casino operation and much else besides, he also hosted a weekly television talk show. It was staged in the Stardust race book, an amphitheatre with the runners at the race meetings displayed around the curving back wall. Ned Day's footage shows Lefty being given a rapturous introduction by a glazed looking showgirl – 'Welcome Mr Fra-a-a-nk Rosenthal!!!' – and then entering shiftily stage right, nervously fiddling with his tie. He sits down behind a desk, a seedy caricature of a talk show host, and tries to engage in small talk. Lefty was so desperately lacking in presence, despite rubbing shoulders with Sinatra and other stars, that he cut a truly comic figure. But there was a sinister underside to his stumble into stardom. 'The fact that he had a talk show and went on the air weekly with celebrities bespeaks the arrogance that the kind of power Rosenthal had can lead to,' commented a federal law enforcement official on Day's programme. He added that the community's acceptance of such a man going on air with a talk show can be seen, with hindsight, as a kind of complicity.

Allen Glick, owner, president and chief executive of the Stardust, a noted contributor to local charities, was honoured as Las Vegas' Man of the Year in 1975. But in May 1976 came the famous raid on the Stardust and the uncovering of the gigantic skimming operation.

Within twenty-four hours of the raid, the Stardust's slots manager disappeared – he knew too much. The bosses in Chicago dared not risk his switching sides and becoming a prosecution witness, always the last resort.

Up to this point, the community had taken the typically Vegan view that you don't look too closely at the people in the casino business because they were helping the town grow. Even a reforming Governor like Grant Sawyer had once sagely observed: 'Our attitude to life, save under the most urgent provocation, is relaxed, tolerant and mindful that if others are allowed to go on their way unmolested, a man stands a chance of getting through the world himself with a minimum of irritation.' Law enforcement and gaming officials might have their doubts and suspicions. But by and large the community considered that Glick was good for gaming. Now the Gaming Commission was stung into action.

Its crucial decision was denying Rosenthal his casino licence. In the most dramatic sequence of Ned Day's report, Rosenthal is seen losing his cool, and berating the chairman of the Gaming Commission, Harry Reid, at a public meeting. Rosenthal, livid with anger, barely in control of himself yet somehow looking ridiculous in a brown porkpie hat and yellow suit, flailed accusations at Reid – whom he accused of reneging on previous favours done on his behalf. He simply could not comprehend that the powers-that-be would give the thumbs down to a man as 'connected' as himself.

In fact, the decision of the Board not to license him proved a life-saver for Rosenthal, because he succeeded in doing what very few people in his line of business ever manage to do: he survived. When a high explosive device was planted under his car, shattering the vehicle and reducing the driver's seat to a mass of burning metal, he was miraculously flung out, alive. When he came to in hospital after the explosion, the FBI was at his bedside. This was their golden chance: but Lefty (who knew about odds) refused the offer of protection in exchange for turning informant. He left town, in one piece, with his cheque-book, and retired to Orange County, taking the precaution of equipping his new home with $30,000 worth of electronic surveillance. He was never charged in the skimming scandal.

Lefty had also suffered a personal betrayal. He may have been as crooked as a corkscrew, but there was one redeeming aspect of his life. He was a devoted family man. Spilotro broke one of the mob's basic commandments: thou shalt not covet thy fellow mobster's wife. Spilotro did not trouble to conceal his affair with Geri Rosenthal: in his crude way, he flaunted it, and the marriage broke up. Rosenthal went so far as to protest strongly about Spilotro's conduct directly to the mob bosses in Chicago.

Allen Glick was forced to stand down from his position at the Stardust. An operator called Al Sachs (approved by the Gaming Commission over the objections of the Control Board) took over. Slit-eyed, he promised there would be no more 'outside influences'. His management proved no better than Glick's. Another raid on the Stardust in 1983 uncovered new skimming. Four executives were indicted, but not Sachs. This was treated as a narrow tax case. Evidence that the money was being shipped to Chicago was not produced. Sachs' license was revoked. And in 1985 the Stardust and the Fremont were sold to the Boyd Group, a privately held company. The Stardust, in a major redevelopment, has grown and prospered. (Though in my fond recollections, conned as I probably was in the poker games of those days, it will always be Lefty's joint.)

Tony the Ant was left as sole ruler, Las Vegas Boulevard his to command. But the public discrediting of the Stardust, a nadir in Mafia handling of its operations, had left him exposed. He grew flabby and more arrogant, and became mistrustful of his followers.

He became so confident that in 1979 he made a new move, to take over mob operations in Los Angeles. The outfit there was so slack it was known as the Mickey Mouse Mafia. After various ups and downs, including the murder of the elder statesman of the mob in LA, Little Tony got control. A small-time hood described as the Mafia's leading light in San Diego, Chris Petti, took over as his second in command. (His importance emerges a little later in the story.) From being regarded as a gofer for the Chicago mob, a minor player of no great weight, Spilotro was by now recognised, and feared, as the undisputed boss of organised crime in Las Vegas. His picture appeared frequently in the papers and on TV news.

Spilotro, however, broke another Mafia tenet, which proved more serious than his ill-judged liaison with his partner's wife. He failed to take care of his men and their families. One of them, Frank Cullotta, sent to gaol, facing a contract on his life, turned informant in May 1982. In a court appearance in Chicago, Cullotta revealed that he had worked for Spilotro since the 1960s, during which time he had been involved directly or indirectly in 4 murders, more than 200 business burglaries, house burglaries too numerous to mention, and about 25 arson jobs. He had a good memory: in his extensive debriefing, he was able to recall details of more than 50 unsolved executions, mostly in Chicago. Spilotro was implicated in several crimes. In response to all these accusations, Cullotta was described by a Mafia defence lawyer as the vilest piece of scum ever to emerge from the Italian ghetto in Chicago.

Dorfman was gunned down in a Chicago parking lot – the mob was afraid he would blab too much in prison. Glick saw the writing on the wall and turned prosecution witness. Geri Rosenthal fell into bad company and went rapidly downhill: she died later in a drugs coma, aged forty-six.

Spilotro was finally arrested in Vegas in January 1983 and extradited to Chicago, where he was later released on bail. But Cullotta never had to testify in court against his former boss. The same fate overtook Little Tony that he had meted out to so many others. Indeed in Mafia terms, his elimination made perfect sense. His organisation had grown sloppy, he was beset by legal troubles and was suffering the embarrassment of front page exposure in the press. Worst of all – from the mob's point of view – there was a suspicion that he was holding back money creamed in Vegas, which should have gone straight to the Outfit. Word was that he was even challenging for the leadership. One fine morning in June 1986 Spilotro and his brother were seen driving off from his suburban home in Chicago as usual. Nine days later their bodies were accidently uncovered in a cornfield in Indiana (not far from convicted Chicago crime boss Joey Aiuppa's farm.) They had been done to death in characteristically brutal fashion, by blows and kicks. At the time of his death Spilotro was suspect in at least 25 murder cases.

The collapse of the Stardust skim, the subsequent gaoling of the Mafia ringleaders and the downfall of Spilotro knocked the stuffing out of the Chicago operation in Vegas. According to various sources, as reported by the Las Vegas *Review-Journal*, the whole town had become so hot that the crime bosses in Chicago ordered a 'hands off policy'. Other families were allowed to move in and take over the franchise, if one may put it that way, paying dividends to Chicago from their own operations. The family from Buffalo in upstate New York was said to be the dominant presence. On one occasion a number of leading figures from Buffalo were tracked in Vegas, holding a meeting with their partners in crime from New Jersey. Remembering how his hubris brought Spilotro down, the new intake of wise guys kept a low profile. At the height of his notoriety, Spilotro's face was seen in the media almost daily. Now there was no identifiable underworld boss in town.

How far, or for how long, Chicago decided to back off is a matter of speculation. 'I just can't conceive that Chicago would walk away from the gold mine that they had in Las Vegas for decades,' was Roemer's view. 'The Outfit is alive and well,' commented the chief investigator of the Chicago Crime Commission (in 'Mob on the Run'); despite its lack of direction, the mob continued its day to day business in both cities. Its strength came from the old standbys of gambling, labour racketeering, political corruption, burglary and cargo theft. 'The inroads are there, they've been there long before you and I were there,' the supervisor of the Chicago FBI's organised crime squad added.

'Because of pressures, because of convictions, they have retreated. But the initial interest they have had out there has continued.' Many of the people who had moved to Vegas from Chicago years ago were still in place.

Some time after Spilotro's death, Chris Petti, the sidekick whom he had recruited in Los Angeles, was arrested on extortion charges. He had been instructed to collect debts still owed to Spilotro in Vegas. Petti's technique of collection was simple: in one instance, the individual was threatened with having his legs chopped off; another debtor was advised that if he planned to go to Chicago, he had better take the money with him – otherwise, he need not bother to buy a return ticket. The extortion case itself was small-time. The significant thing about it, according to FBI agents, was that it showed that the Chicago outfit still had a structure in place. It so happened the FBI knew all about Petti; he was already the subject of an extensive wire-tap. He was later convicted for violating parole in a bookmaking case. In a report to the Permanent Subcommittee on Investigations of the US Senate in 1988, the FBI stated that the Mafia had been significantly weakened in Las Vegas, but was still involved in gambling, labour benefit and racketeering, narcotics and skimming. In these activities, narcotics was up and skimming was down. Secondary activities included fencing and major thefts, loan-sharking, pornography and prostitution.

In 'Mob on the Run' Ned Day compared the Mafia to an octopus whose tentacles reached out into all sections of society. In the federal wire-taps which exposed widespread corruption at the Tropicana, for example, Harry Reid, the Gaming Commission chairman was given the nickname 'Mr Clean Face' and described by the wise guys as 'bought and paid for'. Reid, who went on to become a Senator for Nevada, defended himself against such slurs, claiming that a lot of names were tossed around. Likewise Bob Miller, then District Attorney, was named in the tapes as a friend of Allen Dorfman, the mob associate who had exploited the pension fund. 'Dorfman was a friend of my late father,' Miller protested. 'Can I choose his friends?' Miller was elected Lieutenant Governor in 1986 and Governor in 1990. But Governor Bob List, who had accepted complimentary services from the Stardust when serving as Attorney-General, including so it was alleged 'booze and broads' parties provided by Lefty, was not re-elected. Senator Cannon, whom Dorfman and Williams were caught on tape conspiring to bribe, failed to secure re-election, after twenty-four years in office. As people like Rosenthal liked to say, defending their murky past, licensed gambling in the silver state grew out of illegal gaming: in that sense, everyone was linked to it, like an archaeological pattern of lines etched into the land.

Ned Day's programme wound up with an optimistic view of Las Vegas. The community had been forced to face the evidence of wrong-doing. It couldn't claim that it was all got up by the press or the feds. The convictions set the stage for the State to take control, with licensing and investigation of new applicants. There was no public relations disaster. On the contrary, the fame of Las Vegas spread wider: 'Las Vegas is poised for a great leap forward into a new golden age of economic prosperity. But the price of the future is never to forget the past.'

What a relief to know that the Outfit was no longer an influence in Vegas, quipped a columnist in the Las Vegas *Review-Journal* after the paper published a series detailing the end of the Mafia. Otherwise people might wonder how it was that a group of alleged Chicago mobsters who pleaded guilty to illegal bookmaking in a recent court case, got their betting line from Las Vegas. One of these people was a close friend of Frank Rosenthal, 'the hatted wonder'. With so many wise guys seeking a life of retirement in Vegas, the *Review-Journal* writer pondered where they might choose to live. He came up with a name – 'La Casa Nostra'. Vegas has been a favourite retreat for people involved in organised crime since the 1940s. 'Many underworld figures, attracted by the entertainment, night life, gambling, and plentiful women, have made Las Vegas their vacation playland', as Bill Friedman put it in *Casino Management*. 'Their presence created a great deal of bad publicity for Las Vegas and the Nevada gaming industry, since every time an underworld figure visited a casino, rumours would spread that he was a "hidden" unlicensed owner.'

In order to reduce this harmful publicity, the Gaming Control Board prohibited licensees from catering to or associating with 'persons of notorious or unsavoury reputation'. But licensees were not given any standards or guidelines to determine who was undesirable. Hence the creation in 1960 of the Black Book. This book contained the pictures, descriptions and criminal records of 11 persons whom licensees were ordered to ban from their premises, under threat of license revocation (Spilotro got listed in 1978). In addition to the casino proper, premises included dining and entertainment facilities, hotel rooms, swimming pools and golf courses. One gentleman of unsavoury reputation who was thrown out of the Desert Inn brought a lawsuit against Gaming Control Board officials and the casino for violating his civil rights. It took some years of litigation before the Nevada Supreme Court finally upheld the State's position that it had authority to prohibit undesirable persons from entering licensed gaming premises. The total listed rose to 16 in 1988, with a further 24 individuals under examination by the enforcement division for possible inclusion. By this time a new provision had been made, granting the right of a hearing to any person whom the board proposed to include. Rosenthal's attorney managed to have his name removed in 1990. 'Frank would like to come back to Nevada and start another business,' he explained. 'He would like to be able to go into a casino again.' However, the Black Book's main value, according to Friedman, was psychological, since most under-world figures had a tremendous fear of publicity. (Considering the celebrated John Gotti and others, this may not always apply).

Gaming licences come under two bodies: The Nevada State Gaming Control Board carries out the actual investigations, dealing at present with about 30 restricted licences a month (for

operating up to 15 slot machines without table games) and
between 12 and 24 full casino licences a year. Final authorisation,
on the basis of the Control Board's recommendations, is given by
a higher level, quasi-judicial body, the Nevada Gaming Commission. Members of both the Commission and the Board are
appointed by the Governor. The Commission also sits as a court:
if the Board finds that a licensee has violated the rules, it
prosecutes the offender before the Commission, which also sets
the penalty if it finds the applicant guilty. The Board employs a
large staff with divisions for tax and licensing, investigation,
enforcement, auditing, security, and economic research.

'The people that were coming to Las Vegas were not bishops of
the church or pillars of the community,' recalled Robbins Cahill,
the first State Regulator of the gaming industry. 'They were
people who were gamblers. They were so happy to be where
gambling was legal.' Cahill, who served from 1945–58, including
a four year term as first Chairman of the Gaming Control Board,
drew a distinction between people with backgrounds as boot-
leggers and gamblers, and people with records as gangsters. 'In
Nevada we had to make that distinction. The person who had
been an illegal gambler was not a gangster in the true sense. All he
wanted to do was come to Nevada and do legally what he had been
doing illegally in other states.' It was from this standpoint that
Cahill came to admire Moe Dalitz, whose activities he had
checked out back in Cleveland. Dalitz was a bootlegger and ran
illegal gaming operations, but the games were clean. 'The guys
from Cleveland were silk glove men.' Cahill gave Dalitz a
favourable recommendation, which allowed him to raise the
money to complete the Desert Inn. 'I think the years have borne
out that Moe Dalitz has done more good for the city of Las Vegas
and done more to build Las Vegas than any single man connected
with the industry,' was Cahill's verdict, looking back at age
eighty-five. He took a different view of Benny Binion. His
criminal record in Texas, Cahill maintains, was so extensive he
should never have been licensed, though he liked the man

personally. Benny's fund of ranching and rustling stories so tickled the other members of the Commission that in the end everyone wanted him licensed, and Cahill had to give way.

Several other states are now experimenting with casino gambling as well as lotteries. Despite the challenge, Nevada will maintain its overwhelming dominance of the industry, affirmed Gaming Commission chairman, John O'Reilly. 'We'll see during the '90s that many of these people who buy lottery tickets throughout the country will find that if they had saved up their dollars, they would have received a much better chance for a return on their money if they had come to Nevada. And they would have gotten a vacation besides.' The upbeat tone of comments by people like O'Reilly, who runs a law office in Las Vegas, shows the commitment of officialdom to the gambling industry – (in marked contrast with the Gaming Board in London, which administers casino gambling as if the whole business gave off a slightly bad odour). But the pro-industry attitude of the Commission has attracted its critics, most outspoken of whom is Professor I. Nelson Rose. 'The fight for regulatory control is almost over – the casinos have won', is the verdict of Professor Rose, whose *Gambling and the Law* is an authoritative treatise on the subject.

Rose, who teaches at Whittier College School of Law in Los Angeles, is an academic with his feet firmly planted on the casino floor. His reinterpretation of the long-standing Californian prohibition against stud poker, on the grounds that this referred to an old Victorian card game which had nothing to do with modern poker, was accepted by the courts, and helped to open the way to a new era of expansion for the card rooms around Los Angeles.

Rose takes a very dim view of the Nevada regulatory bodies. 'It may not seem that way, outside of Nevada, on a case by case basis', argued Rose, in an acerbic review of the past decade in 1990, 'but every year the industry gets a little more of what it wants.' In the coming decade, Rose predicted, the Nevada

Gaming Commission will fade away, while the Nevada Gaming Control Board will be little more than a lobbyist for the casino industry. One of the main reasons, he believes, for the industry's 'regulatory triumph' during the 1990s is the economic turbulence in casino growth. Loosening of the rules – in favour of the casinos in Las Vegas and beyond – will be essential, as competition for the gaming dollar increases.

An example of the kind of thing which particularly incensed Rose was the Control Board's approval of blackjack dealers counting cards. This might seem a small thing to carp about, but it is perhaps symptomatic. The casinos' attempt to foil the counters – players who count down the deck in order to gain an advantage – is part of the cat-and-mouse struggle that goes on at blackjack. (I describe the whole process in *Easy Money*.) The most effective counter-measure, which quick-on-the-draw pit bosses do not hesitate to take, is simply to eject counters from the casino. But a *dealer* counting the deck – what is the motive for that? Either to increase or decrease the house odds, answers Rose, which means either the dealer is working in conspiracy with the house or for himself, perhaps with a player. Either way it is wrong. Yet the chair of the Control Board voiced the opinion that there was nothing illegal about a casino counting cards. This seems disingenuous: it would allow the casino to change the odds in its favour in the middle of a game, which is unfair to players, and certainly not within the law. At the same time, casinos remain free to ban counters from the players' side of the table, at will. Rose castigated this sort of attitude as akin to the Atomic Energy Commission arguing that nuclear plants could set their own safety standards, while claiming at the same time that there was nothing wrong with a little radioactive meltdown anyway.

Professor Rose's ire against the Gaming Control Board was especially aroused by a recent case concerning a nineteen-year-old boy named Kirk Erickson who won a million-dollar jackpot on a slot machine at Caesars, but who was then denied the pay-out because he was under age. When I first heard about this case, though I felt sorry for the boy, it seemed open-and-shut to me. Under Nevada law you can't gamble if you are under twenty-one; so if you do, and get caught, hard luck. That was not Rose's view, as Counsel for the Erickson family, which petitioned for judicial review against Caesars and the Control Board. The case came before the Supreme Court of Nevada in 1989. Rose's argument, in brief, was this: When the family checked into Caesars, nothing was ever mentioned to the boy, his younger sister or parents about the legal age of gambling in Nevada, nor were any signs that you had to be twenty-one to gamble seen anywhere by the party, nor was it mentioned in the closed-circuit TV presentation explaining various casino games. Caesars sold the young man tokens to gamble at least six times. (In Arkansas, where they came from, gambling is legal at eighteen.)

Kirk and his parents played 'Million Dollar Baby' slot machines, trading machines with each other; Kirk happened to be the one who pulled the handle when a big jackpot was hit. Kirk and his father pushed the call button for an attendant. When it was confirmed that Kirk was the player who had pulled the handle (all the action in casinos is recorded on video), Caesars ruled that it was not required to pay because he was a minor. The Gaming Control Board supported the decision. The case came down to a single question, according to Rose: when a minor wins a legal slot machine bet from a licensed casino can he collect under Nevada law? If state law and case law requires the casino to pay the winnings, then the decision of the Board was incorrect as a matter of law and must be overturned.

In refusing to address the issues of due process, Rose argued, 'the Board abused its discretion and again showed that it is a captive regulator, more concerned with keeping the casinos happy than with really regulating them'. Rose quoted a comment on regulatory bodies by Justice Douglas in a case in 1972 as directly applicable: 'The . . . agencies of which I speak are not venal or corrupt. But they are notoriously under the control of powerful interests who manipulate them through advisory

committees, or friendly working relations, or who have that
natural affinity with the agency which in time develops between
the regulator and the regulated.' The Board was not a dis-
interested, neutral policymaker. Its informal, unwritten, un-
publicised policy giving casinos unlimited powers to decide when
they would pay minors their winnings and when they would not
was a classic example of a decision made in favour of casinos and
against the players. When a minor loses, Caesars keeps his
money; when a minor wins, Caesars keeps his money. And when
Caesars gets caught gambling with minors, it pays no fine. 'The
laws prohibiting minors from gambling are to protect minors, not
to allow Caesars to exploit children and take their money,' Rose
fulminated. 'This is not gambling, it is cheating, it is fraud. It is
theft.'

It was not surprising that this argument did not wash with the
Gaming Control Board. It turned out that Erickson Senior had
claimed, when first questioned, that he had pulled the handle
himself; it was only the evidence of the video camera which
persuaded him to admit that his son had hit the jackpot – which
seems to imply that the family did know what it was doing. In a
further petition for judicial review, the Supreme Court of Nevada
upheld the original judgement.* It was an interesting case. If the
Erickson family was disingenuous in claiming ignorance of the
law, it is also true that the casinos do not trumpet the fact that
minors are not allowed to gamble. In practice (so I would judge)
the casinos might put it this way: Folks come here to gamble and
have a good time. We're not going to ask every kid for his driver's
license, they're supposed to know the law. If they win a few
bucks, good luck. Who's to say if some strapping great fellow is
twenty or twenty-one? We'd rather they spent their money in our
place than go across the street. But writing out cheques for a
million dollars . . . You gotta be kidding!

*The Ericksons finally lost their case when the Federal Judicial Appellate
court in San Francisco dismissed their claim.

Certainly the gaming industry needs to be well regulated, on behalf of society as a whole, but primarily to protect people who gamble. Even an illegal gambling operation, it has been pointed out, unlike other criminal activity, has to be run properly. The adherents of organised crime already control most of the illegal gambling in the United States. Whatever the extent of illegal gambling (estimated at one-fifth of the total revenues from legal gambling) Vegas is never going to lose its attraction for such operators. It is too rich and too efficient and too tempting. Having met and talked to some of the people working in the regulatory agencies, I felt that any wholesale dismissal of their role and effectiveness was unfair and certainly exaggerated. What is notable is that reaction to specific problems, as they arose, has been the pattern of Nevada licensing. At no time since 1959 has either the Gaming Control Act or the Nevada Gaming Regulations been subject to comprehensive overall revision.

Two dominant theories of the regulatory agency are held in economics, notes a recent study of casino regulation, *An Economic View of the Nevada Gaming Licensing Process*, by Anthony Cabot and Richard Schuetz. The 'public interest' theory holds that regulation is to control the market, and the 'capture' theory that regulation serves the interest groups involved. Among economists who support the latter view was John Kenneth Galbraith, who wrote in 1954, referring to the Securities and Exchange Commission: 'regulatory bodies, like the people who comprise them, have a marked life cycle. In youth they are vigorous, aggressive, evangelistic, and even intolerant. Later they mellow, and in old age – after a matter of ten or fifteen years – they become, with some exceptions, either an arm of the industry they are regulating, or senile.'

The main point made by Cabot and Schuetz is that the Nevada licensing process is in itself the greatest barrier to entry into the casino industry because it is so expensive for the applicants. The onerous process of licensing would seem to bear out the 'public interest' theory of regulation, insofar as it obviates federal intervention and ensures honest gaming. On the 'capture' model, it obviously benefits the existing casinos, though they display little interest in such theoretical issues. On the other hand, the elaboration of licensing can be seen as serving the interest of the regulatory agency, whose expansion and extra personnel are largely paid for by the applicants themselves, rather than from public funds.

During the 1950s the criteria for licensing were fairly simple. The Nevada legislature decided that the following types of applicant were unsuitable: (1) persons convicted of a felony, larceny, narcotics violation or firearms violation within the past five years; (2) persons under 21; and (3) aliens. These guidelines were of questionable use, adds the Cabot and Schuetz commentary, because many crime figures would not have faced a felony conviction or could use front men. So the criteria were abandoned in favour of greater administrative discretion, involving consideration of business probity and financial standing. Through the 1960s and '70s the major focus was on keeping organised crime out of gaming. This was achieved by requiring all casino operators to be licensed: the concern was to block criminal infiltration, on principle, not whether the gaming was honestly run or taxes duly collected. In fact, as Robbins Cahill noted, shady operators, aware of their reputation, might have been even more careful to conduct their business properly. Gradually, as people deemed to be unsuitable found alternative employment in the industry, the regulators required other personnel to be licensed – such as landlords, lenders, junket reps, equipment manufacturers, loan brokers, union officials and people doing business on casino premises.

Thus, beginning in the 1970s, the view of the 'unsuitable' applicant began to go beyond an overt association with organised crime. It made an assessment of bad character. In 1973 the Board set out its licensing guidelines. They included (a) conviction of a felony or misdemeanour involving violence, gambling or moral turpitude; (b) an unexplained pattern of arrests; and (c) a failure to prove good character, honesty and integrity. Another criterion was conduct reflecting discredit upon the State of Nevada or the gaming industry. 'Since 1983, there have not been any serious allegations of significant infiltration of the criminal element nor the slightest hint of potential federal intervention', conclude Cabot and Schuetz. The agencies, therefore, have done their job. But within this process, they add, 'there are risks of capture, agency-generated growth and lethargy.'

In Rose's considered view, the cause of greatest concern in Nevada's regulatory system is its mixing of functions. Only in the world of gambling control, he wrote in *Gambling and the Law*, would you find the same administrative body bringing the initial charges, conducting the investigation, prosecuting the complaint, making the rules for the hearing, judging the hearing, ruling on the case, hearing the appeal of the ruling, deciding on the punishment, and enforcing the decision. 'The gaming boards in Nevada are more than judge and jury, they are judge, jury, prosecutor, police, appellate court and executioner.' As for protection of the public, no provisions are made for setting odds, rates of payout, minimum and maximum betting limits, hours of casino operation or other factors directly related to the impact a casino will have on the people it is designed to attract.* The Nevada authorities, adds Rose, believe that the competition created by the free enterprise system ensures that the public will be treated fairly. This may be true for sophisticated gamblers who know what it means when a casino offers, say, single, double or triple odds at craps. But it is no protection to the amateur or the compulsive gambler.

Steve Wynn, taking a practical view based on long experience of the industry, holds that only those kind of people who were drawn, one way or another, towards the Mafia ever got involved; that is, they were asking to get involved. In the old days, his

---

*Among various technical requirements, I am glad to note that the maximum 'rake' (house cut) at poker is limited to 10 per cent.

mentor E. Parry Thomas, the banker, got his funds from the Mormons. He was never involved with criminal elements, insisted Wynn. Thomas himself explained his policy as a banker by saying he would accept investment from the devil himself if it was legal. By the time Wynn came into the casino business, in 1967, there were only isolated instances of Mafia ownership. As for criminal penetration of casino ancillary services, like food and wine purveyors, Wynn says he has never encountered a hint of it. It's always in the air, though. To take a recent instance, Wynn showed no hesitation in standing up for one of his casino hosts, despite an FBI investigation which showed that the man had a very dubious record, and had been comping players at the Mirage known to be mob associates. He believes that talk of Mafia involvement reflects in part the desire of law enforcement agencies to build themselves up. 'Anyway, Las Vegas gets glamourised. We don't want to look like Des Moines, do we?'

CONCLUSION
Beyond the Pleasuredome

You see things: and you say 'Why?' But I dream
things that never were and I say. 'Why not?'

The Serpent to Eve in *Back to Methuselah*,
George Bernard Shaw

Out on the west side of Las Vegas, on the rocky plain leading up to
Red Rock Canyon and the Spring Mountains which ring the
horizon, is a new kind of development, which runs for mile after
mile after mile, like new housing built on the moon. These houses
stand in clusters, desert-yellow brick under terracotta-red roofs,
all new, clean, silent, a seemingly endless embroidery fringing the
edge of the desert. These new communities for the new Las Vegas
bear poetic names, like Spring Rainbow, or Mountain Shadows;
mile upon mile of sun-kissed dwellings which bespeak peace,
purity, order and, of course, the money to enjoy them.

These houses are where the new arrivals, 5–6,000 a month at
the turn of the new decade, drawn to the bright lights and greener
bucks of the casino industry, will come to live, to settle down and
make a new life. The stillness and elegant repetition of these
homes, in a southern design sometimes known as Spanish
Colonial, offers a soothing contrast to the ceaseless moil and toil
of the casinos in which the house-owners earn their livelihood.
Such houses are probably a third or half the prices of Southern
California. The new housing is part of a development by the
Summa Corporation to transform 39 square miles of desert into a

living, thriving community, complete with golf courses, business parks and schools. The plan is for 30 'villages' with a total of 80,000 homes, a project which will run well into the 21st century before it is finished. The Summerlin project is part of Las Vegas' answer to its extraordinary expansion. No town in the United States, perhaps no town anywhere, has grown from virtually nothing to nearly a million in so short a time.

'Yes, we are an example to the nation,' says Thomas Graham, director of Design and Development at City Hall. Graham sets out his hopes for the city in precise terms, as befits a town planner, but has the enthusiastic commitment of an artist, an impression heightened by his long beard and long brown hair, hippie-style. His desk is a hollowed-out black grand piano, his office an art deco dream, the walls lined with futuristic landscapes of a shiny, space-age city, the new Jerusalem as conceived by his own design team. Graham, who grew up in a pre-revolutionary small town in Pennsylvania, comes from sturdy Scots ancestry. He studied classical architecture for a year in Florence, and could command a job in any city architect's office in America, but he is possessed by a vision of Las Vegas. His vision is focused, first, on the downtown area, which as everyone knows is in trouble. It is old, it is seedy, it is not like the Strip. 'We are in better shape than people perceive us to be, the basic concept is sound,' Graham maintains. 'Every metropolitan centre in the country faces similar problems of blight. This is what happens when you go from a watering hole to a city approaching a million people.' Downtown, in his view, is merely going through a traditional cycle. But it has two basic advantages: it is at the crossroads of the freeways, connecting the interstate roads system like the bloodlines on your hand; secondly, the downtown casinos, which are close together – and ought ideally to be in a pedestrian precinct – remain highly profitable.

The downtown casino operators themselves are desperately searching for a new theme, to rescue the area. 'We need a volcano,' they say, looking wistfully to the example of the Mirage.

Wynn, a leading light in Glitter Gulch as owner of the Golden Nugget, came up with a bizarre suggestion: *canals*, Venetian-style. Despite the water shortage, it was a serious suggestion, not just a way of provoking debate. Wynn's design people built a huge scale model, showing what the downtown properties would look like, lapped by blue water. It was impressive, as even an old-style owner like Jack Binion admitted – but a bit too risky. What would happen if you ripped up all the streets and then found the canals idea didn't work out? Another idea now under study is for a giant awning over Fremont Street, to turn the area into a kind of mall of gambling: the awning would provide shade by day and allow light and laser projections at night. Everyone agrees that something needs to be done. The downtown casinos have been hit by the opening of local casinos on the edge of the freeway. People living in the valley have no need to go all the way in to spend their leisure time, when they can drive straight into the Palace Station at the Sahara exit, or the Gold Coast and Rio at the Flamingo exit, or Sam's Town, a western-style outfit on the other side of town on Boulder Highway, or the Sante Fe on the road out to Reno.

For Graham, taking an architectural overview, the key is transportation. He maintains that downtown has not yet capitalised on its advantages, its link to the freeways and the proximity of the 14 or 15 casinos which comprise its core. In addition, there is the huge 320-acre Union Pacific railroad yard standing empty, behind the Union Plaza. This site, when it is eventually sold, offers an unparalleled scope for new housing, casinos and leisure pursuits, tripling or quadrupling the down-town area. Such a development, which should begin in the next year or two, could give downtown a new thrust and identity, if it's done well. It's a design problem, which needs another Wynn behind it, not an urban development problem, insists Graham. Downtown is not a blighted area: the casinos may be squeezed but they are not losing money. The concept which Graham cherishes – his dream – was inspired by a vision of transport. New, space-age transport, as reflected in the gleam of futuristic drawings on his office walls (over the caption of dreaming about things that never were, cited above). There were two schemes: inner and outer. Neither has happened yet.

Inwards, the idea was to link the downtown area with Cashman Field, the baseball ground and convention centre, by a new kind of vehicle, magnetically levitated, electromagnetically propelled, running on a monorail. A worldwide search for a new system led to a contract with a German firm, which invested half a billion dollars in the scheme. In design it looked truly wonderful – a sleek, fast-moving train, without wheels, suspended by magnetic force from its monorail, driven silently and cleanly and cheaply by electric power. Graham rode the prototype in Germany at 225 miles an hour, and was thrilled. 'The invention of transport without the wheel is as significant a development in the history of man as was the invention of the wheel itself,' he enthuses. Soon pylons were planted down Las Vegas Boulevard South, all the way out to Cashman Field, to carry the monorail. It was costing the city nothing because the manufacturer was paying for it all.

Outwards, the idea was to construct a high-speed train which would whoosh people from Southern California right into downtown Las Vegas, inside say sixty or seventy minutes. Quicker and far more convenient than flying, given the hassle of driving in and out to the airport. Downtown, the monorail system would have carried the travellers on, on lines radiating out to the new communities in the valley. From an environmental point of view, and from an architectural point of view, the whole scheme was a dream. There was just one snag. The snag was that to pay, the monorail had to be extended down the Strip and out to McCarran airport, which in turn required the approval of Clark County. And the Strip casinos did not like the idea of thousands of customers speeding by their properties, heading some place else. They turned it down. 'I lost ten years of my working life on this plan,' Graham laments. The high speed rail link is unlikely to be built either. The financial backing is not there. Then came the Gulf War, and the recession. Graham chooses a fitting western image to express the collapse of these projects. 'We were pioneers that got out too far ahead. We had to be more like scouts. We had to come back to the wagon team, and then lead them forward.'

A realist as well as a dreamer, Graham is not giving up. He regards detailed financial planning as a challenge, as much a part of the creative process as designing new buildings. He has succeeded in erecting one building which aptly reflects his enthusiasm, the grandly named Downtown Transportation Center. This is a small and elegant bus station. Clean and unfussy, compared with the dismal transport terminals of most cities, it offers an open welcome to new arrivals. Originally it was intended as a cornerstone of the city's 'second evolution of growth', to be combined with a city marketplace and festival plaza. This scheme for what was termed a 'cultural-entertainment' corridor around the bus station has not yet happened. Nevertheless, the Downtown Transportation Center demonstrates Graham's basic precept: that because the growth of cities has been dictated by the automobile, not by architects and designers, the top priority in urban planning must be to balance the automobile with human values. He works closely and energetically with City Hall. He sees Las Vegas becoming recognised as a leader in urban design, a city which in barely fifty years has handled unparalleled growth, attracting new people, giving them work, housing them, entertaining them.

Architecture is frozen music, Graham likes to say. Its rhythms and themes are expressed in concrete and steel, its rest bars are the spaces between buildings; his role is to conduct the orchestra or talents which are available to City Hall. One day, the melody of transport and buildings will play against the steady bass of the desert and the mountains in the background to produce a new harmony downtown. 'Vegas isn't burdened by the past, there isn't enough past to weigh it down. It can't follow classical rules, it evokes new rules.'

An instance of what can go wrong when a gambling town runs too fast for its own good is close to hand, ninety miles south of Las Vegas. If you drive past the chemical blight of Henderson, down the narrow highway of US 95, past a long stretch of rocky desert you get to a new, baby-size version of Las Vegas: Laughlin, Nevada, population 6,200, hotel rooms 8,100 (1991). A few years ago Laughlin wasn't even on the map. It sprang out of nowhere, on the Nevada border with Arizona, along a bare stretch of the Colorado river, like a cactus out of the rock. All there was to see on this desolate stretch of desert was a derelict motel and bar. It is now the fourth largest gambling town in the United States, after Las Vegas, Atlantic City and Reno, having overtaken Lake Tahoe at the northern end of the State.

Laughlin offers a snapshot of a gamblin' town in the making, not quite like Vegas the way it was, more of a mining camp after the first lucky strike – a mining town plus neon lights. The strike was aimed at Arizonan gold, at all the folks over there, home on the range, looking for fun and games and the bright lights. Why drive all the way in from Phoenix and up to Vegas for a good time when there was a ready-made gambling town just over the river? Night after night, fairy lights twinkle under the desert sky, eclipsing the stars, outlining in silhouette a riverboat steamer with paddle wheel, the Colorado Belle, and reflecting in the shining water the crazy colours of the casinos. Strains of music, shouts and laughter, the sound of action, drift out over the river. Fleets of gaily lit flat-bottomed boats are waiting to ferry the folks across. How could it miss? We're not talking about nickels and dimes, as in some crossroads township in the wastes of the desert. Despite its bleak location, the gross income of Laughlin's nine casinos in 1989 was over $455m., leaving a net profit of $44.8m. after tax. (Though this sizable sum was 35 per cent down on the year before, due to the recession.) The upward growth in profits is expected to be no more than a pause, as Laughlin girds itself for the next leap forward. Most of the major casino groups are in on the new game.

Laughlin (pronounced Lofflin) took its name, or rather was

given its name, by one Dan Laughlin. Now turned sixty, Laughlin is one of those fast-talking, high-rolling dudes who came out from the east as a brash young man to make his name and fortune, and damn near won the West – a vanishing breed in these days of button-down accountants. He's worth many millions now, maybe a quarter of a billion, but all he had going for him when he started out on this venture was a bright idea. It was from the air that Laughlin prospected his strike. Flying over this stretch of barren land below Davis Dam, one fine day back in 1966, the river marking the border between Nevada and Arizona caught Laughlin's eye: gambling was legal in Nevada but not in Arizona. Dan Laughlin's bright idea was to bring the two together. He bought the disused motel and bar, which was all there was down there, for a down payment of $35,000. 'Naming the place Laughlin wasn't my idea,' he claims. 'The postal inspector said the name I chose, Casino, had been used enough already, so why not give it a good Irish name, like Laughlin? So that was it.'

Dan has always been a gambling man. He quit school back in Minnesota when he was caught running slot machines. He had bought his first slot machine from a mail order catalogue, and by the time he was in ninth grade was making $600 a week from half a dozen machines, placed in stores and taverns around town. He moved to Las Vegas, went to dealer's school, saved money and at age twenty-three bought a restaurant and bar, which ten years later he sold for a ten-fold profit. This provided the grub-stake for his venture into the southern desert. It wasn't long before he opened the Riverside Resort Hotel and Casino. For the first few years he couldn't raise a bank loan (this was before the banks latched on to the casino business) but the place was a hit from the start. The ferries plied all night, bringing eager gamblers over from Bullhead City, the hick Arizona township across the river, and then ferrying them back again in the morning, their pockets emptied. Later on, Laughlin used his money and clout to pay for a new bridge leading straight up to the Riverside, and donated it to the County. His 'gift' pre-empted construction of a new bridge at a less favourable point. Now the traffic streams in all day, much of it RVs, bound for the casinos' vast Recreational Vehicles parks.

For Laughlin is essentially a 'low rollers' resort, a place for senior citizens to park themselves in the winter months, hook up their mammoth vehicles to water and electricity lines, and then . . . misspend their declining years! And why not? It's cheap, it's warm, and their kids are all grown up, busy raising their own families. It's a lot more fun playing the slots and meeting other oldsters for an 'All you c'n eat chicken buffet' price $2.49 than sitting around the porch back home. (Alert to the interests of the older generation, the Riverside once advertised regular Sunday talks on the problems of arthritis.) By happy chance, Dan Laughlin had solved the problem of how grandparents can while away the long days of retirement: recreational gambling. I recall a grey-haired but gamesome lady in a low stakes poker game in Sam's Gold River confiding to me: 'I wish I could catch me a pair of aces.'

'You've got to live right to get aces,' I responded with the old poker saying.

She gave me a look over her granny specs: 'Then I guess I'm never gonna git 'em!'

After the Riverside, half a dozen other places started up. Along the barren shoreline stands a gaudy line of casinos, flashing out their wares. They include, beyond the Riverside, the 2,000 room Flamingo Hilton, the Edgewater and Colorado Belle both run by Circus Circus, the Ramada Express with a front designed like an old railway station just above, the Golden Nugget, and Sam's Gold River owned by the Midby Group, which also launched the Emerald River. This project ran out of money after a golf course and hotel tower were completed, and is now in bankruptcy, underlining the dangers of over-rapid growth.

What made it all possible is the Colorado river, which brightens and lightens what would otherwise be a harsh and utterly inhospitable rocky waste. Dan Laughlin is not thrown by all the competition. For one thing, the Riverside – run by his son Don as vice-president – has the best location. For another, he has plenty of things to keep him amused – like his 61,000-acre ranch in Arizona, with 1,400 head of cattle, which provides all the steaks for his casino restaurant. He is also fond of ballroom dancing. When he sets out on the dance-floor with his chief cocktail waitress as partner a drum roll salutes the first couple of Laughlin. His son Don is not exactly a chip off the old block. A quietly spoken family man, he frankly regrets not having spent more time at university, acquiring a wider education. The company is family run and family owned, with no plans as yet to go public. What happens when Don disagrees with Dan about casino policy? Don smiles. 'We get along pretty well, but I guess Dad usually gets his way as senior partner.' Dad gets his way on most things, including one or two run-ins with the Gaming Control Board. Family troubles arose when a first cousin, working as manager at the Riverside, had his licence suspended in 1989 for alleged facilitation of cocaine dealing out of the casino. Dan dismissed the charges as a smear campaign. There have also been technical disputes, such as failing to update properly the names on the Riverside licence after he bought out his former wife's share for $500,000.

The town of Laughlin is continuing to boom, but the social and environmental problems caused by its over-rapid growth are acute. So many people have been moving in that water supplies are stretched to the limit. There is a school but medical treatment and other services are out of town. Housing for casino employees cannot be built fast enough. Facing all these problems, the town planners have dithered and delayed, with no overall plan of development. Who cares about the future when the present is so much fun, when everyone is having such a good time, making so much money?

One man who seems intent on both spending, and making, more money than anyone else in Vegas in the years ahead is Kirk

Kerkorian. I got that impression from the way men were digging up trees from the rolling green sward of his new property. 'We've got $4 million worth of trees out there. We're moving them all, at a cost of $1.8m.,' said Bob Maxey, in a tone which implied that if you look after the pennies, the millions will take care of themselves. 'Then we'll move them all back in.' We were looking out at the former Tropicana golf course from the site office of Kerkorian's new project, the *new* MGM Grand. The new MGM, a 5,000 room casino-hotel plus theme park, is going to cost an estimated $750m., probably nearer a billion, give or take a few sundries. Maxey is an old casino hand, a specialist on start-up operations. I asked him why Kerkorian, a man in his seventies, with everything he wants and a lifetime of achievement, should want to undertake such a huge new project in Las Vegas. 'Kerkorian doesn't think of himself as old. He plays tennis every day. He's energetic, he's interested, he doesn't look seventy. You'd think he was my brother. He believes he can do it.'

'Kerkorian is a man who stays above all the noise,' says Larry Woolf, who was brought back from 'exile' at Caesars Tahoe to head the MGM team. An amusing and talented man, as happy to direct a multimillion casino as make up the numbers in a five dollar poker game, Woolf's first job was as a guest room attendant in Elko, Nevada. He rose from dealer to casino manager at Harrah's in Reno by the age of thirty; if he had taught American history, as he intended at university, his salary by that time would have been $7,000 a year; now it is into six figures. 'Kerkorian has wonderful judgement of what a business is worth,' explains Woolf. 'Whether it's an airline or an automobile company or a casino, he knows exactly the right price to buy or sell. When the price is right, it's Win, Win, Win! No risk. Zero. Zip. Airlines and movies are very like casinos. In a good year, there's no upside limit, they just take off. Even in a bad year, they look to get better.' For example, Kerkorian bought the Sands and Desert Inn for $160m. in 1981 and sold the Sands for $110m. Woolf was moved across to revive the Desert Inn, which Kirk Kerkorian later bought for $130m. for his private company, the proceeds going to MGM.

There is gossip around town that Kerkorian will not be able to raise the money and the new project will never get off the drawing board. Maxey dismisses such rumours, claiming the company has the strongest balance sheet in the industry, with a debt to equity ratio of only 15 per cent. Kerkorian was also in dispute with Disney over the right to the name MGM. It is not a fast-track job. According to Maxey, it will take two years from approval of all the plans, a stage which was still some way from completion when we talked in spring 1991. The MGM is expected to open early in 1994.

'Our basic reason for feeling confident is that we believe Las Vegas can sustain its growth,' Maxey said. 'Entertainment is a different business today from twenty years ago. The market is so deep you can't even plumb its depths. Vegas has had a 12 per cent compounded annual growth. It goes up in sudden jumps as new properties are opened and new capacity is created. And then there's a pause when revenue seems to slow down. But if you draw a straight line you can see it's onward and upward, compound growth, all the way.' In conception, the MGM Grand is impressive. For one thing the site, at 120 acres, is extremely big. By way of comparison, Maxey gestured towards the mammoth-sized property of the Excalibur, a golf shot across the fairway of uprooted trees, and then jabbed his finger down on the blueprint of the MGM lay-out: the Excalibur would seem to fill hardly more than a couple of bunkers on the MGM plan. The theme park will be its great draw, containing a variety of attractions in the style of a Hollywood back lot. 'Everyone who comes to town will have to see it, everyone who lives here will bring their families and their friends. It's going to cost $120m. and be as big as Disneyland. Can you imagine people coming to Vegas and then going back home to Des Moines and saying: "We didn't see the MGM?" I don't think,' Maxey chose his words, 'that some little old "volcano" is gonna provide much competition.'

But where are all the new customers to come from? The hotel will have 5,000 rooms – it will be the largest in the world. Maxey listed five segments the MGM will draw on. They are (not necessarily in order of importance): (1) The tour and travel market; people on a three-and-a-half-day excursion to Vegas – 'Our product hits them right between the eyes.' (2) The convention market: the MGM will aim for it indirectly, with its 15,000-seat stadium. (3) The 'free and independent traveller': lawyers, engineers, the kind of people who make their own travel arrangements, who might fly or drive to Vegas half a dozen times a year – and who pay full retail prices. (4) The high roller market: this is an expensive sector to attract, limited perhaps to 300,000 people in the USA; exciting because the main if not sole purpose of these guests is high stakes gambling. (5) Local business: with a population heading towards a million, Vegas itself has become a viable base for customers, especially during week-days when the crowds are missing. 'The synergism of energy from all the MGM's attractions makes it bound to succeed.' 'And what about Europe?' I suggest. With cheap fares, it is almost as economical for someone (like myself) living in London to take a vacation in Vegas as it is to fly to Rome or Nice. Bob Maxey's eyes light up like a slot machine.

Entrance to the MGM theme park, through the Emerald City of the Wizard of Oz, will be off the main highway, Las Vegas Boulevard, in order to give easy access to families and children. It is expected to handle from 9,000 to 15,000 visitors a day. As a family-style entertainment, the theme park will stand on its own, separate from the casino (itself twice as big as anything that exists today). The casino in turn will be linked on the far side to the hotel complex, fanning out from the opposite, north-west corner of the site. In the middle will be the pool, sports arena and theatre. The advance notices sound great. If the Mirage began the post-modernist phase in Las Vegas in November, 1989, then the MGM Grand, if it is built as planned, will complete it. In practice, it all depends, Maxey admitted, on how well the theme park is realised. Assuming it all works out, the centre of attraction of Las Vegas will tilt – sharply and dramatically – to its southern end, away from the traditional casinos of the Strip and Glitter Gulch. If, that is, Kerkorian's ambition in deed proves as good as it looks on paper. The test of the new MGM is yet to come.

A similarly optimistic view of Vegas' future is taken by one of the brightest people in the industry, Glenn Schaeffer, chief financial officer of Circus Circus Enterprises. 'We are not in the gambling market any more,' says Schaeffer. 'We are in the tourism business. We are selling entertainment, an environment to have fun in. Our customers come here to visit the fun house. What people are really doing, sitting at a slot machine, is buying time.' Schaeffer, in his mid-forties, came to casinos via the hotel business in Phoenix. Appointed to take over as president in 1991 by the man who built up the company, William Bennett, he has a good overview of the industry – as can be seen in the colourful annual reports of Circus Circus.

Schaeffer is bullish about the prospects for the year 2000. 'Las Vegas is becoming a principal destination resort like Orlando, Florida. And the demographics are exciting. We are in a super region. The seventh largest economy in the world is 250 miles from us. California is now the immigration point for this country. People are coming in from the Pacific, whereas they used to come from the Atlantic. That's good for our business.' In addition, he cites other growth points. 'The generation of baby-boomers is now in its thirties and forties. It's looking for entertainment. The affluent elderly have become a new class. They have play money, beyond their living needs. They are moving into booming desert communities.' What about the falling share prices of casino stocks? Schaeffer observes cheerfully: 'The Wall Street people are wishing their woes on the rest of America. All those grungy, dark buildings in New York! It's not like that out here. We see a consistent growth market, with more and more entertainment.'

Circus Circus and Excalibur are particularly well placed, because they 'control' the freeway exits, where 40 per cent of the traffic comes in. 'We own the most land and parking. The Strip is

2.2 miles long between our two properties. It's a mall. The only original building in the United States in the last fifty years is the suburban shopping mall,' Schaeffer enthuses. 'The question is: how do you tap this?' Despite all the expansion in Vegas, the company is actively looking for new projects, either by developing a new themed entertainment on its frontage on the Strip or by taking over properties in trouble. 'So many people have not taken a vacation in Las Vegas, they will surely come. We are building a "must see" resort here.' To exploit its site at the southern end of the Strip – 'the number one corner for tourism in the world' – the company decided to build a new theme-casino in the shape of a 30-storey pyramid, called Luxor. This play-version of ancient Egypt, costing $300m., is to include a full scale reproduction of King Tut's tomb; hotel guests will be ferried to the 2,500 rooms over the 'river Nile'. Opening is set for October, 1993. Not to be outdone, Circus Circus is tacking on a five-acre water theme park, Grand Slam Canyon, at the other end of the Strip.

Things can go wrong. 'In the 1960s and 1970s, a lot of people thought casinos were immune from downturns in the general economy: Nevada's gross gaming revenue appeared to grow regardless of ups and downs in the economic cycle,' noted Eugene Martin Christiansen, the industry's leading financial analyst. 'It may be, however, that gaming's apparent immunity from hard times was simply a reflection of a grossly under-supplied market. In those days Nevada had the only legal casinos in North America, the major competing gambling industry, pari-mutuel racing, was mature, and lotteries were not really a factor until the late 1970s.'

The US wagering economy is very different today, Christiansen points out. Lotteries won $9.6 billion in 1989 compared with $7.8 billion for casinos. Aggregate gross gambling revenue from legal games – pari-mutuels, bingo, lotteries, charitable games, Indian reservation gambling, everything combined – totalled $23.5 billion; casinos had a relatively large share (25.5 per cent) but they were not the whole show by any means, or even the biggest part of it. Lotteries were. The experience of Atlantic City, whose troubles are deepening, and of Las Vegas, which is attracting new players, Christiansen maintains, shows the great value of entertainment. 'Casino games and non-gaming entertainment enjoy a symbiotic relationship. The games generate immediate revenue, and in the short-term non-gaming entertainment may look like costly overhead. It is not. Non-gaming entertainment values are the essential difference between Las Vegas and Atlantic City.' He predicts that because Las Vegas offers more than casinos it will prosper in the recessionary, more competitive environment of the 1990s.

But although legal gambling continued to spread across the United States at the start of the new decade, no one can be sure how far it will go. Could the trend indeed be reversed if the public was seized by a sudden change of heart? If there was a reversal of moral attitudes? One man who thinks so is Nelson Rose. Looking ahead, taking a historical perspective, he detects 'a whiff of a backlash' at this 'morally suspect' industry. Rose, who likes to strike a slightly puckish note, believes that there will, inevitably, be a swing back away from gambling in the next generation, beyond the year 2000. What he calls 'the third wave of legal gambling' is now sweeping the country, which will be followed by a crash.

The immediate future is for more gambling, more video lotteries, more sweepstakes, more television game shows with phone-in callers, he wrote in *Gambling and the Law*. But the public's desire to gamble will run into more and more legal barriers, set in the previous century. Rose sees the boom and bust of legalised gambling running in seventy year cycles. The first wave came with the American colonies, which were actually founded by lotteries. By the 1820s and '30s lotteries were held in general disrepute. The first crash, by his reckoning, came in the 1820s, ending in a nationwide prohibition on gambling and a tangle of legal debris and anomalies. The second wave came with the Civil War and the expansion of the western frontier. The crash followed in the 1890s, with another nation-wide ban. By 1910 only two States allowed betting, limited to horse racing; even Nevada outlawed all forms of gambling.

The third and current wave began with the Depression. In the 1930s Nevada re-legalised casinos, and twenty-one States opened race tracks. Bingo and social gambling began to be legalised in the 1950s. Today legal gambling is the nation's fastest growing industry. In America legal gambling always self-destructs after a few decades, Rose maintains. 'Perhaps it is our frontier mentality; Americans are always flip-flopping between having the law simply outlaw what everyone agrees is illegal, like murder, and trying to enforce morality, like Prohibition.' The crash will come when the general public comes to feel it's all too much. If the public approval of gambling is changed, it will probably be by scandals, which are likely to occur (human nature being what it is) in the State lotteries; a process which may be speeded up by trouble elsewhere, in sports betting, for example, where the temptation to fix results will descend even to amateur sports, as betting outlets proliferate. If at the same time the nation is experiencing a rebirth of conservative morality, legal gambling will perish, concludes Rose.

I must say there is not the faintest sign of such a change of mood in Las Vegas: what is certainly true of Atlantic City – a surfeit of facilities – has not caused any self-doubts on the Strip, only a determination to step up the appeal. Smaller, less well financed properties will be squeezed out; and down in Laughlin a prudent reassessment of its headlong growth is under way. A decision by Wynn in early 1991, not to proceed with the Golden Nugget's plans to build in Laughlin, points to a period of consolidation. The spread of legal gambling, and especially state lotteries with their gigantic prizes, remains a potential threat to Vegas, but (in most expert opinion) more apparent than real. Riverboat gambling in Mississippi or video poker machines in Deadwood, South Dakota, have local appeal. But they cannot possibly pack the entertainment punch of the capital of gambling.

One can imagine (among many other possible changes) a reborn morality sweeping the nation in the next century, say in the year 2010. Atlantic City is merely an experiment, and when experiments fail they are quickly discarded. But even if a national move against gambling were to develop, southern Nevada could hold out – unless a social and political campaign to outlaw gambling induced Congress to prohibit it completely. That was of course Las Vegas' fear in the 1950s. Rose predicts that a hundred years from today most of the gambling we see now will once again be suppressed, because of the historical swing. (Unfortunately none of us are likely to be around to verify that judgement.) My own guess is that once gambling, like sex, is out of the bag, it won't easily be put back in. People will always gamble, as they always have in the past, and Las Vegas will be there, ready to roll.

The biggest night of the year in Vegas is New Year's Eve. The blaring noise of hundreds of penny trumpets fills the air as the whole town turns into a party. The Casino Center downtown is blocked to traffic; all the Strip casinos put on special shows. The revellers in the streets are decked with paper hats and cut-out tiaras; they wave hot-dogs and beer cans, chant and sing. New Year is the time for everyone's luck to change!

On New Year's Eve of 1991 there was a lot going on in Vegas, mostly shows featuring the same old troupers, warmed over. Thus Caesars offered Little Richard (succeeding Julio Iglesias), Excalibur staged King Arthur's tournament, Wayne Newton was still at the Las Vegas Hilton (the show opened to the reverberating bass of thirty-two loudspeakers heralding the descent of an enormous spaceship), Frank Sinatra, aged seventy-five, now at the Riviera (where the owner had booked his wife Pia Zadora on the same bill), still felt so young, Bally's had an 'outspoken' comedian, whose speciality was to give offence to everybody, the Sands offered Melinda 'first lady of magic', the Stardust presented performing orang-utans, while Bobby Vinton, booked at the Golden Nugget just after New Year, claimed that his song 'Mr Lonely' was the number one request with the US troops in Saudi Arabia.

Resisting the crooners and conjurors, I took to the streets. Downtown, Binion's was jammed wall to wall, a jackpot was being called every other minute. With all the restaurants in town booked out, I dined famously at the 24-hour snack counter on ham and lima bean soup, price $1.35. It could scarcely have been better at the Ritz. Downtown was so overloaded that the gas supply broke down. All the kitchens without emergency power had to switch to cold food. A young kid staggered away from the poker table after losing a big hand and marched blindly around the room, clutching his head, before hitting the street. A large black man in the men's room was shouting, 'A man's gotta do what a man's gotta do.' I fought my way to the bar. 'You get all sorts,' observed the barman, as a cowboy-figure with a sixty-inch belly eased his way past. People literally had to battle their way to the tables to blow their money. When I got back to my car, a guy was urinating against the door. 'No offence, man,' he said.

I drove up to the Strip. A fight was going on at the Mirage outside the Lagoon Saloon, where a man was trying to force his way through the guards to reach his wife. She was shouting, pop-eyed, about twenty paces away, cut off by the immovable throng around her. It was too crowded even to swing a punch. Two green-jacketed security guards were rocked to and fro without moving their feet by the furious party-goer. Finally a big black guard, built like an anti-tank gun, hove into view. The crowd cheered, the combatants subsided, the man was reunited with his spouse. In the convention centre, Steve Wynn had thrown a couple of parties – 1,400 slot players in one room, 850 high rollers in another. A special show, with acrobats and entertainers, had rehearsed for three weeks to entertain the high rollers' party. Japanese in dinner jackets streamed out of the ballroom, on their way back to the baccarat tables. Every young American girl seemed to be wearing a little black dress.

On the Strip, it was bitterly cold. A desert wind ripped through my jacket like a flail. Traffic was stopped. At the four corners of Las Vegas Boulevard and Flamingo, car horns jammed continually. I went into the Dunes, one of the casinos which was in decline and struggling. On this night of all nights, it should have been bubbling, but the restaurant and bar were three-quarters empty. The barman served me a glass of red wine, ice cold. As midnight approached I went out on the Strip again. An aroma of beer wafted over the freezing night air like after-shave. Everyone ignored the traffic lights, cheering and singing. In the Barbary Coast, the band was playing rock and roll as the kids pressed in all the way down the long double line of tables. A shriek of joy went up as the first jackpot of 1991 rang out on a slot machine. A large lady stood gazing in rapture at the screen, moaning in disbelief as the coins tumbled down the chute in front of her. 'Oh, oh oh, I can't believe it.'

I could have killed for a cup of coffee.

A NOTE
ON
SOURCES

I could not have written this book without a great deal of help from many people wiser than myself. People in the casino industry in Las Vegas are, in general, happy to give interviews without fuss, and to talk frankly about their life and work. Although I cannot list everyone I talked to, I append a brief note on my main sources of information. I record my particular thanks to my good friend William Eadington, Professor of Economics at the University of Nevada, Reno, whose encyclopaedic knowledge prevented me from making many errors of fact and judgement. Those that remain are all my own work.

Chapter 1 Interviews with Steve and Elaine Wynn and members of the Mirage team. Particular thanks to Eric Drache for inviting me to the opening of the Mirage. I also drew on cuttings from the Las Vegas *Review-Journal* and Las Vegas *Sun* and other journalistic sources, notably the *Las Vegas City Magazine* (February 1985), filed in the Special Collection of the University of Nevada at Las Vegas. This library is an indispensable source of gambling literature. Students of the subject, in Las Vegas and around the world, are indebted to the collection's cheerful and tireless librarian, Susan Jarvis. In the same spirit, the Gamblers Book Club, run with unflagging enthusiasm by Howard Schwartz, at 630, South 11th St., Las Vegas, Nevada 89101, is an essential port of call on every trip to town (or fax 702 382-7594).

Another useful source of industry news is *The Casino Journal of Nevada*, published monthly; while a sparky record of current events is given by the *Las Vegas Advisor*, a monthly newsletter (Huntington Press, PO Box 28041, LV 89126), which also helped me in preparing the casinos' map.

The Predators' Ball, a masterly account of junk bonds, is by Connie Bruck (New York, 1988). Donald Trump's autobiographies are *The Art of the Deal* (New York, 1987) and *Surviving at the Top* (New York, 1990). *The Boardwalk Jungle* by Ovid Demaris (New York, 1986), is a racy account of how casino gambling came to Atlantic City. Eugene Martin Christiansen directs Christian/Cummings Associates, Inc. in New York, specialising in financial analysis of the casino industry. *Gaming and Wagering Business Magazine* and *Barron's* are both published in New York.

Chapter 2 I drew on the following books: *Life Among the Paiutes: Their wrongs and claims* by Sarah Winnemucca, and *Nevada: A History of Changes* by David Thompson (Reno, 1986), which is an incisive and sensitive record of the times, highly recommended. Also the *Diary and Letters* of Reverend Joseph Cook (Laramie, Wyoming, 1919), *The Readers Encyclopaedia of the American West*, ed. H. R. Lamar (New York, 1977), *Las Vegas: As it began – as it grew* by Stanley W. Paher (Las Vegas, 1971) and *Nevada Towns & Tales, Volume 11 – South*, edited by the same author (Las Vegas, 1982). Two modern books are *People of Chance* by John M. Findlay (New York, 1986), which reviews gambling in American society from Jamestown to Las Vegas, and *Resort City in the Sunbelt: Las Vegas 1930–1970* by Eugene P. Moehring (Reno, 1989).

'Bugsy's Casino and the Modern Casino Hotel' by James Smith, Professor of American Studies at the University of Pennsylvania, was presented to the 7th Conference on Gambling and Risk Taking in London, 1990, available in *Gambling and Public Policy*, (edited by W. R. Eadington and J. A. Cornelius (1991). *The Noel Coward Diaries* are edited by Graham Payn and Sheridan Morley (London, 1982). The movie *Diamonds Are Forever* starring Sean Connery came out in 1971, and *Desert Bloom*, which is really a father – step-daughter conflict, but set in Las Vegas, was released in 1985. Tom Wolfe's essay 'Las Vegas (What?) Las Vegas (Can't Hear You! Too Noisy) Las Vegas!!!!' is contained in *The Kandy-kolored Tangerine-flake Streamline Baby* (New York, 1963). *The Desert Rose* by Larry McMurtrey (New York,

1983) is an everyday story about everyday Las Vegas folk, sort of. *Justice Downwind: America's Atomic Testing Program in the 1950s* by Howard Ball was published in 1985 (New York).

Chapter 3 Interviews with most of the personnel named, plus company reports and casino brochures. I record with thanks the continuous help of Don Payne of the Las Vegas News Bureau. *Fear and Loathing in Las Vegas* is the celebrated record of a drug-filled spree by Hunter S. Thompson (New York, 1971). *The Day the MGM Grand Burned* was written by Deirdre Coakley with Hank Greenspun, Gary C. Gerard and the staff of the Las Vegas *Sun*, (Las Vegas, 1982); *The Green Felt Jungle* by Ed Reid and Ovid Demaris, has become a classic on Las Vegas' early days of crime and corruption (New York, 1963).

Chapter 4 I owe special thanks to architectural-artist Jenny Sparks, resident in London, for setting me in the right direction. *Learning from Las Vegas* by Robert Venturi, Denis Scott Brown and Steven Izenour was first published in 1972 (Cambridge Mass.). 'Relearning from Las Vegas' by Stephen Izenour and David A. Dashiell III, appeared in the *American Institute of Architecture*, (New York, October 1990). The *Architectural Record* article on Predock is from July, 1987 (New York). Other publications consulted: *Cadillac Desert* by Marc Reisner, (New York, 1990); *Saloons of the Old West* by Richard Erdoes, (New York, 1979); 'Las Vegas: Imagery and Mythology of a Frontier Boom Town Restated' is a paper by Frank Reynolds and Dr Hugh Burgess, (Arizona State University, Tempe, Arizona, 1988); Joan Didion's spare and tragic novel *Play It As It Lays* appeared in 1970 (New York). Hunter S. Thompson and Tom Wolfe as cited above.

Chapter 5 There is a varied literature mentioning prostitution, of which I consulted *Daughters of Joy, Sisters of Misery: Prostitutes in the American West, 1865–90* by Anne M. Butler, (Urbana, 1985), *Comstock Mining and Miners* by Eliot Lord, 1881, *Gold Diggers and Silver Miners: Prostitution and Social Life in the Cornstock Lode* by Marion S. Goldman (Michigan, 1981), *Saloons of the Old West* by Richard Erdoes, and *The Girls of Nevada* by Gabriel R. Vogliotti (Secaucus, New Jersey, 1972). *The Nye County Brothel Wars* by Jeanie Kasindorf was published in 1985 (New York). *Dummy Up and Deal* by Lee Stolkey (Las Vegas, 1980), is about dealing blackjack. 'The Organisation of Bell Desk Prostitution' by Loren D. Reichert and James H. Frey was published in *Sociology and Social Research*, (Las Vegas, July 1985). *The Green Felt Jungle* was already cited in Chapter 3. John Gregory Dunne's *A Memoir of a Dark Season* (New York, 1974) describes a sojourn in Vegas to get over a rift in his marriage. *The Best Cat Houses in Nevada* by J. R. Schwartz is available from the Gambler's Bookclub at $5.95.

Chapter 6 Few books have been written about baccarat because there is not a lot to say about the game. I record my special thanks to expert Robin Powell, for explaining how the game is run. Professor Peter Griffin, who teaches mathematics at the University of California at Sacramento, is an acknowledged expert on gambling theory, particularly blackjack. *The Royal Baccarat Scandal* by Sir Michael Havers, Edward Grayson and Peter Shankland, (London, 1977), is an amusing account of the cause célèbre involving Edward VII. *Fools Die*, which seems to take Caesars Palace as a model, was written by Mario Puzo (New York, 1978). *Scarne's Guide to Casino Gambling* by John Scarne is one of many gambling books by this author, (New York, 1978). *No Way Out* by Gary Ross (British title *Stung*) appeared in 1987 (Toronto). Bill Friedman, also quoted in my introduction, is the author of *Casino Management* (Secaucus, New Jersey, 1974), which remains a standard text on casino management in all aspects. *Trumped!* by John R. O'Donnell, formerly president of the Trump Plaza in Atlantic City, appeared in 1991 (New York). *Beat The Dealer*, by Edward O. Thorp, the book which showed how astute players could beat the game of blackjack, first appeared in 1962 (New York). A full account of the subsequent history of blackjack was given in my own *Easy Money*, (London, 1987). An account of experiments to track roulette by computer was described in *The Eudaemonic Pie* by Thomas Bass, (New York, 1985). The casino industry newsletter *Rouge et Noir* is available from PO Box 1146, Midlothian, Virginia 23113.

The dialogue on blackjack comes from *Keno Runner* by David Kranes, (Salt Lake City, 1989): I was determined to quote something from this novel in my book, in tribute to David Kranes, Professor of English at the University of Utah, whom I admire as far and away the best novelist to have written about life in Las Vegas.

On slots, I record my special thanks to Richard Schuetz, an authority on the subject with wide casino experience. My thanks also to Logan Pease of IGM. *Automatic Pleasures*, by Nik Costa appeared in London in 1988. The *Casino Gambler's Guide* by Allan M. Wilson (New York, 1965), is a good introduction to gambling in general.

Chapter 7 Joyce Carol Oates's essay 'On Boxing' appeared in *Reading The Fights*, (New York, 1988). My special thanks for the continuous help received from Michael Roxborough, who runs a leading sports consultancy in Las Vegas. *Lem Banker's Book of Sports Betting* appeared in 1986 (New York). Social psychologist Erwin Goffman's classic essay 'Where the Action Is', may be found in his collection *Interaction Ritual*, (New York, 1967). Professor I. Nelson Rose, who contributed these comments to the monthly magazine *The Card Player*, is the author of a standard work *Gambling and the Law* (Secaucus, New Jersey, 1986). A paper on sports betting by Lange and Roxborough is collected in the journal *Gambling and Commercial Gaming* (Reno, 1991).

Chapter 8 Interviews with Governor Sawyer, John Reilly and other officials on the regulatory bodies. Other sources: *Where I Stand* by Hank Greenspun with Alex Pelle, (New York, 1966); *Man Against The Mob* by William E. Roemer, Jr., (New York, 1989); *Little Man: Meyer Lansky and the Gangster Life* by Robert Lacey (Boston, 1991). *The Last Mafioso* by Ovid Demaris (New York, 1981), has a 12-page appendix listing who was who in the mob. The series of articles in the Los Angeles *Times* by Walter J. Goodman, detailing Spilotro's career, ran in February 1983; other reports from the Las Vegas press, notably by columnist John L. Smith. *The Boardwalk Jungle* is cited above, as is *Fools Die* by Mario Puzo.

My special thanks are due to Anthony Cabot of Lionel Sawyer and Partners of Las Vegas, co-author with Richard Schuetz of 'An Economic View of the Nevada Gaming Licensing Process', in *Gambling and Public Policy* (Eadington and Cornelius, eds. as above); and equally to Professor I. Nelson Rose of Whittier School of Law, Los Angeles, for a variety of articles on legal issues in addition to his invaluable *Gambling and the Law*.

Conclusion Interviews with people quoted, plus back-up material provided by the Department of Design and Development, Las Vegas City Hall. Various casino personnel in Laughlin, and the Chamber of Commerce. Eugene Martin Christiansen's comments were contributed to *The Newsletter of the Institute for the Study of Gambling and*

Commercial Gaming, Volume 2, number 1, an occasional publication, from the University of Nevada, Reno.

If there are other key sources which I have inadvertently omitted, my apologies – with a promise to make amends in any future edition.

Finally I must record my heartfelt thanks to my editor Lesley Bryce for all her care and attention to my text.

INDEX

Of related interest

Published by the University of Nevada Press

Casino Accounting and Financial Management
by E. Malcolm Greenlees

The Last Resort: Success and Failure in Campaigns for Casinos
by John Dombrink and William N. Thompson

Distributed by the University of Nevada Press for
the Institute for the Study of Gambling and Commercial Gaming

Gambling and Commercial Gaming: Essays in Business, Economics,
Philosophy, and Science
edited by William R. Eadington and Judy A. Cornelius

Gambling and Public Policy: International Perspectives
edited by William R. Eadington and Judy A. Cornelius

Gambling Behavior and Problem Gambling
edited by William R. Eadington, Judy A. Cornelius, and Julian I. Taber

Gambling Research: Proceedings of the Seventh International   Conference on
Gambling and Risk Taking
edited by William R. Eadington and Judy A. Cornelius

The Gambling Studies: Proceedings of the Sixth National Conference on
Gambling and Risk Taking
edited by William R. Eadington

Indian Gaming and the Law
edited by William R. Eadington

International Casino Law
edited by Anthony Cabot, William Thompson, and Andrew Tottenham